COMPLETE
BIKE
BOOK

COMPLETE
BIKE
book

CHRIS SIDWELLS

DK Publishing

LONDON, NEW YORK, MUNICH,
MELBOURNE, DELHI

US Editors Margaret Parrish and Christine Heilman
Senior Editor Neil Lockley
Editor Richard Gilbert
Senior Art Editor Kevin Ryan
DTP Designer Rajen Shah
Production Controller Kevin Ward

Managing Editors Adèle Hayward, Sharon Lucas
Managing Art Editors Marianne Markham, Karen Self
Category Publisher Stephanie Jackson
Art Director Carole Ash

Produced for Dorling Kindersley by

Phil Hunt Editorial

64a Marmora Road, London SE22 0RY

Sands Publishing Solutions

4 Jenner Way, Eccles, Aylesford, Kent ME20 7SQ
Editors David and Sylvia Tombesi-Walton
Art Editor Simon Murrell

cobalt id

The Stables, Wood Farm, Deopham Road,
Attleborough, Norfolk NR17 1AJ
Designers Paul Reid, Pia Hietarinta

Photographer Gerard Brown
Photographic Art Director Jo Grey
Technical Consultant Guy Andrews

First American Edition, 2003

Published in the United States by
DK Publishing, Inc.
375 Hudson Street
New York, New York 10014

03 04 05 06 07 08 10 9 8 7 6 5 4 3 2 1

A Cataloging-in-Publication record for this book is available from
the Library of Congress.

ISBN 0-7894-9337-3

Reproduced by Media Development Printing Ltd, UK
Printed in the UK by Butler and Tanner

See our complete product line at
www.dk.com

Contents

HEALTH AND FITNESS

COMPETITIVE CYCLING

MAINTAINING YOUR BIKE

Foreword

I was six years old when I discovered biking. The day my dad let go of the bike, there I was, riding solo, and my whole world changed in an instant. Before long I was riding my bike to school, thrilled that I did not have to fight for the front seat of the car with my five siblings. The bike became my transportation until I discovered cars as a teenager.

I did not get involved in cycling again until my mid-twenties, when a friend of mine saw a magazine article about the Ironman Triathlon and suggested we do it. We survived the Ironman, barely, and for me it was the catalyst for a long career in cycling. From road triathlons I progressed to road racing, then to cyclo-cross, and finally to mountain-bike racing, which I discovered to be my forte, gaining six national titles and a win at the first World Championships. Later I discovered the Xterra Mountain Bike Triathlon and won World Champion titles in 1998 and 1999.

It is easy to see why I am excited about Chris Sidwells' *Complete Bike Book*—it contains a wide variety of cycling information compiled in an easy-to-understand format. Not only do the photographs convey the excitement of different racing disciplines, they are also critical to developing an understanding of riding techniques and mechanical maintenance.

The maintenance section is especially important. Many riders who are new to the sport may not realize the value of tuning your bike. A cycle tuned to your riding style and terrain will not only increase your performance, it will also make your riding safer. Of course, some mechanical understanding while out on the road or trail will give you the satisfaction of making hands-on repairs, as well as save you a long walk home!

The wealth of information here will expand your knowledge of the history of cycling, the bikes, and the races, and will show you how to train and ride faster and more safely. Enjoy!

NED OVEREND

The early years

An improved American velocipede

A patent for a wooden-framed machine with a fixed wheel at the back and a steerable one at the front was first taken out in 1817 by Karl Friedrich Drais von Sauerbronn, a German baron. The draisine, named after him, spawned many similar machines, known as dandy-horses. These were not really bicycles, since they were scooted along by the rider's feet on the ground. The invention that really defined the bicycle was the pedal. In 1839, Scottish blacksmith Kirkpatrick Macmillan built a machine that had its rear wheel powered by treadles, but these proved inefficient.

Creating the velocipede

In 1861, Parisian coachbuilder Pierre Michaux attached cranks and pedals to the front wheel of a dandy-horse, and the velocipede was born. Michaux's invention proved popular, and hundreds of velocipedes appeared in European cities. In 1866, Pierre Lallemet, a former employee of Michaux, took out a patent for the velocipede in America.

Just three years later, on May 31, 1869, in the Parc de St.-Cloud, Paris, the first velocipede race was held; Englishman James Moore won. The first race between towns, from Paris to Rouen on November 7, 1869, was also won by Moore, covering the 76 miles (123 km) at an average speed of 7 mph (12 km/h). The Paris–Rouen race is still held annually.

Designing for speed

Velocipede racing motivated the competing teams to develop faster machines. The first evidence of their effort was a speedy growth in front-wheel size. With the pedals attached directly to the front wheel, the distance a bike can travel during one pedal revolution is dictated by the circumference

▶ **Racing ordinary cycles**
Ordinary (penny-farthing) bicycle races were highly popular, and annual track events are still held by veteran cycling clubs in Great Britain.

History of cycling

Although the contributions of pioneers such as Baron Drais von Sauerbronn, Kirkpatrick Macmillan, and Pierre Michaux cannot be overstated, it is impossible to say with any certainty who invented the bicycle. Indeed, the basic elements of a bike—two wheels, a steerable front, and pedals—came together over a period of several decades. Subsequent refinements of and additions to those elements led to today's bicycle. This timeline charts some of the most important developments in the bike's history.

1800–20

1817 Baron Karl Friedrich Drais von Sauerbronn patents a design for a wooden-framed, steerable machine with two wheels. Called the draisine, it was named after him.

1819 Denis Johnson files a patent for the draisine in Great Britain. Draisines start to appear on British and North American roads.

The draisine

1821–40

1839 Kirkpatrick Macmillan builds a two-wheeled vehicle similar to the draisine but fitted with treadles to propel the rear wheel.

Early sketch of a draisine

of the driven wheel. This gave rise to the ordinary, or penny-farthing, bicycle with its huge front wheel and tiny back one. The rider sat directly over the big wheel, making the machines highly unstable, and there were many falls and injuries. Nevertheless, the machine's potential was instantly recognized, and hundreds were bought by upper-class gentlemen for touring and racing. Cycling by the general populace still lay decades in the future, however, since working people had neither the money nor the leisure time to take it up.

Leaping into the future

A problem with the ordinary was that its wheel size, and therefore the bike's potential speed, was determined by the length of a rider's leg. This, and the design's unenviable reputation for accidents, led to the development of the safety cycle, launched in 1885 by Englishman James Starley. While the penny-farthing had wheels of 4–5 ft (1.2–1.5m) in diameter, the safety cycle was much more manageable on its 30-in (76-cm) wheels.

After the Franco-Prussian War of 1870, bicycle racing on the road flourished in Europe. In 1903, the editor of one of the journals launched to report it, *L'Auto,* held a race around France to promote his paper. The Tour de France was born. The first Tour was 1,510 miles (2,428 km) long, and the winner was chimney sweep Maurice Garin. In the US, racing on steeply banked tracks was growing in popularity, as were six-day track races (Sunday being left out for religious reasons).

In Europe, however, the outbreak of World War I in 1914 was destined to bring this period of huge growth for the bicycle to an end. Nevertheless, the bicycle found a variety of helpful roles on the battlefield, being used by both sides to transport troops, pass messages, and carry munitions.

1841–60	1861–80	1881–1900	1901–14
1845 R.W. Thompson takes out a British patent for a "hollow, air-filled tube." This was the first attempt to create a pneumatic tire.	**1861** Pierre Michaux attaches cranks and pedals to the front wheel of a dandy-horse, calling his invention the velocipede.	**1883** The Cyclists' Touring Club (CTC) is formed in Britain.	**1903** The Tour de France is held for the first time.
	1869 The first recorded cycle race takes place in Parc de St.-Cloud, Paris.	**1885** The safety cycle is launched by James Starley.	**1914** Bicycles are used in war.
	1870s The ordinary (penny-farthing) bicycle gains popularity.	**1880s** The pneumatic tire is invented by John Boyd Dunlop.	
	1874 The first World Track Championships are held in England.		

Early Parisian race, c.1870s

The safety cycle

Competitors in an early Tour de France

After World War I, bike sales fell in the US as people turned to the car, a more convenient mode of transport over long distances. But in England, there was little spare money, and bike use continued to rise.

Racing was resumed as quickly as possible in Europe. In 1919, for the first time in the history of the Tour de France, the rider leading the 3,417-mile (5,500-km) race on overall time was awarded the yellow jersey—yellow after the color of the pages of the organizer's journal, *L'Auto*.

Developing the technology

The resumption of racing restarted the race to build a faster bike. Tire improvements resulted in the development of the tubular tire—a tire cover sewn around an inner tube to create one unit. In June 1927, Italian racer Tullio Campagnolo was racing in snow through the Dolomite mountains in the Tour of Italy when a tire punctured. With his hands numbed by the cold, he could not undo the wheel's wing nuts. He abandoned the race but later invented the hollow axle and quick wheel-release mechanism found on most bikes today. Six years later, Campagnolo created the derailleur gear, a mechanism that allowed several different cogs to be accessed on the rear wheel. Multiple gearing made life easier in hilly terrain.

Competing with the car

Bike use reached its zenith in much of Europe, including Great Britain, on the eve of World War II, when millions of people were using the cycle for both fun and transportation. When Britain was rebuilt after the war, however, it was with the car in mind. Germany, the Netherlands, and Belgium, on the other hand, were rebuilt with bike lanes as part of their transportation systems. In North America, cycling as a mode of transport fell out of fashion due to the increased availability of the car.

Cycling's first true superstar, Fausto Coppi, emerged in 1940 with his victory at the Tour of Italy. He went on to become the first rider to win the Tours of Italy and France in the same year (1949). Meanwhile, cycling was becoming more sophisticated. Technical refinements and vehicles carrying spares meant that a mechanical mishap no longer spelled the end of a race for a rider.

The 1950s saw the rise of Frenchman Jacques Anquetil, the first five-time winner of the Tour de France (1957 and 1961–64). The first women's World Championships were held in 1958; the road race was won by Elsy Jacobs from Luxembourg, and the track races by Russians Galina Ermolaeva and Ludmila Kotchetova.

Racing to new heights

Up until 1960, road racing was largely dominated by riders from mainland Europe. Then Englishman Tom Simpson widened the competition by winning the Tour of Flanders in 1961, wearing the yellow jersey

1918–20	1921–30	1931–40	1941–50
1919 The yellow jersey appears for the first time in the Tour de France. The Tour is won by a Belgian cyclist, Firmin Lambot.	**1920s** Track sprinting is the most popular branch of cycle sport during this period. Dutchman Piet Moeskops dominates, winning five world titles (1921–24 and 1926). **1927** Tullio Campagnolo invents the quick-release wheel.	**1931** Hubert Opperman (later knighted and an Australian cabinet minister) becomes the first Australian to win a Classic bike race, Paris–Brest–Paris. **1933** Tullio Campagnolo invents the derailleur gear. **1938** The 3/32 chain (which is the size currently used) is invented. Named after the width of the roller in each link, this chain leads to advances in the derailleur gear.	**1940** Fausto Coppi wins the Tour of Italy for the first time. **1947** Jean Robic (France) wins the first postwar Tour de France. **1949** Fausto Coppi wins the Tours of Italy and France.

Firmin Lambot

Tullio Campagnolo

Fausto Coppi

in the 1962 Tour de France, and winning the World Road Race title in 1965.

The 1970s saw the height of the career of one of the greatest cyclists ever, Eddy Merckx. In 1974, he won the Tours of Italy and France and the World Road Race Championships. At the same time, cyclists in California were exploring trails on "clunker" bikes, leading to a brand-new sport—mountain biking.

In 1984, aerodynamics technology helped Italian Francesco Moser set a new world hour record. The mid-1980s saw the first Olympic women's cycling events (Los Angeles, 1984), the first American Tour de France winner (Greg Lemond, 1986), and the first mountain-bike World Championships (France, 1987). The late 1980s saw Jeannie Longo from France—arguably the greatest female cyclist ever—become a five-time World Road Champion, a three-time World Time Trial Champion, and a three-time World Pursuit Champion on the track.

▶ **Riding to victory**
Belgian cyclist Eddie Merckx competed in the 1970s and won over 550 races. No one had come close to his domination of cycling before, or has since. Merckx is still seen as the greatest cyclist ever.

1951-60	1961-70	1971-80	1981-90
1950s Professional road racing grows rapidly in popularity.	**1960** TV cameras cover live racing for the first time. Advertising revenue leads to an increase in prize money.	**1970s** BMX, triathlon, and mountain biking are born. These developments resurrect the cycling industry.	**1980s** New training techniques are increasingly used to improve the performance levels of professional cyclists.
1958 The World Championships accepts women entrants for the first time.	**1960s** Cycling loses much of its popularity as a mode of transport in the US and the UK.	Manufacturers create specially built mountain bikes, triathlon athletes buy road bikes, and fitness enthusiasts turn to cycling.	**1980s** Jeannie Longo dominates as World Champion.
		1974 Eddy Merckx wins the Tours of Italy and France and the World Road Race Championships.	**1986** Greg Lemond becomes the first American to win the Tour de France.

1950s road race

1970s mountain bikes

Jeannie Longo

Cycling today

Mountain-bike suspension system

Cycling today is a global and diverse sport, with people of all ages riding and competing on bikes. Mountain biking made it into the 1996 Olympics in Atlanta, and triathlon followed in Sydney in 2000. Both disciplines now have their own World Cup events. There is also a whole new world of multisport events—BMX (Bicycle Motocross) racing has been rediscovered, and new disciplines, such as trials, BSX (Bicycle Super Cross), and dual slalom, have been developed.

Racing to worldwide fame

The jewel in the crown of sports cycling is still road racing, with the Classic races in Europe and the Tours of France, Italy, and Spain attracting media interest from all over the world. No longer do European riders totally dominate, though. In 2002, American Lance Armstrong won the Tour de France for the fourth consecutive time, proving himself to be one of the greatest cyclists of all time.

Australians, Canadians, Germans, Russians, and Colombians are also winning European races, and riders are emerging from Asia and the Middle East to challenge the old order. The racing season now includes additional countries. It starts in Australia with the Tour Down Under, then moves to Taiwan with the Tour of Langkawi, and ends with the Japan Cup. A new race in the Middle East, the Tour of Qatar, was run for the first time in 2002 and was a great success. With major races in North America, Eastern Europe, and Asia, the sport that was born in a Paris park has traveled around the planet.

Cycling in the cities

Perhaps the most important role played by bikes in the modern world is that of freeing up the streets of the world's cities. Anyone who regularly moves around in any city knows that car use has made circulation increasingly difficult over the years. Local and national governments are now increasingly ready to promote cycling and provide facilities for cyclists. They have created cycle lanes, bike traffic lights, and secure bike racks. In cities throughout the world, including Amsterdam and Copenhagen, they have also set up programs in which a bike can be picked up at one point and left at another for a minimal charge.

The ease with which a bike can move in traffic makes sense for other applications, too. For example, paramedics and police can often reach the scene of an incident faster by bike than by car. The bike is also a viable proposition for businesses. Cycle couriers are a familiar sight on city streets, but recently the principles of cycling have also been applied to human-powered taxis and delivery vehicles.

As cities become increasingly bike-friendly, support programs for cyclists are growing. In addition to secure bike racks and cycle lanes,

---

1990–91

1990 Off-road clipless pedals go on sale.

1990 Suspension forks, which help to absorb the shocks of bumpy terrain, become commercially available.

1991 Djamolidine Abdoujaparov, from Uzbekistan, wins the Ghent–Wevelgem road race for the first time. (Eastern-bloc amateurs were not allowed to ride with western professionals until the demise of the Soviet Union.)

Early 1990s suspension fork

1992–93

1992 Full-suspension bicycles are widely available for the first time.

1993 Frenchwoman Anne-Caroline Chausson wins her first World Championship Downhill mountain-bike race. She dominates the field for the next decade, winning eight more times.

1993 Scotland's Graeme Obree sets a new world hour record on a bike with a radical new riding position, eventually leading the UCI to clamp down on bike design and standardize it.

1994–95

1995 World bicycle production rises to 107 million units. In the same year, automobile production is around 37 million units.

Graeme Obree

▼ **Providing help rapidly**
Paramedics and police have established that the quick response time a bike can offer in city centers is making their work easier and saving more lives.

some cities are even offering rescue services for cyclists stranded with damaged bikes. There are also programs to train children and adults in how to cope with traffic and other road hazards.

Encouraging bicycle use

The organizers of facilities such as cycle lanes and traffic-free routes, bike racks, and changing rooms at places of work still have much to accomplish. But governments have seen, at last, that something has to be done about urban congestion, and that the bike just might be the low-cost answer.

The French rail system has a program in which the commuter cycles to the railway station, leaves the bike at the departure point, and then rents a bike at the other end to ride to work. In Belgium, the "Bike + Train" program enables passengers to rent a bike at major train stations, and every station has secure bike parking. In the Netherlands, bicycles may be rented at every major train station. Governments are now encouraging integrated transport policies in which bikes play a pivotal role. "Cycle-then-ride" initiatives clearly demonstrate the bigger role that the bike can play in transportation.

1996–97	1998–99	2000–02

1996 Cross-country mountain-bike racing becomes an Olympic discipline.

1997 EuroVelo, the European cycle-route network, is launched. It comprises 12 long-distance routes across the continent of Europe and currently covers 12,500 miles (20,000 km).

1997 The European Greenways Association is set up at the first European Conference on Soft Traffic and Railway Paths, to encourage nonmotorized transport on Europe's disused railroad corridors, towpaths, and historic routes.

1999 Campagnolo releases the ten-speed cassette.

1999 American Lance Armstrong wins the Tour de France for the first time.

Lance Armstrong

2000 Triathlon becomes an Olympic discipline.

2000 US bike imports rise to a record of 20.2 million units.

2001 It is estimated that the number of bikes in use worldwide stands at 1.4 billion, while the number of cars is 340 million.

2002 The results of the 2000 US census indicate that there has been a nine-percent rise in the number of Americans commuting to work by bike.

Bike park

Discovering the world on two wheels

Urban cycle commuter

Cycling has no equal as a low-impact form of personal transport. If everyone rode a bike, the resulting reduction in pollution and congestion on our roads would create a healthier environment.

The bicycle is a perfect vehicle for all kinds of discovery. Whether you want to explore your own neighborhood or travel in a new country, or pursue a healthier and more environment-friendly lifestyle, a bicycle is the ideal choice. Every year, many thousands of people discover—and rediscover—the joy, simplicity, and convenience of the bicycle.

Appreciating the bicycle

The world of cycling is a huge one. The machine that first saw the light of day in the second half of the 1800s has spread to the four corners of the earth, spawning a multi-billion-dollar industry,

a global sport, and a fascinating pastime. The bicycle can also make a huge difference in the quality of life in the Third World, and it might just be the answer to the transportation congestion that is doing so much damage to the quality of our lives in the developed world.

So, what is it about the bike that attracts people and allows it to play an increasingly important global role? There are several answers. Cycling combines a human fascination with machines with physical endeavor. The bike's simplicity means that it does not exclude anyone; in equal fashion, an entry-level bicycle or a race-level road model will allow you to experience the joy of cycling. Although sophisticated race bikes may seem expensive, they soon appear less so when compared with other high-end sports equipment. Thanks to cycling's increased popularity, good-quality entry-level bikes now represent excellent value for money.

Then there is the bike's convenience and adaptability. It is both a mode of transport and a very good way to exercise. You can also make cycling as social or as solitary an activity as you

▼ **Cycling to the limit**

Some expert cyclists can accomplish spectacular jumps. Despite their daredevil appearance, such leaps can be achieved by using the techniques found in this book. The design excellence of modern mountain bikes also helps to make jumps possible.

▼ **Enjoying the great outdoors**

Whether you ride alone or with friends, cycling quickly improves your fitness, health, and sense of well-being. Cycling outdoors gives direct access to the sights, sounds, and smells surrounding you, which cannot be said of traveling within the confines of a car.

▲ **Choosing an alternative sport**
Trick riding on BMX bikes is fascinating to many young people. The opportunities for gaining personal expertise can make it seem preferable to traditional team sports.

wish—you can take off alone for a contemplative ride or join a group of friends for a gregarious one. It is this flexibility that makes cycling so attractive.

Cycling is something that everyone does as a child, when life has not yet revealed its boundaries and restrictions. As people grow up, they exchange their bicycles for cars, but when they drive they take the cares and worries of adulthood with them. Driving a car, unlike cycling, reflects adult limits regarding where we can go and what we can do.

Making the most of cycling

There is something for everyone in this book, and plenty to help you find your way in every aspect of cycling. For example, if you have not ridden since childhood, this book will guide you through buying the bike you want. You may even get hooked on the sport and decide to take up competitive cycling (*see* pp.156–77). But this book is also about family cycling and the joys of young and old riding together; about parents seeing

cycling as an ideal sport for their children; and about youngsters developing a lifelong passion for cycling. It is also about trying to persuade people to make some journeys by bike rather than automatically using a car.

Looking to the future

In the coming years, the world can look forward to seeing roads made safer for cyclists, as well as greater cycle access to the countryside.

Many cities are actively encouraging cyclists back onto their streets and, as a consequence, cycle use is increasing. What is needed now is more cities to follow suit. An increase in the number of cyclists will mean that governments will be encouraged to build and adapt facilities to accommodate them. This, in turn, will encourage still more people to use bikes, leading to a greater reduction in the transportation problems that can be seen in today's cities. Get out there and ride, and maybe it will happen.

Getting started

People choose to cycle for many reasons, from getting to work to enjoying the countryside. It is important to obtain the right bike, clothing, and equipment for your type of riding. The following pages offer a wealth of useful information, from buying a bike to the basics of riding on- and off-road, and also introduce the concept of cycle touring.

Why cycle?

Cycling is not only good for your health and for the environment, it is also great fun. Cycling can do much to restore your capacity for enjoyment. Additionally, cycling is an affordable and time-saving mode of transport.

Saving time and money

For the past few years, surveys have compared inner city and suburban journey times by car, train, bus, taxi, and bike. The bike has been fastest every time. In cities, where most journeys are less than 2 miles (3.5 km), cycling saves time.

It can also save you money. A bike, some basic tools and clothing, a pump, and a few spares do cost money, but these are one-time payments. No fuel is needed for a bike, and there is never any threat of parking fees or tickets. By adding up these costs, it is possible to see how quickly a bike pays for itself.

Many people who live in cities tend to use public transportation much of the time, leaving the car idle at home. For some of them, selling the car and buying a bike may be a real option.

▼ **Traveling without restrictions**
With a bike you can often visit areas that would be simply impossible to reach in a car—a narrow mountain path, for example. A ride in such a setting can also offer spectacular views and a real sense of adventure.

▼ **Getting in shape**
A bike acts as both an ideal form of transportation and an excellent means of exercising outdoors.

Helping the environment

No one would deny that cycling is beneficial to the cyclist's health, but it also makes a noticeable difference for other road users.

Every person who takes a bike, rather than a car, to work saves a car's space on the road. If, in a given city, 10 percent of its 100,000 daily commuters were to travel by bike, not car, they would free up an area equivalent to 5 miles (8 km) of average road. Suddenly the system works and everyone arrives at their destination on time.

But it is not just a question of congestion—all the noxious substances that cars emit also harm the environment and public health. By making more journeys by bike, people effectively reduce the amount of dangerous emissions.

Regaining fitness

Even if you have not cycled for years, it does not take very long to become proficient on a bike once again. If you have children, you can even take them with you—clearly not a practical option if you go jogging to stay in shape.

Health tips

- Make sure your lower back is covered when cycling. If the muscles get cold, they can become stiff and painful.
- Cycle out of the saddle occasionally during a ride. It will help exercise different muscles and allow your muscles to stretch.
- Change into dry clothes as soon as you can if you sweat or get wet while cycling, to avoid catching a cold.
- Make sure your saddle is at the right height. If it is too high or too low, it will put strain on your knees.
- Wear a cycling mask if you regularly ride in traffic. A mask can also help if you suffer from asthma or hay fever.

Professional cyclists are among the toughest athletes in the world, and they have to be. Most authorities agree that the Tour de France is the most demanding sports event in the world.

Cycling also has something to offer to children. Mountain biking, downhill racing, dual slalom, 4X (Bicycle Four Cross), trials riding, and BMX (Bicycle Motocross) all capture the imaginations of young people, who are thrilled by the fast, close competitions. What other sport, pastime, or form of transportation has as much to offer as cycling?

▼ **Prolonging health**

Because the bike supports your weight and places less strain on the joints than many other sports, cycling is an ideal form of exercise for older people.

▼ **Commuting quickly**

It is much quicker to get around town if you go by bike—it is obviously faster than walking, and it is far better than sitting in a car in gridlocked traffic.

▼ **Carrying loads**

In some parts of the world, the bicycle has a role other than transporting people; it is also used as a means of carrying essential goods from one town or village to another.

See also

Road proficiency skills **pp.30–31** Family cycling **pp.36–37** Health and fitness **pp.140–55**

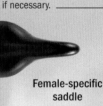

Buying a bike

A bike that will meet your immediate needs, but still suit you if you develop a passion for cycling, need not be very expensive. If it is a suitable type, is the right price, feels comfortable, and you like the way it looks, then go ahead and buy it.

Finding the right shop

The staff of a good cycle shop can take much of the guesswork out of bike-buying, and shop personnel provide advice and support for many cyclists.

The first questions to ask are: do the staff ride, and what kind of riding do they do? It is also useful to know whether the shop is in touch with the local cycling community. Look for evidence of this, such as ads for races or rides in the area.

Regular rides starting from the shop are another indication of a well-respected outlet. Furthermore, the salespeople need to be good listeners.

Selecting the correct size

When buying a bike, it is essential to find one that fits exactly. Bikes are adaptable, but to achieve your perfect position, the frame must be correct from the outset, since it is the part that you cannot adjust.

The correct frame size depends on your inside-leg measurement, taken from the crotch to the floor in bare feet. However, manufacturers use different units of measurement. Mountain bikes, for example, are measured in inches; road-bike sizes are expressed in centimeters; and some

Choosing a bike

If you are new to cycling, the first thing you may notice is just how many bikes are on the market these days. However, deciding on the right bicycle is simple. Think hard about what you want it for now—basic exercise, for example—and what you might go on to do with it later, such as enter a competition. Once you have given this some thought, the examples below will guide you in making your choice.

Road bike
Lightweight materials and narrow tires make this bike suitable for fitness riding, day touring, and competitions. The aerodynamic position afforded by a drop handlebar offers great speed.

Hybrid bike
The hybrid combines lightweight materials with fatter tires, making it perfect for bumpy urban roads. It is ideal for commuting, family rides, fitness riding, and touring.

Mountain bike
The knobbly tires, less-stretched riding position, and specialist brakes make the mountain bike perfect for off-road riding and touring, competitions, and working out.

What to look for

Be wary of a bike that promises a lot of features for little money. It is better to buy a bike made by a company that is known for quality. Even if the bike seems more basic, it will be better engineered.

Saddle
Saddles that feel very soft can be uncomfortable. Look for a firm, supportive saddle that is not too broad at the front. Women should consider a female-specific saddle; ask the shop to change the one on the bike if necessary.

Male-specific saddle

Female-specific saddle

Gears
If you live in a very hilly area, consider a triple crankset on a road bike. Three gears will be fine for a commuter riding on flat roads.

Pedals
Choose your pedals according to your needs (see pp.216–17).

Differences in human anatomy

As well as having different hip structures, men and women have other skeletal differences. Usually, they have longer legs in proportion to their bodies than men do, and they have longer upper-to-lower-leg ratios. This explains why women are morphologically better suited to cycling than men, and why both of these characteristics are also found in the best male bike racers.

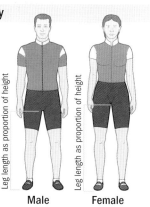

Leg length as proportion of height

Leg length as proportion of height

Male   Female

manufacturers label their bikes small, medium, or large. Refer to the table below to determine your size, but also ask a salesperson for advice.

Although bike shops cannot always stock every size of bike, they should be able to order them on request. If your inside leg is 31½ in (80 cm) and the shop tries to sell you a 20-inch mountain bike simply because it is the only one they have in stock, find another shop.

When buying children's bikes, allow room for growth. For trikes or bikes with training wheels, as long as children can reach the pedals, they will be fine. Once on two wheels, though, a child should be able to put the front part of both feet (not just the toes) on the ground while still in the saddle.

Handlebar
Pick the handlebar suitable for the kind of riding you do. Ask the shop staff for advice.

Choosing frame size

Inside leg measurement	Road frame	Mountain-bike frame	S, M, or L
29½–30¾ in (75–78 cm)	48–51 cm	14–16 in	S
31–32¼ in (79–82 cm)	50–54 cm	16–17 in	M
32½–34 in (83–86 cm)	53–57 cm	17–18 in	L
34¼–35½ in (87–90 cm)	56–60 cm	19–21 in	XL

Frame
Frame fit is more important than lightweight materials. The lightest, most sophisticated race frames are not designed for everyday use.

Brakes
Look for brakes that have plenty of adjustability. Consider either adjustable or small levers if you have small hands.

Wheels and tires
Match your tires to the conditions in which they will be used. For more grip, look for a knobbly tread pattern that continues around to the tire's sidewall. Slick tires roll better than knobbly ones, so they are easier to ride on the road. A multipurpose tire should give good grip, but not compromise the tire's ability to roll along a surface.

Off-road mountain-bike tire

Slick road tire

Multipurpose tire

See also
Road riding: adjusting position **pp.86–87**   Off-road riding: adjusting position **pp.110–11**

Equipment and accessories

Apart from a bike, the only truly essential item needed for cycling is a helmet. Helmet design has improved so much recently that there can be no logical objection to wearing one. They are light and comfortable, and they look good.

There is no immediate need to buy any special clothing. Whatever you wear for other outdoor activities is fine for everyday bike use, but a waterproof jacket and pants for heavy rain are worthwhile purchases if you have no alternative but to ride in the wet.

Reflective belts, vests, and tape that you can stick to your clothing all help increase your visibility at night. If you ride in traffic after dark, you can also buy small LED (light-emitting diode) lights that fit to the backs of your hands, thereby making your hand signals clearer to the road users behind you.

Basic equipment

The basic kit that you should always carry with you includes a spare inner tube, three tire levers, a puncture repair kit, and at least one multi-tool. You will also need a mini-pump. A cycling computer, though not essential, is a useful addition.

Puncture repair kit
The essential elements of a repair kit are adhesive, sandpaper, a piece of chalk, a crayon, and patches.

Inner tube

Tire levers

Mini-pump
A mini-pump will easily fit inside a cycling backpack.

Helmet

A good helmet is an essential item, regardless of the type of cycling you intend to do. Helmets absorb the energy of an impact by crushing and breaking up. Consequently, if your helmet suffers a knock, it will no longer protect you, and you must replace it.

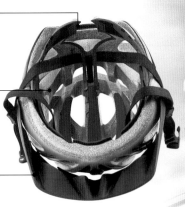

Helmet modeling
The helmet's aerodynamic design reduces wind resistance.

Ventilation slots
Strategically placed ventilation slots divert air over your scalp to keep you cool.

Side view

Retention strap
The strap's length can be altered to achieve a snug fit.

Internal padding
Extra padding is supplied with new helmets to ensure a good fit.

Peak
The detachable peak helps keep the sun and rain out of your eyes.

Inside view

Helmet position
Your helmet should sit straight and level.

Retention strap
This strap secures the helmet on the back of your head.

Chin strap
The chin strap and the behind-the-ear strap adjust for a level fit, preventing the helmet from moving.

▲ **Wearing a helmet**
Wear a helmet according to the manufacturer's instructions. It should be level on your head when standing upright, and tight enough so that it does not move while you are riding.

Backpack
Use a lightweight cycling backpack to carry all you need.

Shoulder strap
The shoulder strap should adjust to a comfortable fit.

Drinking system
This allows you to drink without letting go of the handlebar.

Main pouch
This pocket may be used to keep items away from damp clothes.

Cycle computer
Use this to record your speed and distance.

Wrench multi-tool
This useful tool contains wrenches of several sizes.

Allen wrench multi-tool
This is ideal for undoing Allen bolts of various sizes.

Bicycle attachments

Mudguards are often overlooked, but installing them will help prevent your legs from getting soaked by the spray from wet roads. A pannier rack is essential if you want to try any kind of touring. Since you should always carry a drink with you, a bottle cage is useful.

Mudguard
Avoid being sprayed by water and mud by adding mudguards.

Pannier rack
Panniers allow you to carry luggage on the bike.

Bottle cage
This is used for carrying a water bottle.

Water bottle
A cycling water bottle is an important extra.

Locks and security

A bike lock is essential for any cyclist who occasionally has to leave a bike in a public place. There are many locks on the market but, whatever you buy, make sure it is of good quality and big enough to lock the bike and front wheel to a solid, permanent street fixture. Look for bike racks, lampposts, or solid metal rails.

Cable lock
The flexibility of a cable lock means it can easily secure a bike to odd-shaped objects.

U-lock
Although less adaptable than a cable lock, a U-lock is ideal for securing a bike to solid posts or railings.

▶ **Securing your bike**
When locking your bike, first take out your front wheel. Pass the lock through it and then through the back wheel and the frame. Secure all three parts to your chosen street fixture.

Staying visible on the road

When riding in the dark or in reduced visibility, you must always have a constant white light at the front of your bike and a red reflector at the rear, and your pedals should also have reflectors. Be sure to check whether your area has other requirements or restrictions. For extra safety, consider adding flashing LED lights to your bike and your clothing.

Front light
A white front light is required by law when riding at times of low visibility.

Reflective clip
These are useful extra reflectors that you can wear around your ankles and even your arms if you wish.

Rear light
Ensure that your rear light is red. You must also have a red reflector fitted to the back of your bike.

See also
Clothing for road riding **pp.26–27**   Clothing for off-road riding **pp.28–29**   Repairing a puncture **pp.208–09**

Clothing for road riding

Cycling clothing keeps you warm in the winter and cool in the summer, but some materials also transport perspiration away from the skin—a process called "wicking"—and others repel moisture, block out wind, and allow perspiration to escape.

The two principles to consider when dressing for cycling are protection and comfort. You must protect your points of contact with the bike with padded shorts, gloves, and supportive shoes. For comfort, dress for the weather and use the layering principle.

Layering involves starting with a base item of clothing made from a material with good wicking qualities, and then adding several thin layers on top; these will trap warm air between them. Finally, put on a top layer that is warm or waterproof, depending on the weather.

◀ **Announcing your presence**
When riding in poor visibility or at night, make sure you have reflective strips on your clothing, shoes, and any bags you are carrying. Nothing announces the presence of a cyclist more clearly than reflective strips when they are caught in the headlights of a motor vehicle.

Winter clothing

When dressing for a cold day in winter, wear bib tights over a base layer. Put a waterproof and windproof, but breathable, outer layer over a long-sleeved mid-layer. Wear thermal cycling gloves and neoprene overshoes that cover the cycling shoes for extra protection.

Top layer
A breathable, waterproof top helps keep out the rain and wind.

Gloves
Thermal gloves keep your fingers warm. Buy gloves with long cuffs.

Bib tights
Covering the legs and abdomen, bib tights protect your legs and lower back from the cold.

Headband
A thermal headband fits under your helmet to protect your ears from the cold.

Overshoes
Thermal overshoes fit over your riding shoes to keep your feet warm in cold weather.

Winter clothing items

Base layer
A thick, wicking base layer is essential for warmth in the winter months.

Top layer
A long-sleeved cycling shirt can be used as a mid-layer on colder days, when a waterproof, windproof top layer is added.

Legwear
Bib tights are available in various thicknesses. Leg warmers can be worn on cool days.

Additional top layers
Wear a warm vest in the cold, or a breathable waterproof jacket in the rain.

Extras
Gloves, overshoes, and thermal socks and headbands are useful when it is cold. Use eyewear with low-light lenses on dull days.

Summer clothing

When dressing for summer, the main elements are Lycra shorts, a wicking vest, and a cycling shirt made from a light material with good ventilation. Padded, fingerless track mitts increase grip and protect the hands. Cycling shoes, a helmet, and sunglasses complete the outfit.

Helmet
A helmet is essential no matter how warm the weather. Buy one with maximum ventilation for cycling in a warm climate.

Sunglasses
Eyewear is recommended in summer and winter. Buy glasses with interchangeable lenses for different light conditions. Prescription sports eyewear is available.

Mitts
Track mitts help you grip the handlebar. Their cushioning increases comfort, and they protect your hands from injury in the event of a fall.

Summer clothing items

Base layer
A lightweight, wicking undervest keeps you dry, and reduces abrasions in an accident.

Top layer
A short-sleeved racing top with rear pockets and wicking properties is an ideal top layer.

Legwear
Wear Lycra bib shorts with a padded seat for comfort. Baggier cycling shorts are also fine if you prefer them.

Socks
Cotton or wicking short socks are perfect for summer. Avoid riding without socks, which can be uncomfortable.

Shoes
Wear cycling shoes. Race shoes have stiff, supportive soles for efficient pedaling.

Extras
Track mitts are essential to protect your hands. Eyewear is recommended.

Summer top
A short-sleeved top will help keep you cool. Wear a wicking vest underneath.

Shorts
Lycra bib shorts are ideal for road cycling. The bib protects your lower back from the cold and sunburn.

Socks
There is no cushioning inside racing shoes, so cotton or wicking socks help keep your feet comfortable.

Footwear
Cycling shoes have stiff soles to ensure that all your energy goes into pedaling.

See also
Clothing for off-road riding pp.28–29

Clothing for off-road riding

Ideal off-road riding clothes in summer are similar to those used on the road—apart from shoes and gloves, the clothes are interchangeable. As on the road, you need comfort and protection, and you should follow the principles of layering.

Differences in clothing become more apparent in the winter, or when you are riding in the mountains. The clothing you need in these situations is a little heavier than garments that perform a similar task on the road. Extreme conditions can be encountered at high altitudes, especially in winter. Mountain weather can change quickly, and even

in summer you should take a survival pack of extra clothing with you on any high-altitude ride. A waterproof top and pants, a mid-layer fleece, and a hat that fits under your helmet will fit in a light backpack. You should also pack food, water, a map, a compass, a whistle, and a first-aid kit.

Off-road shoes should have a good tread on their soles and heels. Consider buying a warm pair for the winter, because overshoes do not generally stretch over them. Summer off-road riding gloves have fingers to improve grip and help protect your knuckles.

Winter clothing

Wear a waterproof and windproof top in the winter, as well as bib tights and thermal gloves. You should also buy some protective eyewear—winter light can be hard on the eyes.

Winter top
An off-road winter top is the first line of defense against the cold, the wind, and the wet.

Legwear
Bib tights help keep both your legs and your body warm.

Eyewear
Clear or light-enhancing eyewear protects the eyes on dull winter days.

Gloves
Thermal gloves with long cuffs will keep your hands and wrists warm.

Footwear
Winter boots or shoes are best in cold conditions.

Winter clothing items

Base layer
This should be reasonably substantial, but retaining effective wicking properties.

Mid-layer
Wear a close-fitting, long-sleeved layer. Off-road riders tend to wear fleeces.

Top layer
The top layer should be windproof, waterproof, and breathable. It is often heavier than those used on the road.

Legwear
Bib tights are the best legwear for winter off-road riding. The bib covers the abdomen and helps keep the body warm.

Gloves
Thermal gloves protect the hands, and should also fully cover the wrists.

Extras
Wear a hat under the helmet. Thermal socks are also a good idea in cold weather.

Summer clothing

Off-road clothing for summer wear varies very little from that used on-road. One of the big differences is that mountain bikers prefer looser shorts. If you choose a looser fit, make sure the shorts are suitable for cycling and that they have a padded seat. Ensure they are cut high at the back of the waist, and that they do not ride up your thigh as you pedal.

Helmet
Always wear a helmet when cycling off-road. Helmets sometimes have peaks that act as visors.

Off-road shorts
Often baggy, off-road shorts usually have several pockets. Some people find road shorts equally comfortable.

Eyewear
To protect your eyes, buy glasses that are specific to cycling and will not fog up.

Top
A short-sleeved top over a base layer is ideal. A looser fit allows cyclists to stay cooler when riding.

Gloves
Off-road cycling requires gloves that have fingers to protect the knuckles.

Socks
Ankle socks in a light material help keep feet cool and comfortable.

Shoes
In the summer, wear well-ventilated off-road cycling shoes.

Summer clothing items

Base layer
A lightweight layer with good wicking properties is essential next to your skin.

Top layer
An ideal top layer is a close- or loose-fitting short-sleeved shirt with rear pockets.

Legwear
Wear cycling shorts. Lycra shorts are fine, though looser-fitting designs often have extra pockets with the security of a zipper.

Socks
Light ankle socks ensure foot comfort.

Gloves
Off-road cycling gloves improve grip and offer protection for the hands.

Extras
Sports eyewear protects the eyes from the sun, grit, and insects. Well-ventilated off-road summer shoes allow your feet to breathe.

Road proficiency skills

They say you never forget how to ride a bike. However, if you last rode one some time ago, a lot may have changed. In many areas, for example, there is more traffic than there was just five years ago, giving cyclists a lot to think about on the roads.

Learning to cycle safely

Training is essential for children before they take to the road, and most larger communities have well-established cycling proficiency programs for them. There are also many adult training programs set up specifically to help people who are new or returning to cycling. Find out from your local government or a national cycling group if there is a suitable program in your area. Being able to practice in a quiet spot without wobbling into the path of another road user will give you much more confidence when it comes to the real thing.

Learn how your bicycle works and how to control it at slow speeds. A lot of urban cycling involves precise riding at slow speeds, when you do not have the bike's momentum to help you balance. Try setting off once or twice, then stopping and putting your foot down. Doing slow left and right turns

▼ **Training safely**
Children should ideally only be allowed to ride in traffic after first attending a cycle-training program. At the very least, make sure they get some practice in a vehicle-free environment.

is another good idea, as is staying in a straight line while looking behind you left and right. Again, do this slowly. Once you feel comfortable, you are nearly ready to go on the roads.

Before you start using roads, however, make sure that you know the traffic laws and can recognize road signs. Ignorance is never a defense in the eyes of the law, and understanding what you can and cannot do while riding your bike could prevent conflict with other road users.

Riding in wet conditions

Road hazards become more dangerous, and numerous, in the rain—for example, painted lines can become slippery when wet. Be careful when riding in urban areas in the first rain after a dry spell. Diesel and oil spillages tend to build up in dry weather, and when made wet by the first rain, they create a dangerous, extremely slippery surface.

Practical riding tips

- Hold your handlebar firmly, but not too tightly.
- Keep your shoulders relaxed and use them to make small corrections in your balance.
- Keep your outside pedal closest to the ground when you turn.
- In a series of tight turns, prevent the inside pedal from hitting the ground by backpedaling if necessary.

In the wet, brake before you normally would, because you need to clear the water from your rims before the brakes can take effect. Do not rush—you will not end up any drier. Make sure that your waterproof clothing does not cover your lights when you ride at night. And never use a hood to keep your head dry unless it fits snugly under your helmet—it may restrict your field of vision. Let a little air out of the tires to improve the bike's handling in very wet conditions.

Dealing with hazardous road surfaces

Look ahead for utility covers, sewer grates, reflective lane markers, and potholes. Do not ride over them, but do not swerve toward another vehicle to avoid them. If they are unavoidable, do not tense up or brake suddenly, but keep moving in a straight line.

Avoid riding over the joints between the slabs of concrete roads if they have crumbled at the edges. These create dangerous cracks for a cyclist. Railroad crossings present a similar problem.

Be careful when cornering or descending on cobblestones—it is easy to lose control. If you regularly ride on cobbles, you may need to check more often that nothing has come loose on your bike.

Always ride up a low curb at a right angle to it. As the front wheel reaches the curb, pull the handlebar up slightly to take the weight from the front wheel. Practice away from traffic first. Dismount and lift the bike if the curb is too high.

Responding to fog, ice, and snow

Fog and ice are bad news for cyclists. Fog is unsafe and uncomfortable to ride in; ice is just plain dangerous, so do not even try to ride on it.

Cycling in new snow is reasonably safe if there is no other form of transportation available. However, snow is dangerous to ride on once it has been packed down by other vehicles or after it has frozen. Avoid it completely on the roads. Off-road, though—in the country, for example—snow can be a lot of fun to ride on.

▼ **Taking care in the wet**
When riding in wet conditions, remember to brake sooner than you normally would. Be aware, too, that roads will be more slippery than usual, reducing the ability of the tires to hold the road.

◀ **Using country roads**
The quiet countryside is better than an urban environment for learning to ride, but even country roads may be busy at times, so be careful.

See also
Road riding: cycling in traffic flows **pp.102–03** Making maneuvers **pp.104–05** Cycling with care **pp.106–07**

Sharing roads and trails

Although the majority of people are perfectly tolerant of cyclists, you may experience animosity from other road and trail users. Some drivers, for example, feel annoyed at having to share the road with cyclists because bikes move more slowly than cars. Some walkers may feel threatened by bicycles suddenly zooming past them, especially since they are not warned of their approach by the sound of an engine.

Such animosity exists, but you need not add to it. Although you may experience drivers sounding their horns and even cutting across your path now and then, bear in mind that such drivers are in the minority. Most motorists do not resent your presence on the road; some, especially those who cycle, are particularly conscious of bicycles.

Tolerating all road users

Tolerance can sometimes seem difficult in urban centers, when pedestrians step into the road without looking, for example, or children cross the road between parked cars. Treat pedestrians as you would any other road user—be aware of them and try to predict their actions.

Tips for road hazards

- Scan the sidewalks for children or inattentive adults—they often walk out into the road without looking. With a little experience, you can tell who is likely to step out in front of you.
- Slow down around schools.
- Be alert around factories and bars, especially at their respective opening and closing times.
- Try to anticipate the actions of animals, but expect the unexpected. Cats sometimes bolt between the wheels of a bike, while dogs seem especially eager to chase or race cyclists.
- Be aware that some car drivers will open their door to exit the vehicle without first checking behind them.

Outside of town, you will also have to share off-road trails with many other users, some of whom may cause you difficulties. You should also be aware of livestock, pets, and wildlife.

Steer clear of areas designated for off-road motor vehicles. Motocross and ATV riders, for example, have even more restrictions placed on

▼ **Encountering livestock**
Sheep are easily frightened, perhaps more so than any other livestock, so try to give them as wide a berth as possible. You may have to consider dismounting.

them than cyclists do, so they are likely to become defensive over their off road areas. Respecting their space will help avoid unnecessary conflict.

Do not ride where you are not permitted to ride; if in doubt, check. You may only be allowed to ride off-road on trails and in other specially designated areas, for example. There are plenty of places where cyclists are welcome.

Observing country courtesies

In the country, use common sense when dealing with people and property. Stick to roads or marked trails, and do not trespass on private land. Close any gates behind you. If there is a temporary restriction against using bikes in an area to which you normally have access, observe it. Also, try not to skid your back wheel when riding on a public bike trail, since this erodes the surface—go to an off-road circuit where skidding is allowed.

Riding in rural areas has its own hazards. Although narrow country roads may not have much traffic, what traffic there is can be difficult to avoid. Keep your ears and eyes open. If you hear something coming on a very narrow road, slow down until the other vehicle has gone by. It pays to be particularly careful in agricultural areas because there may be a slow-moving farm tractor just around the next corner.

Tips for off-road hazards

- Stop riding if you see a dog off its leash, and wait until its owner has it under control. If the dog is aggressive, stand still and shout a stern "No!" Put your bike between you and the dog; your tires will probably prove far more interesting than you.

- Always slow down when you see a horse approaching. Conversely, if you catch up with a horse, politely announce your presence to the rider before the horse sees you. This way the rider can be ready to take control of the horse. Approach very slowly.

- Slow down when approaching walkers from behind and announce your presence. If the trail is narrow, stop when you cross paths.

- Ride as far around livestock as you can. Sheep scare easily, bulls may be aggressive, and cows can be unpredictable if they have just calved. Any animal can knock you off your bike.

Avoiding heavy traffic

Finally, ride on main roads with heavy traffic only if there is no alternative. Although cyclists have every right to be on such roads, there are some that are simply far too dangerous for a bicycle. Nor are they any fun. It is safer and more enjoyable to add a little time to your journey and ride on less-traveled roads instead.

Of course, the amount of traffic on a particular road can change dramatically, depending on the time of day. Get to know your area, and avoid roads with schools and factories on them, especially at the start and end of their respective days.

▲ Riding in heavy traffic
Riding a bicycle in a busy downtown area can be dangerous. However, if such an area is an essential part of your journey, be sure to make yourself clearly visible to all other road users and pedestrians.

▲ Cycling in the country
When riding off-road, always get the landowner's permission before you enter private property, and be sure to close any gates behind you.

See also
Road riding: cycling in traffic flows pp.102–03 Making maneuvers pp.104–05 Cycling with care pp.106–07

Teaching a child to ride

Balancing on a bike and pedaling is a lot to ask a child to learn all at once. The method illustrated in these pages depends on your child first learning how to pedal, ideally from an early age.

Starting children early

The best time to teach your child to ride is usually between the ages of four and five. However, before they have their own bike, teach them how to pedal on a tricycle. There are many models on the market—even toy trikes with the pedals attached to the front wheel are fine for beginners.

When the child moves up to a bicycle, note that children's bikes are generally measured by wheel size and come in 12, 16, 18, 20, and 24 inches. See pages 22–23 for guidelines on what size to buy.

Cycling for pleasure

Cycling is a perfect form of exercise for children. It develops their cardiovascular systems without placing too much strain on their growing bones. But it can be difficult to get them interested, especially if they would rather watch television or play computer games.

Consider allowing your child to try sports cycling; some disciplines offer racing for age ten and under. Around the world, schools are discovering that cycling is more likely than other sports to capture a child's imagination.

Teaching and encouraging your child to ride will lead him or her to an understanding of the joy of simple things such as physical effort, and also to a developing appreciation of the environment.

◄ Using training wheels
Children too old for a trike but not yet old enough for their own bicycle can learn to pedal on a bike equipped with training wheels. However, as soon as a child can pedal, remove the training wheels. If you do not, he or she will get used to them and simply lean the bike on them, instead of learning how to balance the bike.

Learning to balance

① **Begin teaching your child to ride** in a park; this is an ideal environment. Choose a quiet, flat path. Remove the bike pedals. Ensure that your child is able to touch the ground with the front part of his or her feet. Before any movement of the bike is considered, first teach your child how the bike's brakes work.

② **Tell your child to scoot** the bike along by using his or her feet. Once he or she has started moving along like this, allow him or her some time to get used to it before moving on to the next step. Let your child practice this type of movement on a flat path first.

③ Find a slight downhill stretch of path once your child is more confident. The slope will help your child to take longer and longer between scoots, and therefore glide more. Once he or she is gliding for long stretches of path, your child has learned to balance.

④ Put the pedals back on. If your child has already learned the principles of pedaling—on a previous occasion using a trike or a bike with training wheels—he or she will now try to pedal and balance at the same time, although tentatively at first.

⑤ Remind your child how to use the bike's brakes. Before long, he or she will be picking up speed and riding as though it is second nature. There will come a point, though, when slowing down is necessary, too.

Child safety tips

- Make sure your child always wears a helmet.
- Buy knee and elbow pads for your child, and insist that he or she uses them on each and every bike ride.
- Buy gloves to protect your child's hands, or mini track mitts if they fit better.
- Make sure that your child can start and stop safely, does not wobble at all, and fully understands the rules of the road.
- Remind your child to focus on what he or she is doing and not play or look around— a child's concentration is easily broken. Cycling should be fun, though, so take frequent breaks between attempts.

See also
Buying a bike **pp.22–23** Maintaining pedals **pp.216–17**

Family cycling

Cycling can bring parents and children—and indeed, a couple—closer together, allowing them to develop a bond based on fitness, an appreciation of nature, and on-the-road experiences.

Preparing the bikes

A child as young as 12 months can sit strapped in a child seat attached to either the back of your bike or its top tube. The latter model is ideal for communication—you can point out things along the way, and the child can look straight ahead. Regardless of which seat you choose, always make sure that the child is strapped in securely.

Trailers are useful for toddlers who are too big for child seats. Pick one with a roll bar. For children who are too old for trailers but too young for their own bikes, there are trailer bikes that attach to the back of your bike, allowing the child to pedal, too. When attaching child seats, trailers, and trailer bikes to your own bike, always follow the manufacturer's instructions to the letter.

Children in seats or trailers should wear helmets that cover their ears, affording more protection to the back of the head. For children on trailer bikes, buy helmets that leave the ears uncovered, so that they can hear and follow your instructions.

Planning your journey

When riding their own bikes, children can usually cycle as far as they want. If they are eager and are used to cycling, children can cover fairly long distances with no ill effects. Many five-year-olds can easily cycle 10 miles (16 km) or more on

Family safety tips

- Only venture onto roads when you are sure your child is ready.
- Keep your child on the inside when other users are on the cycle path.
- On cycle trails and paths, keep to the right and do not wander into the path of oncoming cyclists.
- Do not let your group split up.
- Ride at the pace of the slowest person.
- Watch your child for signs of tiredness.
- Make sure your child eats and drinks regularly.

▲ **Cycling with children**
It is fun to plan cycling trips with your children, suggesting interesting places they might want to see.

a flat route. Always watch them for signs of tiredness, and remember that you might also have to make a return trip. Apart from this, let children cycle as much as they want. Keep an eye on the weather, since children get cold very quickly and dehydrate in warm weather quicker than adults do. Be sure to take extra clothes (including waterproof items), high-energy foods, and plenty of water on your trips together.

Choosing suitable routes

The best places to ride with children are designated cycling trails. In North America, parts of the TransCanada trail are ideal for families, and many US cities are starting to encourage parents and children to ride together. In Europe, many rivers and canals have cycle paths beside them. In Great Britain, many old railroad tracks have been surfaced and provide perfect trails for family cycling. Some countries have networks of lightly traveled roads that are ideal for family trips when the children are older. The British Byways route is a perfect example of these, since it specifically links interesting historical sites.

Protecting your bike

When transporting your bike over long distances by train or airplane, make sure you protect it adequately. You do not want to find that it is damaged when you reach your destination.

Padded bike bags and bike boxes are like large suitcases and will afford total protection to your bike. A cheaper alternative is to ask your bike shop if you can have one of the boxes in which bikes are delivered.

If boxing your bike, you will have to take it apart and pad it with bubble-wrap. For extra security, tie-wrap wheels and other parts to the frame.

Transporting your cycles

Unless you live on a family-friendly trail, you will have to think about transporting your bikes to wherever you will be cycling. There is a huge selection of car bike racks to facilitate this. Trunk racks are very popular, but make sure your bikes do not obscure any of your car's rear lights, including turn signals, or your license plate. If they do, you will have to buy a plate-and-light kit and attach it to your bikes.

Roof racks present no such problems. However, some strength is required to lift bikes onto them. Buy one that holds the bike upside down by the down tube, rather than right side up by the forks. The latter can damage a bike's headset. Remove anything that is not bolted to your bikes before putting them on your car.

▲ **Using child seats**
Children as young as 12 months can sit on a specially designed child seat. Make sure the child's weight does not exceed the manufacturer's recommendations.

▲ **Riding trailer bikes**
The most sophisticated trailer bikes have gears, allowing the child to learn the relationship between gearing and pedaling even before he or she has learned to ride.

See also
Buying a bike pp.22–23 Basic touring pp.38–39 Improving your fitness pp.142–43

Basic touring

Cycling is one of the best ways to experience the world. It is quicker than walking, yet—unlike driving a motor vehicle—it will not cause pollution or trail damage to the environment through which you travel.

Preparing for the ride

Apart from a bike, panniers are the first things that any road—or independent-minded off-road—cycle tourist needs. They come in many shapes and sizes, but regardless of which type of pannier you choose, always remember to split your load between the front and rear of the bike, so as not to affect the bike's handling to any great extent. Fully loaded panniers create a lot of stress on the frame or forks where they join, so add these points to your regular frame checks.

A handlebar bag is essential when touring. This will give you easy access to the items you need throughout the day, such as money, a map, and

Balancing your panniers

When you are packing pannier bags, put heavy items in the bottom of each one, then lighter ones above them, and the lightest on top. A bike is always more stable if you can lower its center of gravity.

Rear panniers
Held high on the bike, rear panniers are clear of the transmission and close to the bike's center of gravity, where they do not interfere with balance.

Front panniers
The effect of front panniers on the bike's handling is minimal, since they are held low down on the bike, near the center of the wheel.

a cell phone. A handlebar bag should have a clear plastic map sleeve on it, so you do not have to keep stopping to unfold your map.

Some tourists who believe in traveling in style carry their luggage in a trailer. This has the advantage that you can unhitch it, set everything up, and leave it at a campsite (provided there is supervision), enabling you to go riding unloaded.

Tours can also be made with a cycling backpack (*see* pp.24–25) big enough to hold a lightweight tent, cooking equipment, food, and spare clothes. The equipment needed for a day tour should also fit in your pack. Some packs benefit from the addition of a bladder drinking system, which has a tube clipped to the pack's straps. Remember to bring water-purifying tablets if you have any doubts about the safety of the local water. An under-the-saddle bag is ideal for tools and spare parts.

All cycling clothing is suitable for touring, as is some outdoor clothing. Make sure all your tops cover your lower back to protect it from the weather.

Setting up camp

There are many practical guides to camping, but it is possible to tour with just a few basics. You need a tent that is just big enough for you (and, if necessary, your partner). It needs to be waterproof and breathable. A head lantern is invaluable for moving around your tent and campsite when darkness falls. Lightweight sleeping bags are available, and you will need a roll-up ground mat on which to put it; this will insulate you from the ground. Lightweight cooking equipment can be found in camping stores. These stores also sell other useful extras: dehydrated foods, multi-tools, canteens, water-purifying tablets, and bungee cords—used for strapping objects together to ensure they do not move around in the panniers.

◀ **Avoiding flooding**
When choosing a place to set up your tent for the night, always be sure to pick a spot on high ground. A heavy downpour of rain can turn any low-lying area into a river. Sudden floods are a particular hazard in mountainous regions.

First-aid essentials

A first-aid pack is required on any tour. Medical professionals, embassies, and tour operators offer advice about special items for particular countries, but this list covers the essentials needed wherever you go.

- Band-aids
- Cloth bandages
- Surgical tape
- Scissors
- Antiseptic wipes
- Painkillers

If possible, it is a good idea to carry some sort of emergency food. If your stove breaks down or you cannot find enough water to cook, you will then have something to keep you going. Also, be sure to keep your matches dry in two plastic bags, and take a cigarette lighter as a backup.

Protecting your health

Eat fresh fruit and vegetables whenever you can, but if you are in a developing country, only eat uncooked foods if they have removable skins. Peel off the skin, then wash your hands and eat. Take a multivitamin each day to make sure you obtain all your nutrients. Try to drink only bottled water; if that is not possible, purify the water first.

Using a map and compass

Navigation depends on your ability to transfer the information on a map to the landscape around you. When road touring, note the first landmark you should pass on your chosen road; if you do not see it when you should, go back and try again. For off-road riding, learn to use a compass with a map, so that you always know which way you are going. To do this, set the map as follows:

Map and compass

1. Turn the compass housing until north corresponds to the direction-of-travel arrow on your compass.

2. Place the compass on the map so that the direction-of-travel arrow is over a north–south grid line (a line of longitude).

3. Turn the map, with the compass still on it, until the red end of the needle aligns with north on the compass dial. The map is now set.

If you need to travel west, for instance, look at west on the compass and note any feature on the map that is in line with west. Locate the feature in the landscape and travel toward it. It must be constantly visible, so try to pick something on top of a hill.

See also
Clothing for road riding **pp.26–27** Clothing for off-road riding **pp.28–29** Making routine safety checks **pp.184–85**

Road touring

A road cycle tour can be whatever you want it to be: a day in a local beauty spot, a week in a different part of the country, or a round-the-world trip. Whether using a prescribed route or going where the inclination takes them, many cyclists simply want to see more of the world they live in.

Touring for one day

The simplest form of touring is the day ride. All you need is a good map of the area, some food, a few tools, perhaps a camera, and some money. Plan with the map beforehand, but do not be afraid to change course if another road looks more interesting. Try to keep to less-traveled roads.

Stay in a low gear, ride within your limits, and eat and drink regularly. Take wet-weather gear, and be careful in the sun. Wear a shirt, even on the hottest day, or your back will quickly burn. Use sunscreen, particularly on the back of your neck and ears, and always wear a helmet.

Making a multi-day tour

A popular choice among cyclists, and an excellent introduction to more self-sufficient touring, is the supported multi-day tour, which you can do either

▼ Loading panniers
Using front and back panniers when touring will leave you unencumbered by extra bags and backpacks. If the weight is correctly distributed, the load will not adversely affect the bike's handling.

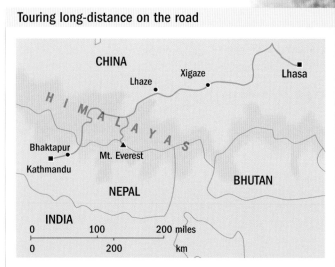

Touring long-distance on the road

CHINA

Xigaze — Lhasa
Lhaze

H I M A L A Y A S

Bhaktapur
Kathmandu — Mt. Everest

NEPAL — BHUTAN

INDIA

0   100   200 miles
0   200   km

This route, along the Friendship Highway across the Tibetan Plateau, is an extreme challenge, and one best undertaken with a tour company unless you have a lot of high-altitude experience. Most of the route is nearly 13,000 ft (4,000 m) high, with the option to visit Everest Base Camp at 18,000 ft (5,500 m) and view Everest's North Face. Extreme temperature changes can occur. May and June are noted for strong winds, and Tibet receives half of its annual rainfall in July and August.

from a base or traveling from place to place. One option is to stay in a central location and tour the region, either with a tour guide or on your own. Alternatively, the company gives you an itinerary, makes hotel reservations, and carries your luggage while you cycle between stops. Either way, you only need to carry the few items you would take on a day tour. The tour operator takes care of everything else, transporting your extra clothes, providing laundry facilities, and issuing city guidebooks, for example.

Touring independently

More self-sufficient cyclists will probably want to arrange the whole trip themselves, and this is where you find the true freedom of touring. Such a tour, especially to a foreign country, requires a lot of planning. Try to buy the maps commonly used in that country before you leave—Cartes Michelin in France, for example—and use these for your planning.

A self-sufficient tour means that you will have to carry all you need with you. Backpacks are ideal for off-road tours, but for road tours, let the bike do the carrying whenever possible. Panniers are the ideal bike-borne luggage system.

▼ Carrying luggage
When on a self-sufficient, long-term road tour, you will have to carry all your necessities with you. Use bike panniers rather than a large backpack and let the bike take most of the weight.

Road-touring essentials

Day touring
The following list contains the bare essentials that you should take with you on any cycling day-trip.

- Basic tool kit
- Spare tube
- Tire levers
- Spare shirt if you plan a stop
- Map
- Saddlebag, or handlebar bag with clear map sleeve on top
- First-aid kit
- Cell phone

Multi-day touring
For a road tour that is scheduled to last several days, you will need to take more items with you—clothes to change into, for example. Here is a guide to some of the most important things you should carry.

- Complete set of both cycling and casual clothes
- Basic tool kit
- Spare tire and several tubes
- Tire levers
- Maps
- Spare spokes
- Spare gear and brake cables
- Link extractor tool
- First-aid kit
- Painkillers and antacid tablets
- Cell phone

Cross-continent tours need serious planning, as well as visas and perhaps vaccinations. The embassies of the countries you plan to visit will help. Read extensively about where you are going so that you can assess potential problems and dangers. Do not forget to take out adequate insurance.

▼ Traveling in foreign countries
One of the most obvious reasons for a tour in a foreign country is to experience cultures and landscapes different from your own. Be sure to take time to stop and absorb your surroundings.

See also
Basic touring **pp.38–39** Off-road touring **pp.42–43**

Off-road touring

Off-road touring offers cyclists the chance to get away from what is, in most cases, their usual riding environment. A good start to off-road riding can be made by exploring the prepared tracks of a mountain-bike center. These are ideal for families and for newcomers to off-road cycling. There is no need to carry much, since many centers have catering facilities and sometimes even a bike shop. You can spend time honing your skills, or trying new things, such as downhill sections.

As with road touring, day trips can be planned and made either alone or with friends. All that you need is a good map showing trails, and a solid understanding of legal rights of way and access, which define where you can ride. Several cycling associations sell good maps of specific on- and off-road routes. National park authorities and tourist offices are good sources of information, as is the Internet (*see* pp.228–31).

Selecting where to go

Many companies specialize in supported off-road multi-day tours, and they will take you across deserts and to remote regions. Some charities run supported bike tours, both on- and off-road, in places such as Vietnam, China, and South America; new destinations are added each year. These tours are useful introductions to do-it-yourself multi-day touring. Many of the tours include camping. The experienced guides will give you useful tips, and you can find out whether you like living, eating, and sleeping in the great outdoors.

Investigate your chosen tour company to see if it or its guides are members of professional bodies. Take out good insurance, and make sure the tour meets the criteria of your insurer.

Carrying your equipment

When touring off-road, you need to consider how to carry your equipment. Using panniers in rough country may result in having to push your bike as much as you ride it. You might be tempted to carry all you need for a multi-day tour in a large backpack. However, this will raise your center of gravity, affecting the handling of your bike and placing strain on your back. Consider wearing properly designed walking boots, not cycling shoes. Switch to flat pedals (*see* pp.216–17), such as the ones downhill mountain bikers use—these will make it easier to put your feet down and keep your balance.

▼ Avoiding dehydration
Make sure you carry sufficient amounts of liquid with you to keep hydrated. This is even more important when touring off-road, where it may be difficult to find refreshments.

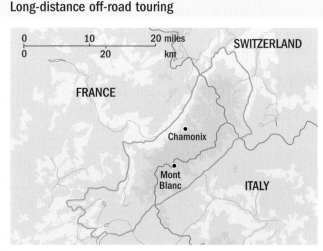

Long-distance off-road touring

SWITZERLAND

FRANCE

Chamonix

Mont Blanc

ITALY

This Alpine route is a circumnavigation of Mont Blanc, the highest mountain in France, using high mountain off-road tracks. The route is around 125 miles (200 km) long and will take you through three countries; to complete it, you must cross three 6,500-ft (2,000-m) mountain passes. The town of Chamonix is a good base. Anybody who is not very experienced in this sort of terrain would be better off riding this route as part of a supported tour.

Off-road-touring essentials

When touring off-road, your essentials should be the same as for road touring (see p.41), but with the addition of the following items:

- Waterproof top
- Waterproof pants
- Survival bag
- Whistle (to attract attention in case of difficulty)
- Compass
- Food and water
- Warm hat and gloves

One solution to the problem of carrying equipment is to set up bases in campgrounds or hotels, making short trips from each base. Doing so will leave you free to use a cycling backpack and carry the bare minimum, following the example of endurance and adventure racers. Cycling magazines list the lightest equipment you can buy.

Lightweight off-road tours can be undertaken in places such as Les Gets, France for the Alps, Andorra for the Pyrenees, and Perth for some Australian countryside. You could also consider the Pennine Way in England or the Arizona Trail. Wherever you go and however you go about your off-road touring, never overestimate your abilities—or underestimate the weather.

◀ Exploring new places
Legal rights of way and access define where you can ride, but legitimate trails and tracks will take you as far into the countryside as you want.

▼ Preparing well
In mountainous areas, the weather can change suddenly from sunny to stormy. Always carry waterproof coverings for yourself and your equipment.

See also
Basic touring pp.38–39   Road touring pp.40–41   Maintaining pedals pp.216–17

Bike gallery

2

From fitness to commuting, competition to touring, whatever your reason for cycling, there is a bike that will meet your needs. This cross-section of the different types of bikes available highlights the particular features that distinguish them from each other and will help you to make an informed choice about which one to buy.

Anatomy of the road bike

The sport of cycling—and, in particular, professional racing—has changed the road bike from a basic form of transportation into the high-tech blend of space-age materials and technology it is today. Carbon fiber, titanium, and aluminum are now commonplace where steel was once the norm. Aerodynamics and computer design have smoothed off the rough edges to form the graceful curves of today's top-of-the-line frames.

However, a chain still drives the rear wheel, and cables still connect the gears and brakes to their controls. And therein lies the beauty of the road bike: it is still, in essence, the machine it was 100 years ago—a highly efficient means of converting energy into forward motion.

Saddle and seat post

Saddle

Seat clamp

Seat post

Rear caliper brake

Brake arm

Centering screw

Quick-release lever

Rear triangle

Seat collar

Seat tube

Carbon seat stay

Chainstay

Rear dropout

Rear wheel

Chainrings

Small chainring

Large chainring

Chain

Front derailleur

Cogs and rear derailleur

Cassette lockring

Cog

Cog

Rear derailleur

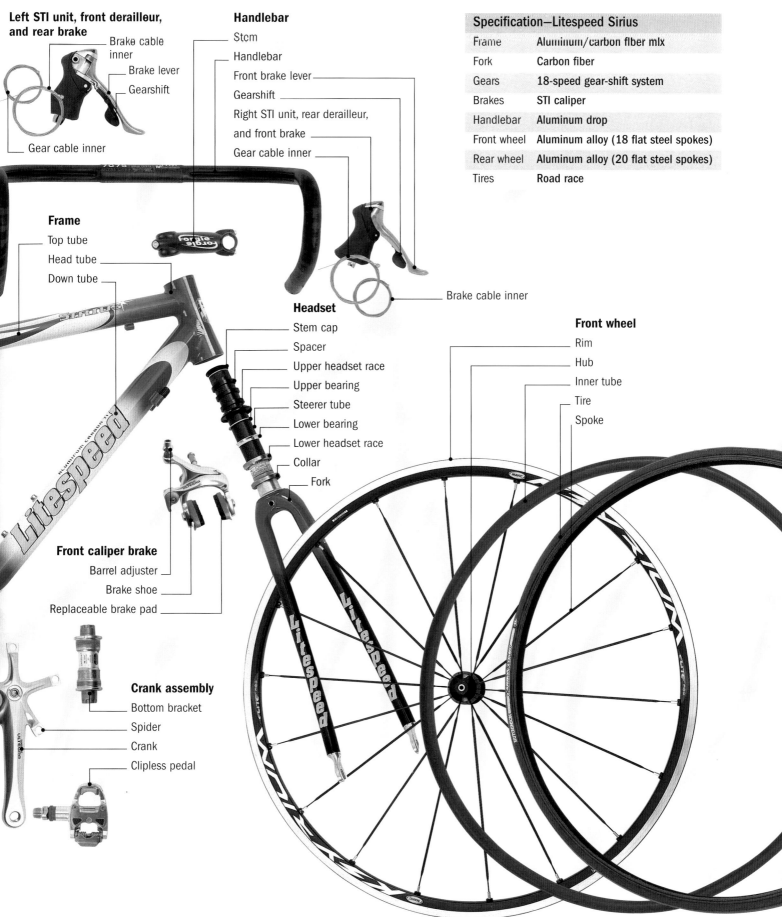

Left STI unit, front derailleur, and rear brake
- Brake cable inner
- Brake lever
- Gearshift
- Gear cable inner

Handlebar
- Stem
- Handlebar
- Front brake lever
- Gearshift
- Right STI unit, rear derailleur, and front brake
- Gear cable inner

Specification—Litespeed Sirius

Frame	Aluminum/carbon fiber mix
Fork	Carbon fiber
Gears	18-speed gear-shift system
Brakes	STI caliper
Handlebar	Aluminum drop
Front wheel	Aluminum alloy (18 flat steel spokes)
Rear wheel	Aluminum alloy (20 flat steel spokes)
Tires	Road race

Frame
- Top tube
- Head tube
- Down tube

Brake cable inner

Headset
- Stem cap
- Spacer
- Upper headset race
- Upper bearing
- Steerer tube
- Lower bearing
- Lower headset race
- Collar
- Fork

Front wheel
- Rim
- Hub
- Inner tube
- Tire
- Spoke

Front caliper brake
- Barrel adjuster
- Brake shoe
- Replaceable brake pad

Crank assembly
- Bottom bracket
- Spider
- Crank
- Clipless pedal

The race-level road bike

Used by professionals in the Tour de France, this bike is also available to anyone who is looking for the ultimate in road-race performance. Every part of the bike is constructed from the lightest material that suits the function it is performing. So, for example, fat tubes of thin-walled aluminum are used to form the main triangle of the frame. These tubes are exceptionally light and stiff, which prevents any energy from being absorbed by the frame and allows it all to go into accelerating the bike. However, the tubes also create a harsh ride, so the fork and seat stays are made from carbon fiber because of its capacity to absorb shock. This provides comfort to the rider and no loss of performance to the bike.

Titanium saddle rails and derailleur parts, and carbon fiber brake levers, are also incorporated to ensure that weight is reduced on the bike wherever possible. Nowhere is this more important than in the wheels—light wheels are easier to accelerate, and fast acceleration is key to successful road racing.

Accelerating away
In a road race, all the riders start together and the first one to finish the course wins. Races are often decided by bursts of speed as the riders try to gain time over each other. These accelerations are helped by a light, rigid bike, which converts all the energy into speed.

Rear view

Seat stay
Carbon-fiber wishbone seat stays are bonded into the aluminum main triangle.

Cogs
Titanium cogs are lighter than steel ones.

Wheel
The wheels have thin-walled rims and a reduced number of spokes, both features lightening the load for the rider.

Specification—Pinarello Prince

Frame	**Aluminum and carbon fiber**
Fork	**Carbon fiber**
Gears	**20-speed integrated system**
Brakes	**Caliper**
Handlebar	**Aluminum drop**
Front wheel	**Spoked (22 spokes)**
Rear wheel	**Spoked (24 spokes)**
tires	**Road race**

Saddle
The minimal but supportive saddle is mounted on light, shock-absorbent titanium rails.

Gearshift
Carbon fiber is used in the gearshift, since it is lighter than metal components.

Front view

Top tube
The top tube's cross-sectional shape, like other tubes on the bike, is not round, but adapted to increase its stiffness.

Saddle rail
Titanium saddle rails flex more than steel, so they add to ride comfort.

Front view

Tire
Race-level bikes often have tubular tires, where the tires are sewn around an inner tube and then stuck on to the rim with glue.

Spindle
The hollow bottom bracket spindle saves weight.

See also
Competing on the road **pp.158–59** Road racing skills **pp.160–61**

The entry-level road bike

The standard of entry-level road bikes improves continually as developments in high-tech racing bikes are incorporated into cheaper consumer models. Better understanding of light and relatively inexpensive materials for frame tubes, together with improved welding techniques, has resulted in light, high-quality, good-value bikes.

The Trek 1000 illustrated here would suit someone wanting a fast, responsive model for fitness cycling and day touring, and would also be suitable for a young racer starting out in the sport. In addition, the triple crankset on this bike makes it suitable for road rides in mountainous regions.

Another application for the entry-level model is as a training bike for anyone who owns a top-end racing machine and wants to keep it specifically for races and special rides. Some expensive bikes can lack durability for heavy everyday use, so a solid workhorse like the entry-level road bike provides a viable training alternative.

Providing a range of opportunities
The entry-level road bike can be used for fitness training or leisure riding in all seasons. The addition of rear pannier mounts to the frame even makes it suitable for light touring. It is an ideal bike for anyone wanting an all-around model to introduce them to road riding.

Saddle
The saddle is contoured to provide extra support.

Cogs
A wide range of gears means that hills can be tackled with ease.

Specification—Trek 1000

Frame	**Aluminum**
Fork	**Aluminum**
Gears	**24-speed integrated system**
Brakes	**Caliper**
Handlebar	**Aluminum drop**
Front wheel	**Spoked (32 spokes)**
Rear wheel	**Spoked (32 spokes)**
Tires	**Racing**

Detail

Crankset
Teeth of a different profile on the chainrings help to pick up the chain during an upshift.

Pedal
The clipless pedal allows a rider to put all his or her energy into the pedal revolution.

Front view

Saddle
The cutaway center of the saddle increases comfort by reducing pressure on the perineum.

Top view

Brakes and gears
Integrated brake/gearshift systems permit a rider to maintain position when braking or changing gear.

Tire
Fatter tires than those found on a racing bike provide a safer ride.

Chainrings
The triple chainrings allow even severe uphill gradients to be undertaken.

See also
Road touring **pp.40–41** Improving your fitness **pp.142–43**

The time-trial bike

Cyclists in a time trial ride alone. To reach the fastest possible speeds, they must present as low and narrow a profile as possible to the air through which they pass. At 21 mph (34 km/h), 80 percent of a rider's force is used to overcome drag. To achieve this, riders crouch as low as they can on the bike and keep their arms in line with their bodies.

A time-trial bike has a special handlebar on which riders can rest their elbows. Riders' arms are then positioned almost in line with the center of their bodies, a little like the stance of a downhill skier.

This position allows the rider to get the front of their body low on the bike, thereby reducing their frontal area still further. Once a time trialist has punched a small a hole through the air, the air that is disturbed has to pass over rider and bike with the minimum of resistance. This is achieved by wearing smooth-seamed clothing and an aerodynamic helmet, and by using aerodynamic components on the bike. The most obvious of these is the lenticular rear disc wheel, which prevents eddies from forming behind the bike and adding a further drag force.

Aero calipers
Small brake calipers are used, since they do not disturb the airflow as much as larger, dual-pivot calipers. However, this results in a drop in brake performance.

Three-quarter view

Emphasizing an aerodynamic profile
In time-trial races, competitors leave the start at regular intervals of one or two minutes. The rider who completes the course in the shortest time wins. Time trialists wear one-piece suits, specially designed helmets, and shoe covers, all designed to smooth the flow of air over them.

Specification—Cougar

Frame	Steel-based alloy
Fork	Steel-based alloy
Gears	16-speed indexed
Brakes	Caliper
Handlebar	Tri-bar mounted on low-profile stem
Front wheel	Spoked (20 flat, radial spokes)
Rear wheel	Disc
Tires	Narrow section time-trial

Handlebar
The wider parts of the handlebar are used for steering through tight bends and climbing steep hills.

Gearshift
Gearshifts are located at the end of the extensions on the aero bar, allowing the rider to change gear without disturbing the airflow.

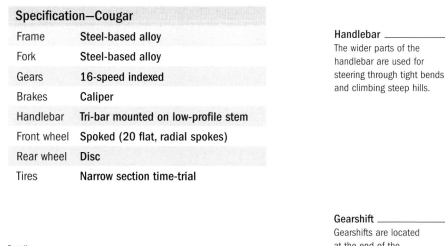

Front view

Detail

Seat post
The flattened section of the seat post smoothes out the airflow over it.

Stem
The sloping handlebar stem allows for a low riding position.

Brakes
Brake levers are positioned on the outer part of the handlebar so that they can be used when cornering.

Spoke
A flat spoke, with its knifelike shape, cuts through the air better than a standard, round-sectioned spoke.

Chainrings
Chainrings are close in size because the bike does not need gears for steep hills.

Rim
The deep, tapered wheel rim smoothes air flowing over the tire.

See also
Triathlon skills pp.162–63

The track bike

The track bike is a racing thoroughbred. The bikes used by sprinters over short distances are designed for maximum speed, aided by the absence of brakes or gears. The spokes are often tied together with steel wire where they cross to prevent any energy from being lost when a sprinter accelerates.

The bike illustrated is an all-around track bike, suitable for scratch races and—with an aerodynamic handlebar added—pursuit racing. In points races and Madisons (*see* pp.164–65), where frequent changes of pace are necessary, the bike would be set up with lighter, spoked wheels.

The single gear on a track bike has no freewheel mechanism and incorporates a fixed gear—when the rear wheel turns, so do your legs. Instead of brakes track riders control their speed by moving up and down the steep bankings, and by applying leg resistance on the recovery part of the pedal stroke.

Working the high-speed track
Track racing takes place on ovals similar to running tracks, but because of the greater speeds cyclists reach, the bends of bike tracks are banked to stop them from careening off. Track bikes are compulsory for track races. Track racing as a discipline is good training for road races, and an indoor track provides an ideal location for winter training for any cyclist.

Securing nut
Track bike wheels are attached with nuts, not quick-release levers. They are more secure under stress and do not cause injury in a crash.

Detail

Disc wheel
A disc wheel can withstand G-forces in bankings. It is, however, more difficult to accelerate than a spoked wheel.

CORIMA

Specification—Corima

Frame	**Carbon-fiber monocoque**
Fork	**Carbon fiber**
Gears	**Single fixed**
Brakes	**None**
Handlebar	**Aluminum track drop**
Front wheel	**Carbon-fiber spoked (4 spokes)**
Rear wheel	**Carbon-fiber disc**
Tires	**Tubular track**

Pedal
Clipless road pedals
are used by many track
riders, with some riders
increasing the release
tension on them so
that their feet are
held more securely.

Handlebar
A track bar is
rounded at the
top because riders
hold the bottom
of the handlebar
for most of
the time.

Front view

Top view

Saddle
A comfortable, supportive
saddle reduces the impact
of the G-forces that
increase pressure on
the perineum.

Frame
A track frame is stiff
so that it does not flex
under the G-forces and
powerful accelerations.

Tire
Tubular tires
are stuck to the
rim with strong
adhesive.

Wheel
The carbon-fiber, spoked
wheel is strong and stiff.

Chainring
The single chainring can
be swapped between
events to obtain a
different gear ratio.

See also
Competing on the track pp.164–65 Track racing skills pp.166–67

The triathlon bike

The bike sections of many triathlons are essentially time trials, so the bikes ridden by triathletes are very similar to time-trial bikes (*see* pp.52–53), but with one major difference—triathlon bikes are not as low at the front. This is because triathletes have to run after the bike ride, so they cannot adopt the very low positions of time trialists, which cause strain in the lower back and hamstring muscles that are essential during the running stage. A triathlon bike should also have two sets of water bottle cage bosses

on the frame, since the bike section is the optimum time in a race for a triathlete to take on liquids.

The illustrated bike is made from oval tubing, which has its long axis at 90 degrees to the front of the bike. This elongation of the tubing smooths out airflow over the bike. There are rules imposed by the international cycling governing body as to how deep these tubes can be, but in triathlon, the rules apply to Elite competitors only. This bike, though, is legal in both cycling and triathlon.

Riding in a triathlon
The first official triathlon—the swim, cycle, and run sport—was staged in 1978. Cycling makes up a large part of the event; a competitor can spend as much time riding as on the other two sections combined.

Cassette
Close-ratio gears such as this are only needed for a flat course. On a hilly race, riders swap the cassette or block for one with bigger cogs.

Detail

Disc wheel
Disc wheels are used for races on the flat, since they are heavier than spoked wheels and require more effort uphill.

Specification—Sigma Kronos

Frame	**Aluminum aero tubes**
Fork	**Carbon fiber**
Gears	**18-speed indexed, bar-end control**
Brakes	**Caliper**
Handlebar	**Integrated tri-bar and lo-profile set**
Front wheel	**Spoked (16 flat, radial spokes)**
Rear wheel	**Disc**
Tires	**Narrow section road-race**

Gearshift
The handlebar-mounted gearshifts enable the rider to adopt an aerodynamic tuck.

Front view

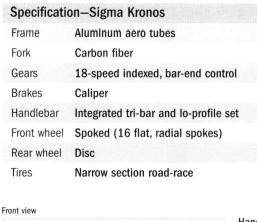

Handlebar
Adjustable handlebar allows a rider to set up his or her ideal riding position.

Front view

Brakes
The dual-pivot caliper brakes provide effective stopping power on all types of triathlon courses.

Frame
Deep-section frame tubes produce maximum aerodynamic effect.

Chainring
Solid chainring improves airflow.

Wheel rim
The aerodynamic, deep-section rim helps smooth airflow over the front wheel.

See also
The time-trial bike pp.52–53 Triathlon skills pp.162–63

Anatomy of the mountain bike

Once cyclists ventured off-road, a bike was needed to cope with a new, often hostile, environment. Mountain-bike design has resulted mainly from the need for a low center of gravity, to assist in technical, low-speed maneuverability, and a fast dismount time, which is why mountain bikes have low frame heights. Also, the need for traction, powerful brakes, precise control, shock absorption, wide ranges of easy-to-use gears, and sealed bearings have all contributed to a very successful, still-developing design.

Early mountain bikes were heavy and unwieldy, but as they developed, so did the materials and methods of connecting them, leading to elegant off-road bikes.

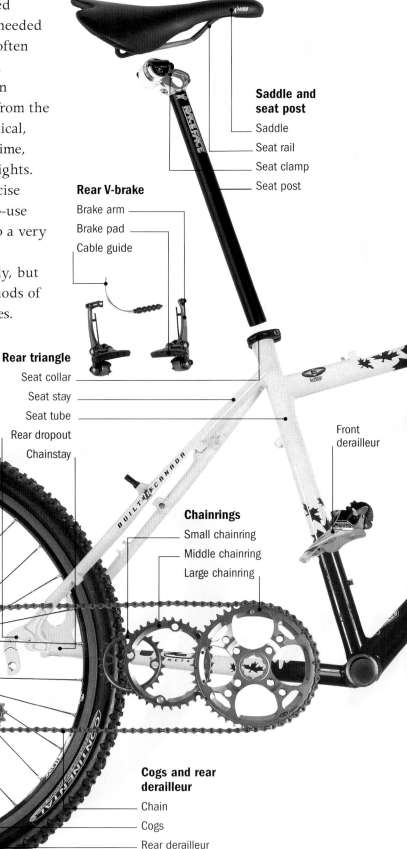

Saddle and seat post
Saddle
Seat rail
Seat clamp
Seat post

Rear V-brake
Brake arm
Brake pad
Cable guide

Quick-release mechanism
Rear axle
Quick-release lever
Rear wheel

Rear triangle
Seat collar
Seat stay
Seat tube
Rear dropout
Chainstay

Front derailleur

Chainrings
Small chainring
Middle chainring
Large chainring

Cogs and rear derailleur
Chain
Cogs
Rear derailleur

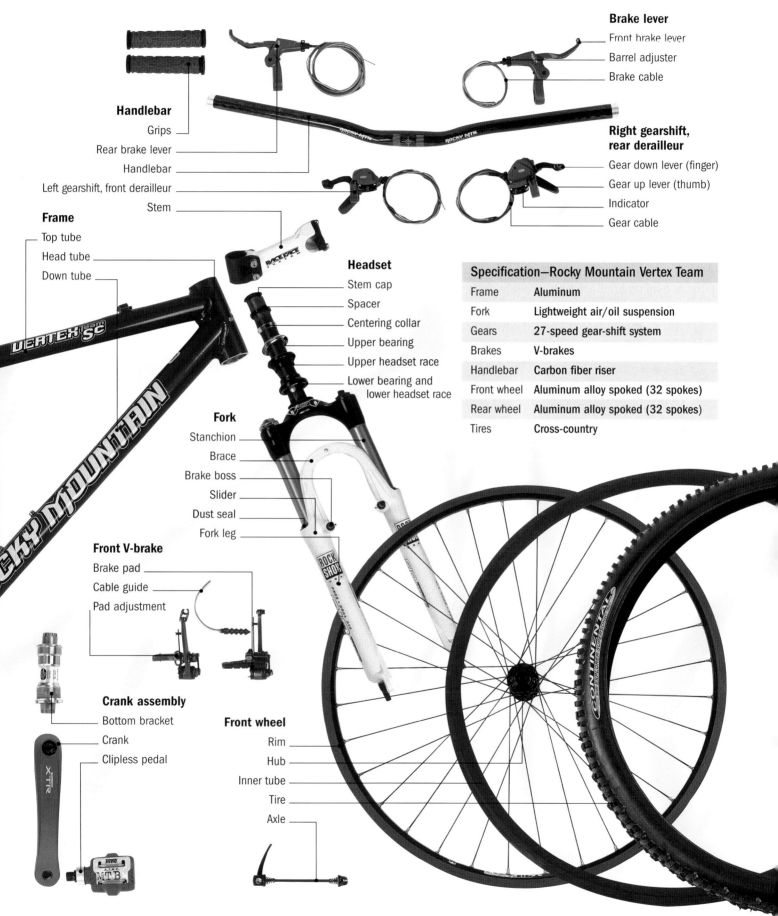

Brake lever
Front brake lever
Barrel adjuster
Brake cable

Handlebar
Grips
Rear brake lever
Handlebar
Left gearshift, front derailleur
Stem

Right gearshift, rear derailleur
Gear down lever (finger)
Gear up lever (thumb)
Indicator
Gear cable

Frame
Top tube
Head tube
Down tube

Headset
Stem cap
Spacer
Centering collar
Upper bearing
Upper headset race
Lower bearing and lower headset race

Fork
Stanchion
Brace
Brake boss
Slider
Dust seal
Fork leg

Specification—Rocky Mountain Vertex Team	
Frame	**Aluminum**
Fork	**Lightweight air/oil suspension**
Gears	**27-speed gear-shift system**
Brakes	**V-brakes**
Handlebar	**Carbon fiber riser**
Front wheel	**Aluminum alloy spoked (32 spokes)**
Rear wheel	**Aluminum alloy spoked (32 spokes)**
Tires	**Cross-country**

Front V-brake
Brake pad
Cable guide
Pad adjustment

Crank assembly
Bottom bracket
Crank
Clipless pedal

Front wheel
Rim
Hub
Inner tube
Tire
Axle

The race-level cross-country mountain bike

One of the most important developments in mountain bike design has been suspension. Front suspension came first, and nearly every new bike today is equipped with a suspension fork. These bikes are known as "hardtails," reflecting the fact that suspension is only at the front. Despite this, hardtails still reduce shock from rough surfaces and improve bike handling on rough sections of trail.

The next step was full suspension, developed so that the rear wheel could better absorb shocks. This first found its way onto downhill bikes, where full suspension meant that bumps could be taken at higher speeds. Now, improved rear suspension and lighter components are revolutionizing the cross-country (XC) racing scene.

Recent research has proved that though full suspension bikes might feel slower, especially on hills, they are actually faster over an average cross-country race circuit, since they enable the rider to negotiate technical sections at higher speeds. The new generation of intelligent full-suspension systems can distinguish between the bounce a rider puts into the bike by pedaling, and the lumps and bumps of the trail.

Testing off-road endurance skills
Cross-country races comprise a number of laps—depending on age and ability—of a countryside circuit that is designed to test both the fitness and off-road riding skills of the competitors, who all start together. Many types of natural obstacles feature in this endurance sport, which lasts from 30 minutes for the youngest competitors, to marathons of over three hours for the professional men's races.

Rear shock
Full suspension cross-country bikes are equipped with lightweight, adjustable, air/oil rear shocks that sometimes have a "lock-out" facility. This turns the shock unit off and is useful for channeling all energy to the pedals when riding across flat, easy terrain.

Three-quarter view

Cogs
The cassette has a wide range of cog sizes to provide a gear ratio for any situation.

Tire
Cross-country tires are quite knobbly. Semi-slicks are used on some courses, especially on the front wheel.

Specification—Marin Mount Vision

Frame	**Aluminum with rear suspension**
Suspension Fork	**Short-travel cross-country**
Rear shock	**Air/oil**
Gears	**27-speed integrated system**
Brakes	**V-brake**
Handlebar	**Flat**
Front wheel	**Spoked (32 spokes)**
Rear wheel	**Spoked (32 spokes)**
Tires	**Cross-country**

Brakes and gears
Gearshifts and brake levers can be used without the riders taking their hands away from the handlebar.

Pedal
Double-sided clipless pedals secure the feet but are easy to engage and disengage.

Front view

Riding position
Cross-country race bikes usually have a long reach between saddle and handlebar, giving a stretched riding position.

Suspension fork
The suspension travel on a cross-country fork is shorter than that on a downhill bike.

Pivot system
The rear triangle, which goes back to the rear axle, rotates on a pivot above and forward from the bottom bracket.

Side view

See also
Competing off-road **pp.168–69** Cross-country racing skills **pp.170–71**

Mountain bikes at this specification have benefited enormously from the material and component advancements that have filtered down from the very top of the sport. In fact, these bikes are lighter—and function more efficiently—than the models that leading professionals were using in the early 1980s.

In particular, the suspension fork on the illustrated bike is far more sophisticated than would have been found on quite recent entry-level bikes.

Lighter materials—aluminum is used for the frame, handlebar, and stem, and in some of the transmission parts—are also incorporated, along with more effective gears and brakes; these are features resulting from high-end bike development.

With the addition of slick tires and mudguards, this bike would easily convert to a rugged commuter bike. Day touring is also suitable for this bike, since it incorporates pannier rack bosses.

Saddle
A supportive saddle suits an upright bike position, but women riders should consider buying female-specific models.

Three-quarter top view

Cogs
A wide selection of gear ratios means that all types of terrain can be tackled.

Cycling for fitness and pleasure
The entry-level mountain bike is an ideal bike for the fitness or pleasure cyclist. It would also make a good first bike for a junior racer. Many avid road racers buy bikes such as this to bring some variation to their training, and to enjoy the experience of riding off-road.

Tire
Off-road tires can be swapped for slicks to turn the bike into a capable commuter bike or road tourer.

Specification—Marin Palisades Trail

Frame	**Aluminum**
Suspension Fork	**Short-travel**
Gears	**24-speed integrated system**
Brakes	**V-brakes**
Handlebar	**Riser type**
Front wheel	**Spoked (32 spokes)**
Rear wheel	**Spoked (32 spokes)**
Tires	**All-terrain**

Three-quarter view

Fork
A relatively sophisticated suspension fork is included as standard on entry-level mountain bikes.

Cable housing
The ideal amount of brake and gear cable housing creates this shape of curve. Too much cable housing increases friction on cables and adversely affects braking/shifting performance.

Brakes and gears
Integral brake levers and gearshifts are easy to use.

Front view

Boss
Pannier rack bosses allow the bike to be turned into a touring model.

Chainrings
The triple chainrings increase the range of the gears.

See also
Off-road touring **pp.42–43** Improving your fitness **pp.142–43**

The downhill mountain bike

Racing downhill at high speeds over rough and twisting terrain requires a special bike. Having the technique to ride like this is essential, but only a bike that can absorb large impacts at high speed and still stay in contact with the ground will allow a rider's skill to be used to maximum effect.

Heavy-duty, reactive, and supple full suspension is what defines the downhill bike. This means suspension with plenty of travel, but also plenty of control. It is pointless if the suspension absorbs a major jolt but then springs back just as severely. Sophisticated damping controls this springing, as do other features that keep the suspension in contact with and reacting to the ground.

The downhill bike is similar to a track bike in that it can only be used in the application for which it was designed. Because of the safety margin built into each component, downhill bikes are so specialized and heavy that riders have to push them, or take a ski lift, to get back to the top of a run.

Taking gradients at high speed
Downhill races take place on courses that are similar to downhill ski runs. Each competitor tackles the course individually, and the rider with the fastest time wins. Many owners of downhill bikes do not actually compete, but are attracted to downhill riding just for the thrill of watching it.

Saddle
A low saddle position keeps a rider's center of gravity close to the ground to provide stability in corners, though downhillers rarely sit on their saddles.

Three-quarter view

Suspension
Rear suspension can be adjusted to suit each type of downhill course. Factors such as gradient and the condition of the trail determine the stiffness of the shock unit.

Tire
The tires found on downhill bikes are more knobbly than cross-country varieties. They provide traction and help deliver the stopping power of the large disc brakes.

Specification—Kona Stab Primo

Frame	**Aluminum with rear suspension**
Suspension Fork	**Long-travel coil/oil**
Rear shock	**Spring type with oil damping**
Gears	**9-speed integrated system**
Brakes	**Hydraulic discs**
Handlebar	**Riser type**
Front wheel	**Custom, spoked (32 spokes)**
Rear wheel	**Custom, spoked (32 spokes)**
Tires	**Downhill**

Fork crown
By continuing the fork stanchions up to a second fork crown, the stresses are shared along a greater distance than on a standard fork.

Handlebar
The riser bar offers increased control for the downhill rider.

Suspension
The long suspension travel on a downhill bike allows severe impacts to be absorbed relatively easily.

Pedal
The pedals are an SPD-flat pedal hybrid—an SPD mechanism holds the foot inside the frame of a flat pedal.

Front view

Brake disc
The large-diameter rotor provides massive braking power.

Chain retainer
Rollers prevent the chain from falling off, which would be disastrous on a downhill run. Chainguards on either side of the chainring perform the same task.

See also
Off-road riding: descending **pp.126–27** Downhill racing skills **pp.174–75**

The slalom mountain bike

Slalom racing and its younger offshoot Bicycle Four Cross (4X)—sometimes known as Bicycle Super Cross (BSX)—developed out of downhill racing, so slalom bikes share a number of characteristics with downhill models. The similarities include the high level of safety features that have to be built into slalom bikes, including double seat-pin clamp bolts and solid-machined stems. The two types of bikes also share flat pedals and suspension forks with reasonably long travel.

The differences between the bikes include their respective weights. Slalom and 4X races are short, requiring agile handling and relatively light, responsive bikes that can be easily positioned on the course. Consequently, slalom bikes are lighter than downhill models. These only require suspension at the front, since the prepared routes are not composed of the natural boulder- and tree-root-strewn surfaces found on downhill and cross-country courses.

Saddle
The low saddle position lowers the center of gravity in corners and increases stability.

Brake disc
Hydraulic discs provide more stopping power than V-brakes.

Riding head-to-head
Dual slalom races are run on short, downhill courses with riders riding next to each other on separate, prepared tracks. 4X races take place on courses similar to BMX tracks that run downhill. Four riders go in each heat, all on the same track. The winner of each heat progresses through the event until the final race.

Rim
The lightweight wheel rim can be used with disc brakes, making the bike easier to accelerate.

Specification—DMR Trailstar

Frame	4130 chromoly steel
Suspension fork	Medium-travel
Gears	8-speed integrated system
Brakes	Hydraulic discs
Handlebar	Riser-type with brace
Front wheel	Spoked (32 spokes)
Rear wheel	Spoked (32 spokes)
Tires	Heavy-duty

Brace
A handlebar brace prevents the handlebar from flexing.

Seat clamp
The double clamp bolt holds the seat pin with extra security.

Detail

Stem
The short stem offers the rider an increased level of control.

Gusset
This bike has a reinforcing gusset that strengthens the frame.

Front view

Forks
Slalom forks have more travel than cross-country forks but less than downhill versions.

Chainring
The bike has a single chainring because downhill events such as the slalom only need high gears.

Detail

Tension device
A chain tension device prevents the chain from coming off.

See also
Off-road riding: bermed cornering **pp.120–21** Extreme riding **pp.176–77**

Anatomy of the hybrid bike

The designs of road and mountain bikes meet to form today's hybrids, cycling's all-arounders. With their mountain-bike, "head-up," traffic-friendly riding position, easy-to-operate gears on flat handlebars, light frame materials, and ultralight road wheels and tires, they are ideal for commuters. They are also ideal for the fitness cyclist, since higher ratio gears than those on a mountain bike, combined with narrower tires, mean that riders can easily cover long distances.

Because hybrid bikes are not designed for heavy off-road use, they do not need either suspension or heavy-gauge frame tubing. They usually have wheels of the same size as road bikes, while the tires have less tread, making them easier to ride on the road.

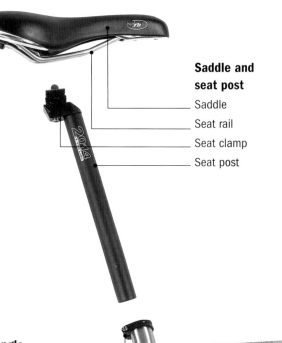

Saddle and seat post
Saddle
Seat rail
Seat clamp
Seat post

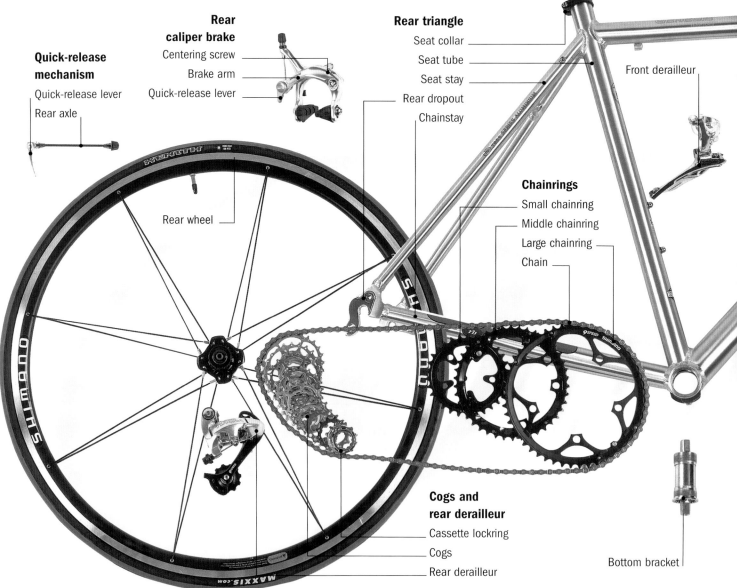

Rear caliper brake
Centering screw
Brake arm
Quick-release lever

Quick-release mechanism
Quick-release lever
Rear axle

Rear triangle
Seat collar
Seat tube
Seat stay
Rear dropout
Chainstay

Front derailleur

Rear wheel

Chainrings
Small chainring
Middle chainring
Large chainring
Chain

Cogs and rear derailleur
Cassette lockring
Cogs
Rear derailleur

Bottom bracket

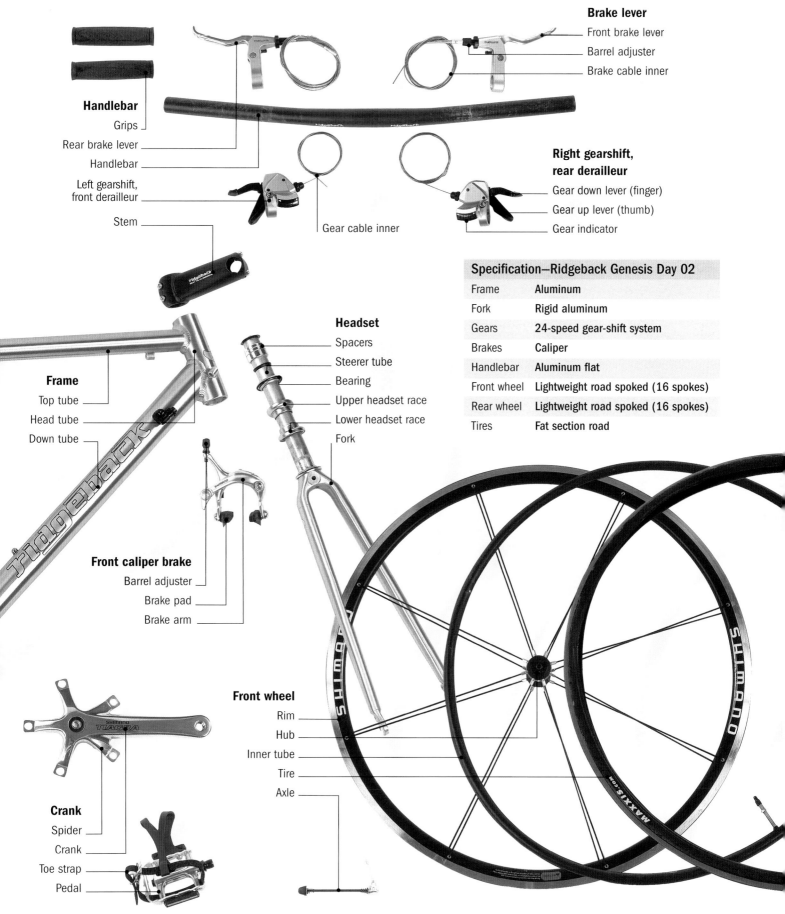

Brake lever
Front brake lever
Barrel adjuster
Brake cable inner

Handlebar
Grips
Rear brake lever
Handlebar
Left gearshift,
front derailleur
Stem

**Right gearshift,
rear derailleur**
Gear down lever (finger)
Gear up lever (thumb)
Gear indicator

Gear cable inner

Headset
Spacers
Steerer tube
Bearing
Upper headset race
Lower headset race
Fork

Specification—Ridgeback Genesis Day 02	
Frame	Aluminum
Fork	Rigid aluminum
Gears	24-speed gear-shift system
Brakes	Caliper
Handlebar	Aluminum flat
Front wheel	Lightweight road spoked (16 spokes)
Rear wheel	Lightweight road spoked (16 spokes)
Tires	Fat section road

Frame
Top tube
Head tube
Down tube

Front caliper brake
Barrel adjuster
Brake pad
Brake arm

Front wheel
Rim
Hub
Inner tube
Tire
Axle

Crank
Spider
Crank
Toe strap
Pedal

The folding bike

Folding bikes are ideal for commuters, and for people with little space in which to store a standard bike. A number of different types are available, but all of them can be quickly folded into a package that is easily carried or stored, and can then be reassembled into a serviceable bicycle without the use of tools.

The bikes vary in their sophistication, from basic single-speed models to bikes with multiple gears, built-in lighting systems, and carrying capacity.

There are even folding mountain, road race, and time-trial bikes available. All have small wheels, which are essential to the design because wheels cannot be folded. One disadvantage of small wheels is that they give a harsh ride; some bikes overcome this by including a suspension system.

Of the two bikes illustrated, the Moulton has full suspension and the Brompton only has rear-wheel suspension, though its upright stance places most of the rider's weight over the back of the bike.

Using flexible transportation
Folding bikes are perfect for commuters who also travel on public transportation. There are a growing number of innovative new bikes available in response to the demand from commuters, or people who just want to get away from using their cars.

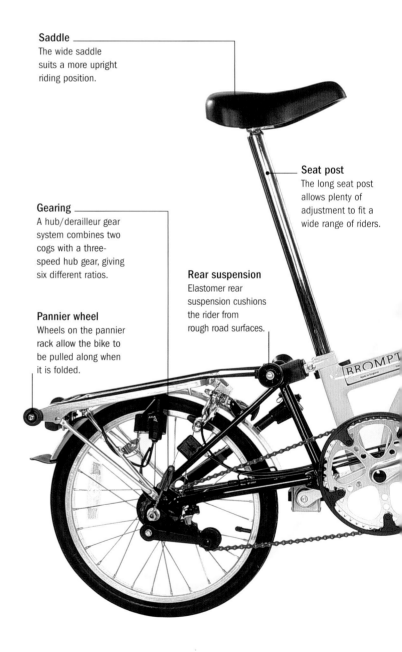

Saddle
The wide saddle suits a more upright riding position.

Seat post
The long seat post allows plenty of adjustment to fit a wide range of riders.

Gearing
A hub/derailleur gear system combines two cogs with a three-speed hub gear, giving six different ratios.

Rear suspension
Elastomer rear suspension cushions the rider from rough road surfaces.

Pannier wheel
Wheels on the pannier rack allow the bike to be pulled along when it is folded.

Moulton folding bike

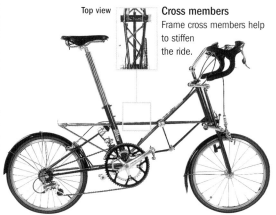

Top view

Cross members
Frame cross members help to stiffen the ride.

Ride on, ride off
Its small wheels and easy assembly make the Moulton an ideal bike to take on trains and planes. Large chainrings are needed because the small wheels require lower gear ratios. A racing saddle reflects near-road-bike performance.

Gearshift
Hub gearshifts require very little maintenance, since they are shielded from the elements.

Handlebar
The handlebar has a high level of adjustability to give the rider a tailored fit.

Hinge
The frame hinge must be locked before the bike is ridden.

Lighting
Front and rear lights are powered by a generator.

Wheel
The small wheels provide a rough ride, but the bike's overall design compensates.

Specification—Brompton

Frame	Folding steel with elastomer shock
Fork	Steel
Gears	6-speed
Brakes	Caliper
Handlebar	Hi-riser
Front wheel	Spoked (28 spokes)
Rear wheel	Spoked (28 spokes)
Tires	Medium section road

Folding the Brompton

1 Unfolded, this bike is well suited for riding in traffic. Its upright riding position gives the rider good control and all-around vision.

2 Disengage the rear section and swing it around. Then push the front section around and lower the seat post.

3 Use the handlebar to push the bike along like a cart when it is partly folded. The rear carrier acts as a bike stand.

4 Release the handlebar assembly and fold it away so that the bike can be carried by its saddle.

See also
Road riding: cycling in traffic flows **pp.102–03**   Road riding: making maneuvers **pp.104–05**

The touring bike

A touring bike must be a comfortable, balanced load-carrier with a wide range of gears and robust equipment. Fat tires and an upright position provide enough comfort to ride in the saddle all day, day after day. Front and rear panniers allow the rider to carry everything needed for a self-sufficient, multi-day tour, and spread the load evenly over the bike.

Because touring is essentially about personal freedom, and individuals take different things out of the experience, touring bikes are one of the few remaining varieties of bikes that use custom frame-builders in their manufacture. Mass-produced touring bikes are available, but a custom-built example, made by a specialist frame-builder, can be tailored to individual needs. This is useful if riders are considering an adventurous tour, and have a good idea of their specific requirements. In a similar way, bikes can be designed to suit the rider's build and riding style, which vary from one rider to another.

Fully loaded bike

Cogs
The large number of cogs and the triple crankset provide a wide range of gears.

Choosing the route as you ride
Touring is cycling for those who want total freedom. You simply plan your destination, and take the most interesting route to get there. Specialist touring bikes are also suitable for commuting, general riding, and fitness training.

Tire
Fat tires are comfortable, with the thick treads helping to prevent punctures.

Specification—Chas Roberts Custom

Frame	Steel-based alloy of several metals
Fork	Steel-based alloy of several metals
Gears	27-speed integrated system
Brakes	Cantilever
Handlebar	**Dropped**
Carry capacity	**2¾ cubic feet (76 liters)**
Wheels	**Spoked (36 spokes)**
Tires	**Fat section touring**

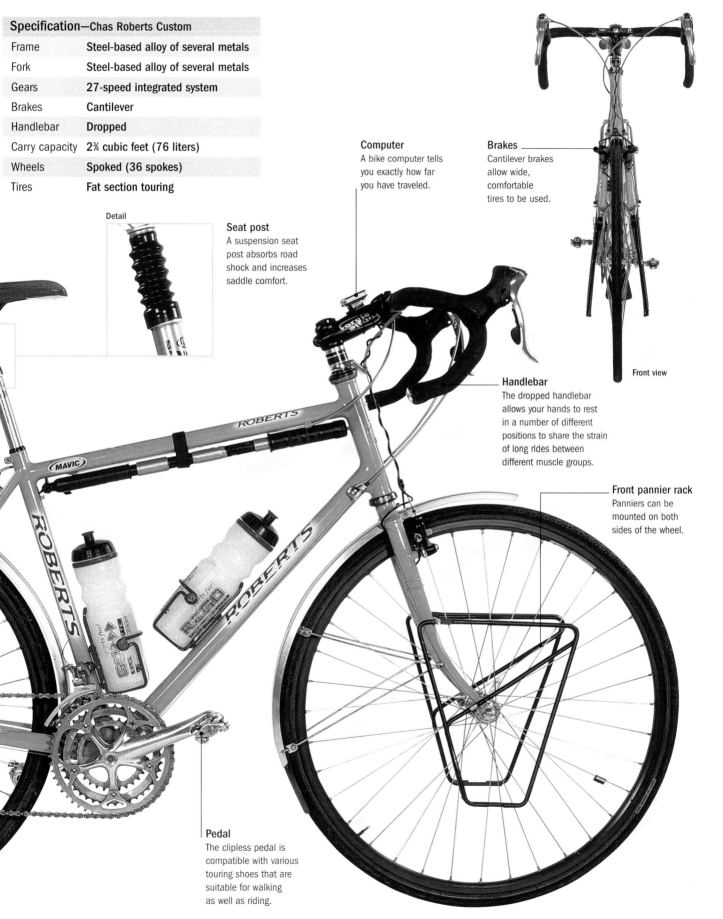

Detail

Seat post
A suspension seat post absorbs road shock and increases saddle comfort.

Computer
A bike computer tells you exactly how far you have traveled.

Brakes
Cantilever brakes allow wide, comfortable tires to be used.

Front view

Handlebar
The dropped handlebar allows your hands to rest in a number of different positions to share the strain of long rides between different muscle groups.

Front pannier rack
Panniers can be mounted on both sides of the wheel.

Pedal
The clipless pedal is compatible with various touring shoes that are suitable for walking as well as riding.

See also
Basic touring **pp.38–39** Road touring **pp.40–41**

The Audax bike

Audax riders cover a particular route within a preselected time limit. Although they prefer bikes similar in design to road bikes, an Audax bike may have more space under the fork crown and rear brake bridge to allow fatter tires, which add to comfort. A triple crankset is a practical addition, since using low gears on hills conserves energy.

It used to be an Audax rule that all bikes were equipped with mudguards and lights, regardless of whether there was nighttime riding on the route.

Now this requirement is left up to an event organizer's discretion. However, mudguards can add to your comfort if the roads are wet.

Some events cover such great distances—the 746-mile (1,200-km) Paris–Brest–Paris is the ultimate example—that packing a spare set of clothing, especially waterproofs if wet weather is forecast, can be worthwhile. A pannier rack allows all kinds of bags to be carried, from a single large saddlebag to touring panniers.

Riding a long-distance event
Audax riders cover great distances within specified times, from about 62 miles (100 km) upward. Some events are so long that riders have to cycle through the night. Audax bikes make ideal training bikes for road racers and are also suitable for day tours and all types of fitness cycling.

Saddle
A comfortable, supportive saddle is more important than a lightweight one.

Pannier
The rear pannier rack helps carry everything needed on a long ride. The rear light should be mounted in a position where it is not obscured by any bags.

Tire
Fatter than road-racing tires but narrower than touring ones, Audax tires are a balance between comfort and speed.

Specification—Dave Yates Custom

Frame	**Steel-based alloy of several metals**
Fork	**Steel-based alloy of several metals**
Gears	**27-speed integrated system**
Brakes	**Caliper**
Handlebar	**Dropped**
Lights	**Dynamo-powered double front**
Carry capacity	**1¾ cubic feet (48 liters)**
Wheels	**Spoked (36 front, 32 rear spokes)**
Tires	**Medium section road**

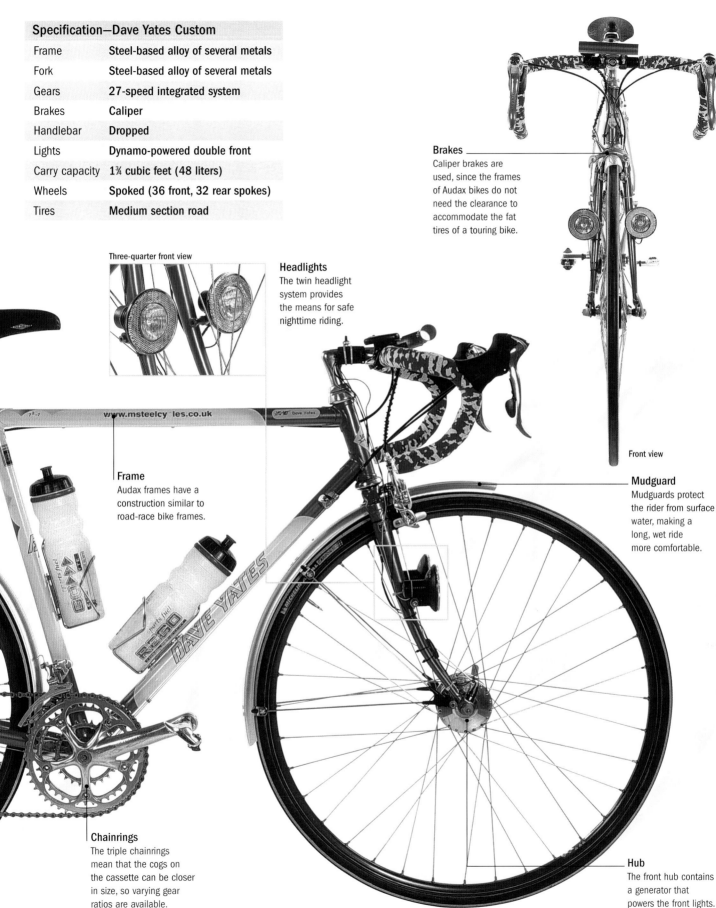

Brakes
Caliper brakes are used, since the frames of Audax bikes do not need the clearance to accommodate the fat tires of a touring bike.

Three-quarter front view

Headlights
The twin headlight system provides the means for safe nighttime riding.

Front view

Frame
Audax frames have a construction similar to road-race bike frames.

www.msteelcy les.co.uk

Dave Yates

DAVE YATES

Mudguard
Mudguards protect the rider from surface water, making a long, wet ride more comfortable.

Chainrings
The triple chainrings mean that the cogs on the cassette can be closer in size, so varying gear ratios are available.

Hub
The front hub contains a generator that powers the front lights.

See also
Road touring **pp.40–41** Competing on the road **pp.158–59**

The cyclo-cross bike

Cyclo-cross races take place during the winter, so mud can be a problem. To counter its effects, cyclo-cross bikes are equipped with cantilever brakes, because calipers collect mud from the wheels and clog up. The bikes are also equipped with fat, knobbly tires for extra grip, and a wide range of gear ratios to cope with the different conditions likely to be found on a given circuit.

Cyclo-cross bikes also have to be light, because during these relatively short events, it is often quicker to run up steep hills carrying your bike on your shoulder than to ride up them. This is why cyclo-cross bikes rarely have sloping top tubes like some mountain and road bikes do—if they did, it would make them difficult to carry.

Cyclo-cross races also differ from mountain bike disciplines in that competitors are allowed external mechanical assistance, and can even change bikes during the race if they wish. In fact, top riders often do. In a muddy race they will swap a dirty bike for a clean one on each lap, leaving an assistant to clean the original one in time for the next swap.

Racing in the winter
Conceived as cycling's equivalent of winter cross-country running, cyclo-cross races last about an hour for Elite competitors. Riders lap circuits—between 0.9 and 1.25 miles (1.5–2 km) long—made up of varied terrain. The winner is the first rider to complete the number of laps that the organizers have estimated will take one hour to cover.

Brakes
Cantilever brakes allow any mud that collects on the tires to pass between their two arms, so that they do not become clogged.

Three-quarter rear view

Wheel and spoke
Light wheels make the bike easier to carry. Fewer spokes than on a standard wheel means that less mud is picked up.

Specification—Rocky Mountain Rail

Frame	**Aluminum**
Fork	**Aluminum**
Gears	**27-speed integrated system**
Brakes	**Cantilever**
Handlebar	**Dropped**
Front wheel	**Lightweight aerodynamic spoked (16)**
Rear wheel	**Lightweight aerodynamic spoked (16)**
Tires	**Cyclo-cross**

Handlebar
The drop handlebar
helps on the short,
fast courses of
cyclo-cross races.

Three-quarter rear view

Stem
For increased control,
cyclo-cross riders sit
a little more upright
than road racers,
so they position their
handlebars higher.

Saddle
A light saddle is
used, since cyclo-
cross races are short
and do not demand
comfortable seating.

Pedal
Off-road clipless
pedals are
preferred, since
they do not
accumulate mud.

Front view

Tire
Fat, knobbly tires are
used for increased
grip and traction.

Chainrings
The triple chainrings are a common
feature, but some cyclo-cross
riders use double and even single
chainrings to save weight—it is
quicker to run and carry your bike in
situations that require a very low gear.

See also
Cross-country racing skills pp.170–71

The tandem

There are a variety of tandems available to suit a wide range of cyclists. These include off-road tandems, tandems that allow a child to ride behind an adult, hybrid tandems, and even racing tandems; tandem sprinting on the track was an Olympic event until 1972. The tandem illustrated is a 27-speed touring model with pannier racks.

The tandem's association with racing was at its peak in the years before World War II, when tandem-paced events on the track were popular. In these races, competitors on solo bikes raced against each other while in the slipstream of pacing tandems. This made for a faster race speed because, on the flat, a tandem can go faster than a solo bike.

The tandem's popularity has waned as motor traffic has increased, which is not surprising, considering the amount of skill needed to ride the bike, from both the pilot and the person sitting at the rear. Even so, there are still tens of thousands of owners worldwide, and many of them are members of clubs that hold special rallies and events to celebrate their unique form of cycling.

Riding a bicycle built for two
Tandems are an ideal way for two people to cycle together. Riding them requires some practice, since both riders must work in unison, especially when climbing hills. Although there are not as many tandems on the roads as as there used to be, tandems still have many fans all over the world who would not cycle any other way.

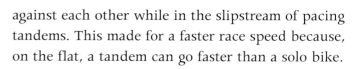
Three-quarter view

Cranksets
The triple crankset offers a wide range of gears, which help tandems to get over hills. The system of having a crankset on each side is known as a "crossover drive."

Rack
Pannier racks are the best way to carry luggage on a tandem.

Specification—Dawes Galaxy Twin

Frame	Aluminum
Fork	Chromoly steel
Gears	27-speed indexed system
Brakes	Cantilever
Handlebar	Dropped
Carry capacity	2¾ cubic feet (76 liters)
Wheels	Spoked (48 spokes)
Tires	Fat section touring

Tire
Fatter tires than
on standard touring
bikes are used to
support the greater
weight of two riders.

Front view

Three-quarter front view

Rear handlebar
The fixed rear
handlebar supports
the rider at the back
and is attached
to the front rider's
seat post.

Pedal
The front pedals
turn a chainring on
the off-side, which
is connected to a
chainring on the
rear off-side.

Gearshift
The front rider controls the
brakes and gears. Bar-end
shifters are used because
they are best suited to the
long cables on tandems.

Tube
Heavier gauge tubing than
found on solo bikes is
used to better withstand
the stress of two riders.

Top view

Chain
The chain is kept tight by
adjusting the front bottom
bracket, which can move
eccentrically in its shell.

Spoke
Tandem wheels have
more spokes than
usual because they
have to support the
weight of two people.

See also
Road touring pp.40–41

The bicycle motocross bike

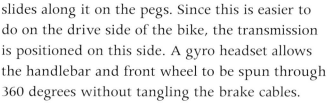

A freestyle bicycle motocross (BMX) bike is specifically designed to carry out stunts, either in competitions or just for the fun of performing them. Its basic configuration is very similar to the racing BMX (*see right*), but stunt pegs attached to the wheel nuts, transmission on the opposite side from a racing BMX, and a gyro headset are features designed to assist in performing tricks and jumps.

Opposite transmission allows "grinds" to be performed on the stunt pegs. Here, a rider jumps the bike onto a surface such as a wall or rail, and slides along it on the pegs. Since this is easier to do on the drive side of the bike, the transmission is positioned on this side. A gyro headset allows the handlebar and front wheel to be spun through 360 degrees without tangling the brake cables.

Racing BMX bikes are tough, single-speed models designed for quick acceleration from the start gate of the BMX racing track. They need to cope with takeoffs and landings, and the occasional crash, in short, eight-rider heats. Everything on these bikes is built for strength.

Expressing a rider's individuality
The crossover is one of many spectacular midair tricks that skilled freestyle BMX riders can do. Using half-pipe tracks, or anything they can find, the best exponents are able to execute extraordinary stunts. Often used to express individuality, freestyle BMX is a growing sport.

Peg
Stunt pegs are used for standing on and performing grinds.

Front view

Top view

Spoke
Extra spokes are used to improve wheel stiffness.

Wheel
This bike has a special rear wheel and freewheel that do not unscrew while pedaling.

Racing BMX—Haro Backtrail

Wheel
Small wheels allow super-quick acceleration.

Handlebar
The wide riser bar provides good leverage.

Riding at speed

Everything on a race BMX is set up to ensure that all the rider's energy goes into forward motion. Races are so short that just one gear is needed.

Fork
The chunky fork and frame tubing add rigidity to the bike.

Specification—Haro Mirra Pro

Frame	**Chromoly steel**
Fork	**Chromoly steel**
Gears	**Single-speed, opposite-side drive**
Brakes	**Caliper**
Handlebar	**Braced high-riser**
Front wheel	**Spoked (48 spokes)**
Rear wheel	**Spoked (48 spokes)**
Tires	**BMX**

Grip
Solid handlebar grips are used—spongy grips do not provide the instantaneous response needed when pulling the handlebar.

Saddle
The saddle is robust and supportive to survive the scuffs from numerous falls.

Front view

Headset
A gyro headset keeps the brake cables straight even when the wheel is spun through 360 degrees.

Three-quarter view

Left-hand chainring
Transmission is on the opposite side from that found on a standard BMX bike to optimize the ability to carry out grinds.

See also
Extreme riding pp.176–77

The trials bike

Trials bikes must be light, easy to balance, and responsive. There is no need for suspension on these models, since obstacles are taken at a slow pace and the bike must react instantly to the slightest rider input, which suspension might otherwise absorb.

Strong brakes are required, since trials riders have to hold the bike still while lining it up to make a move on an obstacle. Low-ratio gears help instant acceleration when the rider is ready to go for the obstacle. In addition, the frame must be stiff so that no energy is lost by frame tubes bending while making a move.

A wide riser bar helps the rider to control the bike, and provides extra leverage when making a move or picking the bike up in a jump or wheelie. Trials riders rarely sit on their saddles during moves over obstacles or tricks, so they are set very low or removed from the bike altogether, to keep them out of the way.

Three-quarter view

Brakes
This rear brake is a hydraulic caliper; rear cable brakes are not as strong as front ones because the cable length absorbs some of the power. An effective braking system is vital to a trials rider.

Gearing
Multiple gears allow the selection of a particular gear required for a trick or part of a course.

Cycling at the extremes
Trials competitions require riders to negotiate obstacles, losing points if they put a foot down to steady themselves. There are also jumps competitions to see how high riders can jump their bikes. Some riders shun competition and use their bikes just to perform extraordinary feats of control and agility.

Tire
Fat tires provide firm grip. Trials riders often use very low tire pressures to improve traction.

Specification—Pashley TV Series

Frame	**Steel-based alloy of several metals**
Fork	**Steel-based alloy of several metals**
Gears	**9-speed integrated system**
Brakes	**V-brake front, hydraulic caliper rear**
Handlebar	**Extra-wide riser bar**
Front wheel	**Spoked (32 spokes)**
Rear wheel	**Spoked (32 spokes)**
Tires	**Fat section, medium tread**

Handlebar
The wide riser bar assists control and provides leverage for wheelies and jumps.

Front view

Saddle
The ultra-low saddle height means that it does not obstruct the rider during a competition.

Frame
A rigid fork is more controllable and responsive than a suspension fork.

Detail

Chainring
The single, small chainring provides instant response through low gearing.

See also
Extreme riding **pp.176–77**

Better cycling

To get the most out of cycling, there are various techniques and strategies you can learn that will help you to cope safely and efficiently with every situation that you may come across on the road or the trail. The advice in this comprehensive step-by-step guide will enable you to work in perfect harmony with your bike.

Road riding: adjusting position

To get the most from your bike, it needs to fit you perfectly, so that you and the bike are a biomechanically efficient unit. With a road bike, this means finding the optimum saddle height that allows all your leg power to go into turning the pedals, then making sure that you are as comfortable and aerodynamic as possible.

If the saddle is set too high or too low, you will not be positioned efficiently, because muscles work best in the middle of their range of movement. And sitting upright, also a consequence of a low saddle, is not particularly aerodynamic. Another element to consider is the handlebar—if it is not wide enough, your breathing can be constricted, and you will feel uncomfortable while riding.

The length of your cranks can also affect riding efficiency. Cranks of varying lengths are available, and having the correct length optimizes the power that is transmitted to the pedals. Crank length is based on inside leg measurement, which is crotch-to-floor distance, without shoes. As a guide, the optimal crank lengths are 170 mm for an inside leg of 29–31½ in (74–80 cm); 172.5 mm for 32–34 in (81–86 cm), and 175 mm for 32–34 in (87–93 cm).

The steps outlined here are based on scientific studies of optimum road-bike riding positions, and they should get you close to your ideal riding position. You will need someone to help you check that everything is lining up as it should, and it will be necessary to put the bike in a turbo trainer or support it against a wall for Steps 4 and 5.

Pro tips

- Only make any adjustments to your existing position in small increments of about a quarter-inch (0.5 cm) at a time. Big changes can cause problems—especially with your knees.

- Never position the handlebar so low that you have difficulty breathing when holding the bottom of the bar. Road racers tend to set the handlebar low to improve aerodynamics, but leisure riders should position it at a comfortable height.

- Be aware of increased pressure on your hands and arms—this could be an indication that the handlebar is set too low.

David Lloyd Coach and former professional rider

Setting your riding position

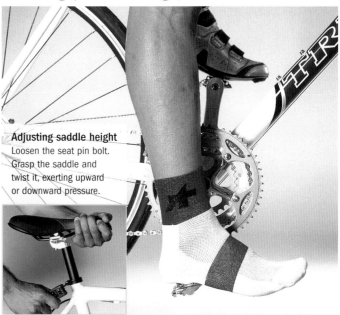

Adjusting saddle height
Loosen the seat pin bolt. Grasp the saddle and twist it, exerting upward or downward pressure.

1 **Enlist someone to help** hold the bike. Remove one shoe and place your heel on the pedal spindle. For your optimum saddle height, your leg should now be straight, so raise or lower the saddle until it is. It is important to sit absolutely straight in the saddle when doing this test and not to lean on the leg that your helper is checking.

Line of sight
Look down— the handlebar should obscure the front hub.

4 **Sit on the bike** and take hold of the bottom of the handlebar. Now look down at the top of the handlebar at the point where it intersects the handlebar stem. Check to see the position of the front hub in relation to this point. If it is in front, you need a longer stem. If it is behind, then you need a shorter one.

Checking for movement
Ask your helper to check for movement in your hips while you are backpedaling.

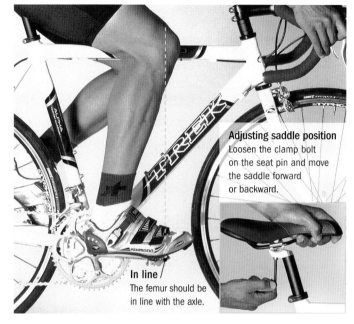

Adjusting saddle position
Loosen the clamp bolt on the seat pin and move the saddle forward or backward.

In line
The femur should be in line with the axle.

② **Put your shoe** back on, engage the pedals, and begin to backpedal. Your helper should stand behind you and make sure that your hips are absolutely level throughout each pedal revolution. If they rock at all, your saddle is set too high, and you will have to go back to Step 1 to check the height again.

③ **The widest part** of your foot should be directly over the pedal spindle; adjust the cleats on your shoes as necessary. Then, with the cranks parallel, the end of your femur (the depression in the side of your knee) should be directly above the spindle. Adjusting the fore and aft position of the saddle will allow you to achieve this.

Pivoting the saddle
Undo the clamp bolt to pivot the saddle up and down on the seat pin.

Visualizing a line
Run an imaginary line from your shoulder joints to the edges of the bar.

⑤ **Place a level on** the saddle to check whether it is flat. If it is not, undo the seat clamp bolt as in Step 3, and the saddle will then pivot up or down. Before you do this, position the level along the top tube just to make sure the bike is level. If it is not, take the bike out of the trainer and continue with it on the floor.

⑥ **Pick the bike up** off the floor. Ask your helper to check where the outer edges of the handlebar line up with your arm/shoulder joints—they should be absolutely level. If your shoulders are wider, the handlebar will constrict your breathing. If they are narrower, then a narrower bar would make you more aerodynamic.

See also
Road riding: climbing **pp.96–97** Road riding: pedaling efficiently **pp.100–01**

Road riding: braking and changing gears

Braking and changing gears is all about anticipation. It is also about timing. Always brake when your bike is going straight, since applying the brakes on a corner is likely to make the bike unstable. It is a good idea to change gears just before you need that gear so that you do not lose speed.

Gear changes should reflect every difference in riding conditions—wind direction, gradient, and road surface changes—so that you can keep pedaling at the optimum rhythm (cadence) for the conditions. This is usually between 70 and 80 revolutions per minute on the flat, a little less on climbs, and much less when climbing out of the saddle. Some riders are more comfortable at a higher cadence, some at lower; the most important thing is not to labor inefficiently in too high a gear or spin too fast in a low one.

It is important to use your gears efficiently. Chains are at their most efficient at transferring energy when they work in a straight line. Avoid using gear combinations of the biggest chainring with the biggest cogs, and the smallest chainring with the smallest cogs, since these ratios can be achieved with better combinations. Anticipation is especially important on hills. At the start of an ascent, choose which chainring you will use to ride up the whole hill. If you get this wrong and have to change from a big chainring to a smaller one because you have no more cogs to go lower, it will completely upset your rhythm.

Pro tips

- Be careful to avoid pulling the brake lever back when you shift to larger cogs or chainrings on a Shimano system. It could cause the brakes to come on if you do. This can be a problem if you have small hands. Experiment with the position of your brake levers and the angle of your handlebar to eradicate it.

- Avoid shifting to a smaller chainring and cog at the same time, since this can cause the chain to jump off. If you suddenly have to change to a low gear, change to a smaller chainring first, then fine-tune your gear selection with the rear derailleur.

Dave Marsh National Masters Circuit Race Champion

Using brakes and gears | Skill rating ■■☐☐☐

Hands on hoods
Positioning your hands on the hoods makes it easy to operate the brakes and gears.

1 **The brakes on road bikes** can be operated from two riding positions. In the first position, the rider applies the front brake—which is the most powerful—with a hand on the brake hood. This is an ideal place to have your hands when riding on the flat, uphill, or in traffic. It is comfortable and allows quick access to the brakes.

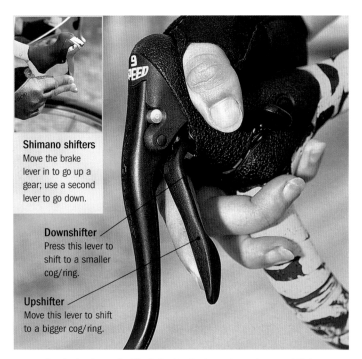

Shimano shifters
Move the brake lever in to go up a gear; use a second lever to go down.

Downshifter
Press this lever to shift to a smaller cog/ring.

Upshifter
Move this lever to shift to a bigger cog/ring.

3 **Push the lever behind the** brake lever inward to upshift (to larger cogs/chainrings) on a Campagnolo brake/gear system (*main image*). Downshift (to smaller cogs) by pressing the lever on the brake hood. Shimano manufactures the other main system.

② **Apply the brakes from** the drops (*above*), where the hands have more leverage and power. This second position is ideal when going downhill. Squeeze the brake lever gently and never grab at it. For both positions, always apply the brakes progressively instead of snatching at them.

④ **Keep pedaling** whenever you shift gears with derailleur gears, since this keeps the chain moving.

⑤ **While riding** out of the saddle, you can change to lower gears if you have an integral brake/gearshift system.

See also
Road riding: cornering on the flat **pp.90–91**   Road riding: hairpin cornering **pp.92–93**

Road riding: cornering on the flat

Although cornering may seem simple, there are techniques that can help you steer your bike with precision and speed. More importantly, these techniques will enable you to come out of the corner on the correct side of the road, so that you are not in the path of any other traffic.

The key to efficient cornering is maintaining speed through the corner, but doing so safely. If you are cycling in a group, always drop back a little from the rider in front of you on a corner, unless you absolutely trust their cornering ability. Pay close attention to the road surface before you turn. Any loose surface or water will have an effect on the line you choose. Also, try to avoid crossing painted road markings in the wet, since they can be very slippery. You can often visualize a line through all these situations, but if you cannot, reduce your speed.

90°

Getting the correct cornering angle
Throughout any corner, keep your head at right angles to the road. This tricks the balance mechanisms in your inner ear into thinking your body is still upright, and helps prevent any possible disorientation.

Pro tips

- Keep your body low while you are in the corner. This lowers your center of gravity, and helps the tires to grip the road.

- Press your weight onto your outside leg as you lean into the corner. This shifts weight to the outside of the bike and provides more stability.

- Do not brake if the corner is tighter than you thought. Try moving your shoulders over your outside leg, since this transfers even more weight to help keep you upright.

Dean Downing National Circuit Race Champion

Riding a corner on the flat Skill rating ■■■□□

Be aware
Watch out for brake lights ahead; they could mean that the corner is tight.

Turning your head
When looking over your shoulder, relax that arm.

Placing hands
Positioning your hands on the bottom of the handlebar increases stability.

1 **Assess the corner** well before reaching it, checking exactly how tight the bend is. Be aware of traffic in the corner and also any after it, and check whether the road climbs or descends when the road eventually straightens out.

2 **As you get** closer to the corner, look behind to check the traffic conditions. When looking over either shoulder, there is an automatic tendency to steer in that direction; be conscious of this and try to avoid doing it.

3 **If the traffic is** clear, move toward the center of the road—this position will allow you to take a straighter line through the corner. Now brake and shift to a gear that will enable you to accelerate quickly out of the corner.

4 **Lean the bike** into the corner. Keep your inside foot at the top of the pedal stroke to avoid catching the pedal on the road. Move your weight over your outside leg and point your inside knee into the corner.

5 **Aim the bike** to brush the inside apex of the corner, or on busier roads a point just after it. This will ensure that you do not end up too far out in the middle of the road after the corner.

6 **Once out of the** corner, straighten up the bike, stand up on the pedals, and accelerate away. If you have come out of the corner a little wide, move back in to the side of the road right away before you accelerate.

See also
Road riding: braking and changing gears **pp.88–89** Road riding: hairpin cornering **pp.92–93**

Road riding: hairpin cornering

Hairpin corners require care because you are turning for much longer than with open corners, so you have to leave your brakes alone for longer. The speed at which you enter the corner must reflect this. The quickest line through a hairpin involves entering wide, crossing close to the inside apex, and exiting wide. This could leave you close to oncoming traffic when you exit the corner, so you must stay alert and only take this racing line when you can see that the road ahead is clear.

Once the technique is mastered, taking a hairpin bend on a descent safely, and at high speed, can be an exhilarating experience. It is a skill that requires plenty of practice, a good feel for your bike, and an appreciation of all the forces you have to contend with when cornering.

Hairpin corners often have a different gradient on the inside than they do on the outside, and this must be considered when picking your line around one. On some hairpins, this differential is quite marked and the insides are very steep. When you take such a corner on a descent, avoid the inside of it, since the sudden change in gradient will throw you off line.

Pro tips

- Take note of the road camber as you approach the corner, and check the road surface for gravel, sand, or water. The line you take should use the camber, but must avoid everything else.
- Only get out of the saddle to pick up speed out of the corner when you and your bike are upright. If you try to acclerate before this, you will be off-balance and could fall.
- Grip into and pull on the handlebar on exiting a hairpin descent. Sit solid in the saddle, and pedal to accelerate.

Barry Hoban Tour de France multi-stage winner

Inside line | Inside apex

Taking the hairpin line
Oncoming traffic severely modifies the line you can take around a hairpin—you cannot take the "out–in–out" racing line. Instead, reduce your speed and stay on the inside throughout the corner.

Negotiating a hairpin bend Skill rating ■■■■☐

Ready to brake
You can keep two fingers ready on the brake lever.

① **Assess the hairpin** before you reach it, obtaining as much information as you can. In particular, check what is coming the other way. If you cannot see, do not guess.

② **Look behind you.** If you do not think anything is likely to pass you before the corner, move out to take the racing line. Do your last braking now.

③ **Lean the bike** into the corner, inside leg up and knee pointing into the corner. Aim to ride across the inside apex. Do not brake, though your fingers can be in place.

④ **Keep your body down** low and press down on your outside leg while in the middle of the corner, and riding across the apex. At this point you do not want to turn any more, so shift your inside knee back toward the bike. Keep your head at 90 degrees to the road.

⑤ **Out of the corner** the bike will drift out from the side of the road slightly. If your entry position and speed were right, this drift should be manageable; if not, stick your inside knee out again to help bring the bike in. Once straight, pedal back up to speed.

See also
Road riding: braking and changing gears **pp.88–89**   Road riding: cornering on the flat **pp.90–91**

Taking hairpin corners at speed requires skill, confidence, a clear road, and fully functioning brakes and gears.

Lean into the corner

Press down on your outside pedal

Cross the apex of the bend

Brake and change gear before entering the corner, and lean your bike into the turn to keep your pace and momentum.

Keep your body low

Control your drift out of the corner

Road riding: climbing

Hills vary in shape, size, and gradient, but climbing them comes down to gear selection and technique. The choice of how you climb a hill depends on its length and gradient, and what is going on around you. For example, sitting in the saddle pedaling in a low gear is the best way up long hills, but short hills, and short sections of a long hill in a race, need to be tackled out of the saddle if speed and keeping up with others is your main concern.

The steps illustrated here will help you to tackle a long climb, and also contain elements that will get you over short, steep ones. One golden rule on any hill, though, is not to ride too hard too early.

Pro tips

- The secret of climbing is breathing. Breathe in and out fully, making the most of every breath. Concentrate on this at the start of a climb, and you will stay in control of your breathing.

- Use a lower gear than you think you will need at the start of a climb while you get your breathing under control, then switch to a higher one if you want to.

- Train as much as possible. You do not have to live near mountains; you can climb the same hill a number of times, sometimes seated, sometimes out of the saddle, but practicing every situation.

Lucien Van Impe Overall winner and King of the Mountains in the Tour de France

Enjoying the ascent
On long hills, or on multiple shorter hills, it is a good idea to ride within yourself, especially early in the ride. It is easy to dig too far into your reserves and turn an enjoyable ride into a grueling journey.

Tackling a climb   Skill rating 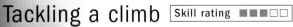 ■■■□□

Changing gears
Shift to a gear you feel comfortable riding in.

Holding the bar
Do not squeeze the handlebar when climbing—it wastes energy.

Hand position
Moving your hands apart helps your breathing.

① **Start a long climb** conservatively. Sit fairly high in the saddle with your weight well back and your hands close to the center of the handlebar. Find a comfortable pedaling rhythm.

② **Shift to a gear** that you can still turn easily but make good progress in as the distance and/or gradient increases. Move your hands to the outer edges of the bar to open your chest and help you breathe.

③ **Place your hands** on the brake hoods. As an alternative hand position to the one in Step 2, it is an ideal way to tackle corners, since the wider hand placement helps you steer the bike.

Pull up

Push down

④ **Concentrate on your** pedaling dynamics; slower cadences on hills make it vital to get the most from each revolution. Pulling with alternate arms helps each leg deliver more power to the pedals, but be careful not to let this affect your steering.

⑤ **Use all your body weight** to push down on the pedals, and pull up forcefully with your arms (*left*) when riding out of the saddle on steep hills. Subtle alterations of your body and bike position help you get all your power into each pedal thrust (*right*).

See also
Road riding: braking and changing gears **pp.88–89**   Road riding: rough surfaces **pp.108–09**

Road riding: descending

Descending a mountain road, professional cyclists can reach speeds of up to 55 mph (90 km/h) on the straights. Riding a bike this fast requires good control, excellent observation, and exceptional anticipation skills. Descents can be used to gain time in a race or increase the average speed of a ride, so it is worth knowing some of the techniques the professionals use to add extra speed, and some of the ones they use to control it.

You can also learn how to control your speed so that you do not have to rely too much on your brakes before arriving at a corner. This is particularly important with a fully laden touring bike because heavy braking can cause wheel rims to overheat and inner tubes to explode.

Riding a descent safely relies on keeping everything smooth and making adjustments in good time. You must also watch out for vehicles on side roads. Even if a vehicle is stationary, reduce your speed in anticipation of what it might do. Above all, build up your confidence as slowly as you feel comfortable with, and be extra-careful descending in unfamiliar areas.

Riding a descent | Skill rating ■■■□□ |

Covering the brakes
On any descent, keep your hands next to the brake levers.

1 **Rest your hands** on the brake hoods so that the brakes are easy to access if you need them; this is an ideal riding position for a short, shallow descent. If you are freewheeling, keep the cranks parallel so that you can easily raise yourself from the saddle in order to let your legs help absorb any road bumps.

2 **To increase speed,** lower your body. This decreases your frontal area and thereby reduces drag. If speed is your goal, then pedal. Shift up until you are in the highest gear possible, but do not pedal faster than feels comfortable—past this point, the action of pedaling will upset the airflow over you and your bike.

Pro tips

- Be relaxed on a descent—a stiff body transfers any bumps in the road to your bike, making it difficult to control. Relax, but stay alert, so that you can plan ahead.

- Stay in your comfort zone. That means only going at a speed you feel you can handle. Do not blindly follow others. Also, if you do not know the terrain, exercise caution.

- Pedal down hills if the gradient is not too steep. A hill after a long descent can be a shock to your legs, so pedaling downhill keeps them in tune for the climb.

Melanie Szubrycht Commonwealth Games competitor

Pedal periodically
Pedaling prevents your legs from becoming stiff.

Air braking

Reduce your frontal area further to go faster. Do this by adopting an aero crouch, with your arms and legs tucked in. You cannot pedal in this position, so do not hold it for too long because your legs will stiffen up.

If you hit a flatter stretch, or a head wind, you will need to resume pedaling in order to keep your speed up. There is no point in losing speed when a little effort is all that is needed to maintain it.

You can reduce speed by changing your body position instead of using the brakes. Sitting up has some speed-reducing effect, as does sticking out your elbows and also your knees.

See also
Road riding: braking and changing gears **pp.88–89**   Road riding: hairpin cornering **pp.92–93**

Road riding: pedaling efficiently

Cyclists refer to correct pedaling technique as "pedaling in circles." It is not just a simple up and down thrusting motion with your legs, since this would only allow you to put power into the down phase of each pedal revolution—this accounts for just 40 percent of the total revolution. Subtle changes in the angle of your foot to your lower leg allow each leg stroke to power much more of every revolution. Correct technique also increases the number of leg muscles you use during each rotation. For example, as well as using your thighs, you will also use your calf muscles and hamstrings.

These steps show you how to pedal efficiently with both legs—constantly monitor your action to see if you are following them. Practicing the correct technique also helps you to think about the stroke of each leg; it is surprising how many cyclists do not power the bike equally with both.

The best exercise you can do to improve pedaling efficiency is one-legged pedaling with your bike mounted on a turbo trainer. Pedal normally for a few minutes on the trainer, shift into a low gear, and unclip one leg from a pedal. Begin to pedal again with the connected leg, concentrating on the circular action outlined in these steps. To move the pedal around each full revolution you will have to use the technique shown here. Do this for a few minutes each week, switching legs every 30 seconds, until you have perfected the technique.

Pedaling technique   Skill rating ■■■□□

Slight forward motion

1 **Push the pedal forward** a little when your foot is at the top of each stroke to help it past this point, which is known as "top dead center." Pushing directly down on the pedal from this position will do nothing at all.

Push

3 **As the stroke continues,** your toes drop below the level of your foot. This is the phase of highest power—nearly every muscle in your leg contributes to it if you pedal properly. At the end of this phase your toes should be pointing downward.

Pro tips

- Do a few seated accelerations. Keep your body as still as possible, and accelerate purely by using your legs and feet. Exaggerate the foot position changes to help you to learn the correct technique.

- Try a few seated, low-gear sprints. At first you will bounce in the saddle. Concentrate on preventing this bounce, because to do so, you have to learn to relax your recovering leg.

- Ride off-road hills. Mountain-bikers are good at getting the most from each pedal stroke—they learn to apply power evenly while climbing in the saddle on steep, loose-surfaced hills.

Russell Downing National Track Champion

Pull

5 **Relax the muscles in your** recovering leg instead of pulling the rising pedal up when pedaling fast. This is perhaps the most difficult phase to master. When spinning slowly, or out of the saddle, there is more of a pull to this phase. Pedals that hold your feet securely will help you pull.

See also
Road riding: braking and changing gears pp.88–89 Maintaining pedals pp.216–17

Push

2 **Drop your heel below the** level of the pedal, and push forward, then down, as if you were sitting on the floor and pushing something away with your foot. This will help to get downward force on the pedal early in the stroke.

Pull

4 **This is the bottom** of the revolution, where you cannot push down any more. You need to pull back. Imagine scraping something off the sole of your shoe. Pulling back with your leg imparts power into a phase of the revolution that otherwise would have none.

Pull

6 **Toward the end of** the stroke, begin to apply the forward push. However, do not do this too early or you will create tension in the muscles of the recovering leg. This technique of "pedaling in circles" is a skill worth mastering, but have patience, since it may take a little time to perfect.

Road riding: cycling in traffic flows

Riding in traffic can be intimidating if you have little experience of it. Get used to riding your bike, and practice road proficiency skills (*see* pp.30–31) before you ride on busy roads. There are also some basic rules that you must be aware of. The first is to always wear your helmet. Next, familiarize yourself with all road signs and always obey them. You must also learn the hand signals to give whenever you want to change lanes or make a right or left turn; these are illustrated on pages 104–05. Finally, always ride with courtesy and respect for other road users.

Staying in control

When cycling on the road the first rule is to be confident, not timid. You are riding a road vehicle, and you have as much right to be on the road as anyone else. This does not mean that your rights will always be respected, which is why you must be more careful than other road users. A car offers its occupants some degree of protection, with a good chance that they will not be badly injured in a slow-speed collision. A cyclist involved in a similar incident is more likely to be seriously hurt.

Using your full field of vision

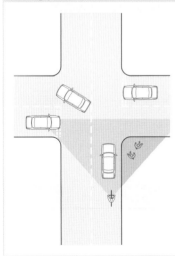

Your most important survival aid is your visual awareness. Illustrated is a typical cyclist's field of vision. To improve peripheral vision, think about it while cycling and consciously monitor the edges of your view. Move your head around to help you scan as wide an area as possible. Monitor the road constantly, looking out for potential hazards such as vehicles turning across your path or waiting to enter from a side road, and pedestrians on the sidewalk who may step out in front of you.

Keeping watch ▶

Stay alert at all times. Mirrors can be mounted on the handlebar to help with rear vision, but you must still turn your head around to check on traffic. Consider wearing protective eyewear—it keeps out dust and flies and stops your eyes from watering, all things that impede your vision. Always wear glasses if you would wear them when driving.

Good bike control is essential. Do not waver or wobble—it makes drivers impatient, and they will be anxious to get past you. Never venture into traffic unless you are able to look over both shoulders and still maintain your riding line. A useful tip when looking behind you is to let go of the handlebar on the side you are looking; you are then less likely to take the bike off-line as you look around.

Imposing your presence

Do everything confidently. Other road users respect this, and it imposes your presence on their consciousness. However, confidence must be tempered by defensiveness. This means never taking for granted what other road users are going to do.

If, for example, you are at an intersection waiting to turn right onto the main road, and a car coming from your left is signaling to turn right into your road, do not move out until that car has begun to turn. Do not rely on the car's turn signals—the driver might decide at the last minute not to make the turn. Act only on what you know is happening, not on what you expect to happen.

Road positioning in heavy traffic

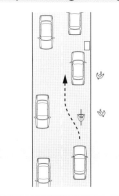

In heavy, slow-moving traffic, join the vehicle flow and ride farther from the edge of the road than usual. This will stop motorists from passing and squeezing you to the side of the road. You will also avoid hazards such as gutters and pedestrians, who may not hear or see you and step out into the road. Drivers can still pass when conditions allow, and all vehicles traveling behind will have a better view of you.

Road positioning when turning right

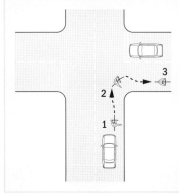

To ensure that following and right-turning vehicles do not force you to the side of the road while cornering:

1 Check behind you for passing traffic and signal left
2 Move out into the lane slightly
3 Assume a safe position on the road you have turned into

Moving left slightly (**2**) stops vehicles from moving past you.

▲ **Setting off**
Look over your shoulder to check for traffic every time you move off. Once there is a gap in the traffic big enough for you to fit in, indicate with a hand signal that you intend to set off into the traffic, then make your move.

▲ **Riding steadily in a traffic flow**
Move with good speed in a traffic flow—not so fast that you become a hazard, but at a speed that keeps you balanced and prevents you from wobbling, especially when you are changing directions.

▲ **Covering the brakes**
Cover the brakes with two or three fingers on a mountain bike, or place your hands on the brake hoods if you have a drop handlebar. This way, you will not have to move your hands very far if you have to brake quickly.

See also
Equipment and accessories **pp.24–25** Road proficiency skills **pp.30–31** Road riding: making maneuvers **pp.104–05**

Road riding: making maneuvers

Successful maneuvering in traffic combines competent observation skills and bike control with clear signaling to other vehicles to let them know what you are about to do. Correct gear selection is also important, as are certain skills that you can practice, such as moving your feet quickly onto your pedals, and riding slowly without swaying from side to side.

Hand signals help impose your presence on the road and create respect for your space from other road users. The two signals you need to know are "I am moving left," indicated by extending your left arm at chest height, and "I am moving right," where the same movement is done with your right arm. Use these signals whenever you are changing lanes, as well as when turning into a road.

Checking behind you

Indicating the direction you wish to turn with a hand signal should make your intentions clear to traffic behind you, but it is still important to look

behind you to see if your signal has been noticed. Practice your hand signals on a quiet stretch of road until you are comfortable with them.

You will have to make frequents stops and starts when riding in traffic. Consequently, you need to be able to remove your feet from the pedals quickly so that you can support the stationary bike while you wait to move on. Never do track stands (*see* pp.112–13) or hold on to other vehicles while waiting. Equally, if traffic is stationary, do not weave in and out of it to avoid stopping; just ride slowly, and if you have to stop, put one or both feet down and wait.

▲ **Preparing to maneuver**
Select a low gear before you stop—this will help you to accelerate away in a straight line. Make sure that you can support yourself with one foot on the ground while stationary. When the road ahead is clear, glance over your shoulder, and if it is safe to do so, move off.

▲ **Keeping your distance**
Stay behind a motor vehicle whenever possible. If you have to pass, do so on the vehicle driver's side. Never pass between a vehicle and the curb—one of the biggest causes of accidents is car passengers opening their doors into passing cyclists.

Signaling before every maneuver

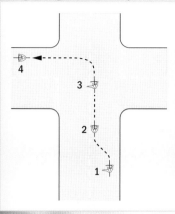

When moving out in front of traffic before making a left turn, always:

1 Check behind and signal left
2 Take up your new position in the center of the road
3 Signal left for the turn
4 Assume a safe position on the road you have turned into

Reinforce the second signal (3) with eye contact and movement of your head, and signal even if you do not think there is any traffic.

◀ **Signaling before turning right**

Making multiple direction signals means that you must be comfortable riding at a wide range of speeds while holding your handlebar with one hand. Anticipate what speed you need to be doing and brake well before you make your signal. Also, when you look behind to check on traffic, it is easy to veer the way you are looking. Be conscious of this and steer straight; relaxing the arm that is in contact with the handlebar helps.

▲ **Checking behind before maneuvering**

Make clear signals, but still check what is happening behind you by turning your head. Every time you make a turn or change your position on the road, you must check before signaling your intentions; then check again before you execute the maneuver.

See also
Road riding: cycling in traffic flows **pp.102–03** Road riding: cycling with care **pp.106–07**

Road riding: cycling with care

While you do need to be cautious as a cyclist, other road users are not your enemy—they will respect your right to be on the road. What motorists require are clear signals from you when you want to change direction; you, in turn, need to be sure that motorists have seen you. This is why eye contact is vital to riding safely in traffic.

Try to make eye contact with other road users by looking directly at them. Once you have made eye contact, a glance in the direction you are going can be very effective. Making eye contact with other road users reassures you that your presence has been noted. You must still make any hand signals necessary, but at least now you know that the other person will see them.

Avoiding potential dangers

Roundabouts, turn lanes, and on- and off-ramps all make the blind spots on motor vehicles—around door frames, for example—much larger, because they sometimes meet roads at sharp angles. Be aware of this and prepare to yield, unless you see that the driver has seen you and has acknowledged your presence. With experience, you will be able to tell when they have. Until then, or if you are unsure, ride slowly and steadily, and always yield.

The majority of road users who do not mind you cycling on public roads are worth working with. Never do anything to lose their respect, or you risk adding to the minority who resent cyclists. When pushed for time, some cyclists are tempted to jump their bikes up onto the sidewalk, ride through a red light, or go the wrong way down a one-way street. Though it may seem appealing, resist the temptation. Not only are you breaking the law, but anyone who sees you will lose the respect for cyclists that all your good, courteous cycling has helped to build.

Cycling with care also means avoiding potential hazards. If you see another road user who is not concentrating on what they are doing, do not try to interact with them—slow down if possible and let them get out of the way. You will come across other hazards (*see* pp.32–33), but the best way to ensure your safety is to treat everything as a potential danger until you can verify that it is not. Ultimately, never take anything for granted.

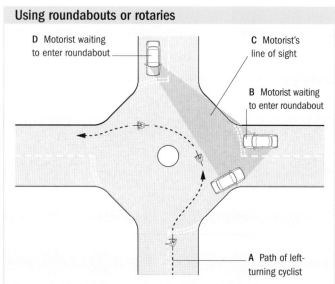

Using roundabouts or rotaries

D Motorist waiting to enter roundabout

C Motorist's line of sight

B Motorist waiting to enter roundabout

A Path of left-turning cyclist

Eye contact is important on roundabouts, particularly when turning left (**A**). Often, motorists are used to the higher speed of motor vehicles, so they may not look at traffic on the roundabout. Instead, they may look at what is about to enter the roundabout (**B**). As a cyclist, you are a small object and may not enter the motorist's line of sight (**C**). Look at drivers waiting to join (**D**) and take note of where they are looking. If they are not looking at you, take extra care. Be sure to emphasize your actions and clearly signal which exit you are taking.

▲ **Cycling with assurance**
Riding confidently and decisively, but also defensively, builds respect, especially among professional drivers in taxis and commercial and public service vehicles. But it is private cars that are involved in most accidents with cyclists, so be on your guard no matter what kind of traffic you are riding in.

Anticipating the path of vehicles with trailers

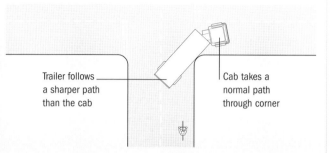

Trailer follows a sharper path than the cab

Cab takes a normal path through corner

Be aware that when cornering, vehicles with trailers take a different path than cars, motorcycles, and bicycles do. Stay well behind them, since the trailer and cab take two different paths, with the cab moving toward the center of the lane before turning left, and the trailer's path following at a sharper angle, often cutting the corner.

Avoiding blind spots

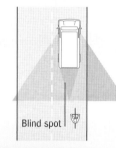

Blind spot

Vans and trucks have a blind spot to the rear of the vehicle, where the height of the rear section blocks the view from the side mirrors. Keep your distance at all times, and take special care when the vehicle has no rear windows. Remember that if you cannot see the mirrors, the driver cannot see you.

◀ **Using your head**
You can still make eye contact if you are wearing sunglasses with light lenses. Remember, the first thing you are looking for is whether the other road users have seen you. When you are certain of this, nod your head to emphasize the contact with them. You can then make your hand signal to indicate your intentions.

See also
Sharing roads and trails **pp.32–33** Road riding: cycling in traffic flows **pp.102–03** Road riding: making maneuvers **pp.104–05**

Road riding: rough surfaces

Road riding is not always a smooth process. From time to time, you will have to negotiate rough surfaces, and even hazards such as potholes and railroad crossings. Paved roads can break up, and minor roads often have an uneven surface. Cobbled roads are still found in many parts of the world. In Europe, some of the world's most prestigious bike races actually seek out these roads, and the ability of champions to ride over them is so revered that the roads have preservation orders placed on them.

Rough pavement or cobbles both require the same technique to get your bike over them. Once you see the surface ahead, shift into a higher gear than you have been riding in, sit well back, and power across. Hold your handlebar firmly, but not too tight, and guide, rather than steer, the bike where you want to go. Let your arms flex to absorb the shocks.

Look for a good line. Cobblestones do not wear evenly—they are easier to ride over where heavy traffic has worn them down. However, wet cobbles are slippery, and sometimes you cannot ride on the part of the road you want to. Just go where the bike leads you, and ride wet cobbles with an extra-light touch. Broken pavement and rough country roads also have smoother lines through them. Look ahead, pick a line, and guide your bike lightly through it.

Negotiating potholes | Skill rating ■■□□□ |

Flexing your arms
Get your arms ready to pull up on the handlebar.

① **Potholes are best avoided,** but never swerve out in front of another vehicle to do so. As you approach one, get out of the saddle and crouch slightly over your handlebar.

Kicking your heels
Kick your heels up to flick the back wheel over the hole.

② **When the front wheel** reaches the edge of the hole, pull up on the handlebar with your arms to lift the front wheel over the pothole. Moving your weight back slightly will help.

Riding various rough surfaces

Cobbles deliver jolts and can become slippery, so they need to be ridden with care. Just before the cobbles, get out of the saddle, keep your weight back, and let your arms and legs flex to absorb the bumps. If you slow down, keep flexing, sit lightly on the saddle, and pedal.

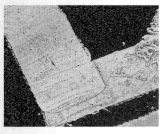

Painted road markings are particularly slippery in the wet. If you are cornering, try to avoid crossing the markings. If this is not possible, slow down. Try and use gaps between the markings to cross, but if not, cross them as close to 90 degrees as possible.

If a wheel gets trapped in a railroad crossing like this, you will crash, so avoid them whenever possible. In the event that you are forced to cross one, do so at a 90-degree angle. Be careful, but not tentative. A little speed helps to get over crossings safely.

Pro tips

- Try to stay seated to put weight over the back wheel when climbing on wet cobblestones. This gives the back tire more traction.
- Even on a dry day, cars can splash water from puddles onto cobblestones. This is extremely dangerous on corners because you are not expecting the wet conditions, so beware.
- Try to get as far to the front as possible if you know there is a rough-surfaced, narrow hill coming up in a race—if a rider in front of you misses a gear, getting past them could be a problem.

Scott Sunderland Professional road racer

Shifting your weight
Move your weight over the saddle to stop the back from lifting.

③ Flex your arms and legs to absorb the shock of landing. Modulate all your movements to the size of the pothole. Just do enough to clear it comfortably.

See also
Road riding: cornering on the flat **pp.90–91**　Road riding: climbing **pp.96–97**

The optimum off-road riding position differs slightly from that for a road bike. Because of the generally slower speeds off-road, aerodynamics are not such a concern and therefore positions are less stretched. This also increases the level of control you have over your bike.

Weight distribution is especially important. If your position places too much weight on the front wheel during steep descents, it will make your bike unstable, particularly under braking. If you have too much weight over the back wheel, you will tend to lift the front when climbing steep hills while sitting in the saddle. On the other hand, too little weight reduces the traction of your back tire.

As with a road bike, the saddle should not be too high or too low, or your leg muscles will not be working through the most powerful part of their range. Exact crank length is not as important when riding off-road, since cadences tend to be less. You should use the longest cranks available (175 mm) because long cranks provide more leverage. However, if your inside leg is less than $31\frac{1}{2}$ in (80 cm), you might be better off with 170-mm cranks. If you also have a road bike, it is a good idea to have the same crank length on both bikes.

The steps here illustrate how to set up a general off-road riding position, but the setups can vary. Downhill riders, for example, have their saddles set far lower. Refer to the Bike Gallery (*see* pp.44–83) for positional differences on various specialty bikes.

Pro tips

- Ask someone to observe you from the side while you are sitting on the bike with your arms straight to check on your reach. Your arms should form a 90-degree angle with your body.
- Try replacing a riser bar with a flat one, or using a zero-degree stem if you would like a more stretched-out position. Some cross-country racers prefer this arrangement.
- Fit a riser bar if you are uncomfortable in a stretched position, or want to do more general trail riding—it is generally wider than a flat one. You can also try a shorter stem.

Wayne Bennet Single-speed champion cyclist

Setting your riding position

Adjusting the saddle
Raise or lower the saddle until your leg is straight. Do not lean over on this leg to make it straight.

1 **Remove one shoe.** Then, with the bike on a turbo trainer or leaning against a wall, sit straight in the saddle and place the heel of your shoeless foot on the pedal. Get someone to observe you, to see if your leg is absolutely straight in this position. Do not influence the leg being checked by leaning on it.

Bar end
These attachments fit onto the ends of the handlebar by means of Allen clamps.

4 **Bar ends can help** when climbing on a mountain bike. You will find the best position to suit you after riding with them for a while. Generally, having them at too flat an angle pulls you too far forward, reducing the traction of the rear wheel. If they are set too high, you cannot get enough pull on them to make them effective.

Level hips
Your hips must remain absolutely level while you pedal.

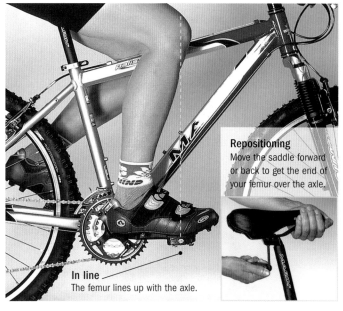

Repositioning
Move the saddle forward or back to get the end of your femur over the axle.

In line
The femur lines up with the axle.

Put your shoe back on, engage the pedals, and start to pedal backward. Your helper should stand, or ride, behind you to check that while you are pedaling, your hips do not rock. If they rock at all, the saddle is set too high. Carry out Step 1 again, concentrating on not leaning on your straight leg.

Adjust your shoe cleats until the widest part of your foot is positioned directly over the pedal spindle. With your foot engaged in the pedal and the cranks parallel, check where the end of your femur (the depression on the side of your knee) is in relation to the pedal spindle. The optimum position is for them to be in line.

Maximum reach
You should be able to hook your fingers over the brake levers, not just touch them.

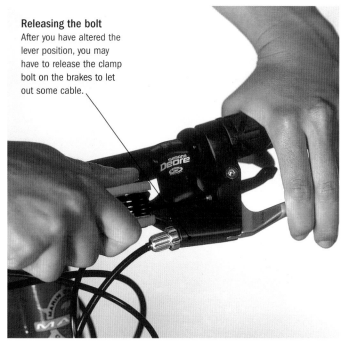

Releasing the bolt
After you have altered the lever position, you may have to release the clamp bolt on the brakes to let out some cable.

Set the brake levers at an angle to the handlebar so that you are pulling in line with your arms and your muscles are working in the line of maximum strength. You should also be able to reach the levers easily with two fingers. Reaching too far reduces the power you can apply to the brakes.

Turn the adjusting screws on the lever hoods if your reach to the brake levers is too far. You will have to undo the brakes to do this. Simply screw the adjuster in until your reach is similar to that seen here. If no more adjustment is available because it has reached its maximum travel, fit smaller levers. Reset the brakes.

See also
Road riding: adjusting position **pp.86–87** Adjusting brakes **pp.198–205**

Off-road riding: improving your balance

There are two invaluable techniques that you can learn to improve your balance and generally help in your day-to-day riding. Riding off-camber deals with negotiating difficult terrain, and the track stand is a skill you can use while assessing a tricky piece of ground or setting yourself up for a complicated move. Both require a certain degree of balance and an appreciation that you can work with your body weight and the terrain to keep making progress.

The key to crossing adverse cambers is to avoid steadily dropping down the slope, using your bodyweight to help prevent you from doing this. The essense of the track stand is to balance your bike against its brakes or a slight slope. This is something worth practicing whenever you can, since it is useful to be able to pause like this occasionally as you figure out what to do next. The track stand is also an integral part of some of the more advanced techniques covered later on.

The principles of weight redistribution that are used in mastering these techniques are repeated many times in off-road riding. When riding on the road, the generally higher speeds help to keep you upright. Because you are often riding slower off-road, particularly when tackling difficult terrain, you do not get this help, and you have to use your body to help keep your balance. The principle is similar to walking a tightrope—if you feel your bike moving one way, you move your body the other way, using it as a counterbalance.

Pro tips

- Keep your knees slightly bent when doing a track stand, and try to keep as centrally positioned over the bike as possible. This will help to keep an even weight over the drivetrain.

- Release the brakes a little occasionally when doing a track stand so you can exert a small amount of pedal stroke into the bike to help stay upright. Do not release pressure on the levers all the way, just a little so that your wheels can move slightly.

- Always wear a helmet, even if you are just practicing track stands in your backyard.

Mark Barrie Professional trials rider

Riding off-camber   Skill rating ■■■□□

1 **Pedal across** on a gentle slope. Aim at a point on the other side of the slope and try to keep the bike level by steering to correct any tendency to slip down the incline.

2 **Build up speed** if the slope is so steep that the up pedal hits the ground, and then freewheel across. Keep your weight over the down pedal to help prevent you from slipping down.

3 **Push off the up-slope** with your foot if you slow down, but keep your weight over the down pedal. Though it might look ungainly, you will make more progress than walking across the slope.

Performing a track stand   Skill rating ■■■□□

Staying in control
Do not exaggerate your movements.

Looking ahead
Look slightly ahead and do not focus on your front wheel.

1 **Use the brakes** to reduce your speed to a crawl as you approach the location where you want to stand. Get out of the saddle and steady the bike under you.

2 **Apply the front** brake and turn the bars slightly. With the cranks parallel to the ground, press on the forward one, just enough to balance the bike against the brake.

3 **Straighten the** handlebar and release the front brake when you are ready to move off. Push down on the forward pedal and continue riding.

See also
Off-road riding: riding singletrack pp.118–19   Off-road riding: riding a dropoff pp.132–33

Off-road riding: braking and changing gears

When cycling off-road, efficient braking and correct gear management add significantly to a positive riding experience. Anticipation is everything—the best off-road riders never lock up a wheel when braking, and rarely get caught out by gradients. The reason is that they are aware of the condition of the trail well in front of them, and they act in good time on the basis of what they see.

Reaching this level of competence takes experience, but the basic principles outlined here will provide enough knowledge to enjoy off-road riding from the start. The two most basic principles to remember are to brake in a straight line whenever possible, and to keep changing gears so that you never have to struggle in too high a gear or ride ineffectively in too low a gear.

Pro tips

- Be prepared to start shifting up as a descent levels out. You can concentrate so much on riding a descent that you are then caught in a high gear at the bottom, with a big climb to face.

- Treat modern mountain bike brakes delicately—their power means that it is easy to lock up a wheel if you are too heavy-handed. Brake extra-early on loose surfaces, and apply the brakes progressively.

Daniel LLoyd XC racer and professional road racer

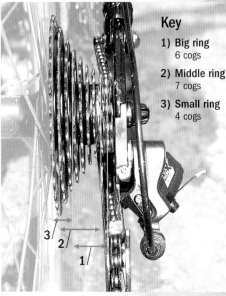

Key

1) **Big ring**
   6 cogs
2) **Middle ring**
   7 cogs
3) **Small ring**
   4 cogs

Chain line
Chains are most efficient when they run straight. Visualize the cogs as being in three sections, each working with one chainring, so that the chain runs as straight as possible.

Using brakes and gears

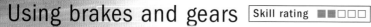
Skill rating ■■□□□

Shifting up
Press the lower lever with your thumb to shift the chain over to larger cogs.

1 **Do most of your** braking with the front brake on flat trails because it is the more powerful one. Use the rear as a backup. Apply the brakes with two fingers, leaving two to hold the handlebar.

2 **Use more of** the rear brake as the descent gets steeper. Riding descents tends to load the front of the bike, and relying too much on the front brake causes a further imbalance in weight distribution.

3 **Shifting with** Rapidfire levers is easy. The lower lever of the right-hand shifter moves the chain to larger cogs, and that of the left hand to larger chainrings. The upper lever of each shifts the chain back.

Tooth profile
Different-shaped teeth help catch the chain on shifts to bigger chainrings.

4 **Reduce the** amount of pressure on the pedals when shifting from smaller to larger chainrings, just until the shift is complete. But do not stop pedaling.

5 **You can shift gears** while riding out of the saddle, but ease off on the pedals until the gear has shifted. Do this on both the up- and the downshift.

6 **Extreme angles** like this one from the largest chainring to the largest cog are inadvisable. As well as being inefficient, they place undue stress on the chain.

See also
Road riding: braking and changing gears **pp.88–89** Replacing hybrid and mountain bike cables **pp.188–89**

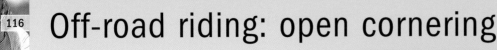
You can really let yourself go when cornering off-road. The absence of traffic means that you should be able corner using the "out–in–out" racing line that road riders use on hairpin bends (*see* pp.92–93). Cornering is about keeping as much speed as possible through a corner so that you can quickly pick up speed after it. Practice cornering techniques at moderate speeds first to build up confidence, but try not to go too slow; slow-speed cornering requires different skills.

Much of the technique of steering around corners comes from the hips rather than the hands. By concentrating on this technique, you will get a feel for how far you can lean your bike in any situation, and what is happening underneath it.

Pro tips

● Focus on your line, not on any obstacles you are trying to avoid. Stay relaxed to help absorb any bumps through the front wheel.

● If you have trouble "steering from the hips," you need to understand how your bike steers. To do this, push your bike forward with your hand (representing your hips) on the saddle. Tiny movements on the saddle will steer the front wheel left or right.

Hannah Reynolds Cycling coach

Ride berm on outside of corner

Change line

Ride berm made by vehicle tire

Flat corner— take racing line

Accelerate away

Exploiting the terrain

Trail awareness will help you take corners better. This rider uses the natural features of the trail to maintain speed. He rides a berm at the top, rather than the racing line, because berms are always faster. Deep troughs left by vehicle tires—like the one halfway down— can provide the same effect.

Riding an open corner
Skill rating ■■■☐☐

Checking behind
Look behind to see if anything is about to pass.

1 **Assess the corner.** First check for any obstructions on the exit. Then check how tight the corner is and whether the trail rises or descends after it. Start to brake now if you need to.

2 **After adjusting** your position to get the best line of attack for the corner, finish braking and make any necessary gear-changes. Look into the corner and visualize your line through it.

3 **Lean into the turn.** Shift your weight to your outside leg. Aim the bike across the apex of the corner. Focus on your line, but maintain an awareness of other things going on around you.

Relax your arms
Stiff arms transfer trail bumps into the steering.

4 **Keep your outside** leg down farther into the corner so that you do not catch a pedal on the ground, and keep your weight over it. Point your inside knee into the corner to help you round it.

5 **This corner** incorporates a trough with sides like a berm, formed by heavy vehicle tires. By carefully picking your line, it is possible to use the sides of the trough to get through the corner faster.

See also
Road riding: cornering on the flat **pp.90–91** Off-road riding: bermed cornering **pp.120–21**

Off-road riding: riding singletrack

Riding singletrack requires precise bike-handling skills, subtle shifts of body weight, and a good sense of balance. Essentially, you have to steer your bike much more with your arms and shoulders, rather than with your hips as you do when negotiating faster corners.

The balance gained from practicing the track stand (*see* pp.112–13) comes in handy on singletrack, and the skills needed can be practiced whenever you are riding slowly. Although you must focus on the terrain just in front of you when riding singletrack, remember to keep looking to see what is coming up. Also, try to maintain your awareness of what is happening behind you.

Ride unfamiliar sections of singletrack slowly at first, but maintain enough momentum to take you over obstacles such as rocks and roots. Once you are more confident, taking singletrack more quickly is one of the thrills of off-road riding. But try to ride smoothly—repeated braking and acceleration makes the bike difficult to control.

Riding downhill singletrack Skill rating ■■□□□

① **Use the brakes** to control your speed. Do not rely too much on the front brake; on steep descents, it weighs down the front wheel and causes shocks to compress. During races, riders tend to bunch up on singletrack, so practice with others.

② **Ride out of** the saddle to help shift your weight around on technical sections. Steer with your handlebar and adjust your shoulders to keep your balance. Do not concentrate on the rider you are following—you may make the same mistakes.

③ **Keep the back** brake on to control speed, but not so much that the rear wheel locks; this rips up the trail and harms the environment. Use the front brake as well. Riding in line improves your reactions, since the rider in front obscures much of the trail.

Climbing on singletrack

Keep your weight balanced between the front and rear wheels. Shift your shoulders to help steer the bike and to move weight over the driving leg. Cover the brakes so you do not roll back if you stop. Steer with your arms and shoulders, not your hips.

④ Take advantage of any straight sections to pick up speed. Here you can just sit down in the saddle and enjoy the ride. With the singletrack successfully negotiated, look ahead to the next difficult part of the track. You could even try the section again. Riding the same piece of singletrack builds skills and is good training for all the muscles needed to achieve better control over your bike.

Pro tips

● During a race, try to reach a section of singletrack before your nearest competitors do. If you ride singletrack well, then this is part of the course on which you want to press home your advantage, so that you do not get held up behind someone who is not as good as you. If singletrack is not your strong point, it is a legitimate tactic to try to take the lead so that those behind you have to ride at your pace, and you will not lose ground to them.

● Do not panic if, while riding singletrack, you find yourself in a rut that goes in the same direction you are traveling in. Simply dab your foot down onto the ground and lift yourself out and back onto the good track.

● Try powering over flat singletrack in a reasonably high gear. Sit very lightly on the saddle, or just above it, so that your bike can move to absorb knocks, but you still maintain good traction from the back wheel.

● Use a wider handlebar, or a riser bar if your bike has a flat one, to help you gain more control. A shorter stem can also be beneficial.

Ian Wilkinson Professional XC racer

See also
Off-road riding: improving your balance **pp.112–13**   Off-road riding: adverse trail surfaces **pp.138–39**

Off-road riding: bermed cornering

Berms are like the bankings in track cycling—
they allow you to take a corner at a much higher
speed than if you were riding on the flat.
Frequently found on BMX, BSX, and downhill
courses, they also occur naturally—where vehicle
tires have eroded forest roads, for example.

To get the maximum speed benefit from a berm,
it is vital to follow the steps highlighted here.
If you go too low when you enter the berm, you
will not benefit from all of its speed-preserving
potential. You should also complete all your
braking before you get to the berm; braking in
any corner tends to make your bike go upright
and steer straight ahead. If this happens in a
berm, you could ride over the lip.

As with other skills, it is best to practice berms
at moderate speeds and then increase as you gain
confidence. Do not approach the berm too slowly,
though—you still need enough speed to get up onto
the face of the berm. Your objective is to ride the
berm with your bike at 90 degrees to the face of it.
This way, you keep the most speed going through
the berm because in effect, your bike is on the flat.

If you feel that you are going too fast, you can
reduce speed by dragging your inside leg lightly
along the ground. This can also help guide your
bike, and is a technique often used by motocross
riders. Watch out for the tops of berms—they are
often weak and can have a crumbly consistency, so
could give way. Look for the line that others have
taken and stay on the high side of it.

Pro tips

- Keep your weight centered. Do not put too much emphasis on the
front or the back wheels. If you have too much weight on the back
wheel, for instance, the front could lose grip and you might crash.

- Preserve speed by pedaling around a deep berm. Stay high,
keep your weight over the outside pedal, and keep it centered.
If you start to drop down, though, stop pedaling. Dabbing down
your inside foot can help you back up.

- Stay loose. If something knocks you off-line, do not fight the
bike, but guide it back in line gently.

Jamie Newall Professional XC racer

Riding a bermed corner | Skill rating ■■■□□

① **Brake early** and adjust your speed. Cover the brakes in case of trouble. Then go in high—riding around the top of a berm has a slingshot effect on your bike because the bike loses no energy in turning. Get out of the saddle, ready to shift your weight as needed. Keep your arms flexed and relaxed, ready to lower your body as you go through the corner. Feel the forces acting on you to build up an understanding of them.

Positioning your head
Keep your head at 90 degrees to the ground to prevent disorientation.

Position pedal
Keep the inside pedal up until you start to pedal again.

② **Keep your head up,** with your eyes focused on the line you are taking through the berm. Do not look too far ahead, but do not look too close in front of you, either. Concentrate on your line.

Centering your weight
Get your body weight centered over the outside pedal.

③ **Keep the** outside pedal down in the middle of the berm; apply pressure through this pedal. Getting your weight over the pedal and lowering your body helps you to keep to your line.

Riding high
Stay high, but avoid the top of the berm—the ground could be unstable.

④ **Start to look** out of the berm as you reach the end of it. Maintain the same body position you had in the middle of the berm, but now begin to be aware of what is coming up next on the trail.

⑤ **Start pedaling as** you approach the exit, but stay high; this way, you gain extra speed as you run down the face of the berm on to the flat again. Once upright and going straight, you can brake if necessary.

See also
Off-road riding: open cornering pp.116–17 Downhill racing skills pp.174–75

To ride a berm smoothly, quickly, and fluidly, you must have balance, timing, and good bike-handling skills.

Enter the corner high on the berm

Keep your body low

Use the angle of the berm to carry your speed through the corner by leaning your bike over into the turn.

Use your inside leg for control

Off-road riding: climbing

You will be amazed at the steep hills you can conquer once you have learned the correct techniques for climbing on your mountain bike. The way to tackle gradual inclines is very similar to the technique on a road bike. However, climbing steep hills is very different. Off-road, it is not just a case of getting out of the saddle and powering over—your power must be applied in a certain way. It requires a delicate touch.

On steep hills, it is important to use your weight to get sufficient traction from the back wheel. You also have to be very careful that you do not lift up the front wheel. The whole procedure requires an empathic feel for your bike and what is going on under its wheels. Just as vital is the ability to react quickly to any changes that may take place.

Tackling a hill requires a positive assessment of what gear you will need before you reach it. This can only come from experience. Think ahead and observe the terrain—correct gear selection can mean the difference between getting up a steep climb or not. For example, you could come to a halt in too high a gear; and too low a gear makes it difficult to modulate the power you put into each pedal revolution, resulting in loss of traction.

Complete mastery of hill-climbing only comes with plenty of practice, but practicing without applying correct technique is a pointless exercise. Concentrate on your technique every time you ride and it will eventually become faultless, and no hill will be able to defeat you.

Pro tips

- Move your weight back if you feel your rear wheel slip. If the front lifts, move your weight forward. But make these moves subtle ones—the difference between having traction or not can be as little as a body shift of half an inch (1 cm).
- Try using a tire with a larger cross-section and a bigger tread to bite into the surfaces if you have trouble getting traction from your rear wheel. Alternatively, run the tire at a lower air pressure.
- Attempt to ride a hill again in a higher gear if you wheelspin during a training climb.

Jodi Vickery National mountain bike series winner

Tackling a climb

Changing gear
Change gear before the climb. On a long climb, use a low gear until your breathing is under control.

Staying seated
Stay almost in the saddle to keep your weight over the back wheel.

1 **Gentle off-road** climbs can be undertaken sitting in the saddle and spinning a comfortable gear. Keep your weight over the back wheel and your elbows out to allow deep breathing.

2 **Use your upper** body to help you pedal as the climb steepens. Pull on the handlebar, but try to keep your back straight so that you do not constrict your breathing.

3 **Ensure that your** pull on the handlebar is directed backward as the gradient gets steeper. Do not pull up— you might lift the front wheel. Moving forward in the saddle helps prevent this.

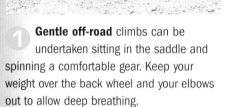

Rising up
As you rise up, keep your weight back to maintain rear-wheel traction.

Keeping straight
Keep your bike and body in line and straight up.

4 **The steepest parts** of the climb might require you to get out of the saddle to use your whole body to power the pedals. If you do, keep your body low and maintain the backward pull on the handlebar.

5 **Keep pulling back** on the bar with a rearward weight bias, and do not rock from side to side—off-road, out-of-saddle riding is all about preserving traction. Do not let your arms constrict your chest.

6 **Sit down smoothly** and keep riding in a low gear for a few seconds when you reach the top. This helps clear lactic acid from your legs. Then shift up through the gears as you build up speed.

See also
Exercising off the bike **pp.146–47** Cross-country racing skills **pp.170–71**

Off-road riding: descending

Using correct technique, even the most spectacular descents can be managed. By applying a number of basic rules, you can make the most of every downhill you come across and ride down the steepest rock- and root-strewn gullies.

A light, confident touch is the key. You need to quickly shift your weight to respond to changes in gradient and trail surface. By learning to relax on the bike, your arms and legs will help absorb shock; if you do not relax, every bump will knock you off-line. Choosing the line of least resistance down a trail is another factor to consider, as is the ability to be aware of terrain well ahead of you. This twin-focus technique comes with experience.

Finally, trust your bike. Modern mountain bikes have evolved so much from the experiences of thousands of off-road riders who have gone before you that they can cope with the most severe types of surfaces found on a trail.

Flexing your elbows
Keep your elbows flexed to help absorb shocks.

Flexing your knees
With your knees flexed and your body out of the saddle, the bike moves beneath you.

Adjusting your center of gravity
On a descent, it is vital to keep your center of gravity between the two wheels at all times. As the trail steepens, the distance between the wheels effectively shortens, so you must move your center of gravity farther back. This means shifting your weight back over the saddle.

Pro tips

- Stay relaxed and let yourself go with the bike instead of fighting it. This is an important element of successful descending off-road.

- Take the direct route. It is often the best line, especially on slippery surfaces, since it saves having to change direction. Do not drag your brakes on such surfaces—just brake and release.

- Sometimes when you pick a line you may be knocked off course by the terrain. If this happens, relax your arms and legs, cover the brakes, and use your momentum to rejoin your chosen line farther down the slope. Trust your instincts to deal with the situation.

Tracy Moseley International Downhill race winner

Riding a gentle descent Skill rating ■■□□□

1 **At the start of** the descent, pick the line you are going to use for the whole route, or at least the part of it you can see. Performing a track stand at the beginning of each section helps.

2 **Ride out of the** saddle as you begin the descent, ready to move your weight farther back if the gradient steepens. Stay relaxed and let your arms and legs allow the bike to move beneath you.

3 **Cover the brakes** with two fingers. Your braking should come more from the back brake, but learn how to use both front and back brakes together for best effect. Apply the brakes smoothly.

Riding a steep descent Skill rating ■■■□□

1 **If the trail** suddenly steepens, stop, do a track stand, and pick your line through that section. Then adopt the same position as in Step 2 for Riding a Gentle Descent, but with your weight farther back.

2 **Control your speed** by braking before you start descending too quickly. Relax and let your bike move; you could fall off if you are too tense on a trail that is covered with rocks and roots.

3 **Start looking ahead** at the bottom of the descent. During the descent, most of your focus should have been on your line down it. In a race, begin pedaling as early as you dare.

See also
Off-road riding: riding singletrack pp.118–19 Downhill racing skills pp.174–75

Off-road riding: bunny-hopping

The bunny-hop is a dynamic technique for jumping a bike over obstructions lying in the trail, such as logs, boulders, or tree roots. It can also be used for jumping the drainage culverts that sometimes dissect forest roads, and for potholes, both on and off-road. It is a particularly useful skill to have.

A successful bunny-hop requires timing, good bike control, and a feel for the right speed at which to tackle each obstacle. These are not things that come naturally, so it is a good idea to practice in a controlled environment. A low obstacle placed in your driveway, or in a local park, is a good way to practice the basics of the bunny-hop. You can increase the height of the obstacle as your skill develops. Be careful when practicing, but do not be too tentative. As with many other cycling skills, you need a bit of speed to execute a successful bunny-hop.

Bunny-hopping can be particularly useful in racing situations. If you have to stop, get off, and lift your bike over an obstacle, you can lose seconds, or even minutes if there are a number of obstructions. Bunny-hopping takes a fraction of this time, but be careful, because fatigue and the buildup of lactic acid in the later stages of a race can badly affect your coordination.

Remember to keep your cranks parallel to the floor throughout this maneuver. You do not have to cover both brakes; just a finger on one will do—the rest of your fingers are better employed securing your grip on the handlebar.

Pro tips

- Takeoffs depend on how good your approach is. Keep your line straight by focusing on a tree or another feature on the other side directly in line with where you want to land.

- If you have flat pedals, the way to lift the back end of your bike is to point your toes down and push back to keep pressure on the pedals. You will then be able to flick up the back of the bike.

Simon Harvey Professional trials rider

Executing a bunny-hop

Skill rating ■■■■□

1 **Get out of the** saddle and crouch down a little over the handlebar as you approach the obstacle. At this point, you must have reached a sufficient speed to clear the obstacle.

2 **Pull sharply upward** on the handlebar to lift the front wheel just before the front wheel hits the obstacle. At the same time, move your body backward. This helps lift the wheel.

3 **Complete takeoff** is required for the back wheel to clear the obstacle. To do this, lift the back wheel by kicking your heels up and backward. This is much easier to do with clipless pedals.

Flexing your arms
Flex your arms to help absorb the landing.

4 **Try to land with** both wheels together, or at least the rear one first. To be sure this happens, you should lift the front wheel with more force than the rear one. Bend your arms and legs to help absorb the landing.

5 **Make any corrections** to the direction of your bike if you have not landed straight. Then start pedaling again. Focus much farther ahead now. Look for the next obstacle and plan early for it.

See also
Off-road riding: riding a dropoff **pp.132–33** Off-road riding: trail jumping **pp.134–35**

Bunny-hopping over obstructions on the trail involves a combination of physical strength, agility, and timing.

Pull up on the handlebar

Approach the obstacle quickly

Lift the handlebar, tuck your feet, and bend your knees in a fluid sequence of movements to cushion the landing.

Tuck your feet up underneath you

Off-road riding: riding a dropoff

When riding your mountain bike, provided it meets a minimum standard and is in good working order, you will be able cope with almost any kind of terrain encountered on a trail. Even particularly tough descents littered with roots, rocks, and steplike vertical dropoffs can be taken in stride by following a few basic principles and putting in a bit of practice. As with all techniques, you should start with small dropoffs and build your confidence slowly. If you try a difficult maneuver too soon, your bike can quickly run away from you, leaving you in a heap on the ground. And nothing damages your confidence quite like a heavy fall.

A dropoff such as the one seen here is a relatively slow-speed maneuver, just like coping with singletrack (*see* pp.118–19). You will need to have a delicate touch and control your bike much more with your arms and shoulders. Experience in executing track stands (*see* pp.112–13) is very valuable in situations like this.

Take time to set yourself up for this kind of dropoff, pick a line, and go for it. Your actual move over the dropoff must be quite dynamic—having second thoughts on the edge and hitting the brakes is a guaranteed way of ending up on the ground. As with descending, when riding a series of dropoffs you must use the dual-focus technique of concentrating on what you are doing while being aware of what is coming up.

Pro tips

- As a rule, keep your weight slightly rear of center on the bike through all phases of the dropoff.
- The distance you look ahead depends on your speed. A big dropoff requires speed to get over, so focus some way ahead.
- Stay off the brakes as much as possible on this type of terrain; rolling wheels are far easier to control.
- Try to land into the gradient of the slope on bigger dropoffs. Landing heavily on the front wheel should be avoided, but landing too much on the back wheel will make the bike difficult to control.

Ross Tricker Professional dual slalom racer

Negotiating a dropoff

Skill rating ■■■□□

Positioning your hands
Cover the brakes with a couple of fingers.

Pulling smoothly
If you brake, do it smoothly. Do not grab.

① **Focus on the** separate parts of the trail once you have picked your line down a technical descent like this one. Take it slowly, stay alert, and just let the bike move under you.

② **Approach the dropoff,** slow down, and line yourself up for it. If you need more time, perform a track stand. Visualize your way over the dropoff, calm yourself, and mentally prepare for the descent.

③ **Pedal forward and** as the front wheel crosses the lip of the dropoff, pull up on the handlebar. As you do so, move your body weight backward to help lift the front wheel.

Flexing your limbs
Keep your arms and legs flexed and the cranks parallel to the ground.

④ **Move your weight farther** backward as the back wheel clears the lip of the dropoff, so that you do not land heavily on the front wheel. Ideally, you should land on both wheels together, but this is not always possible on slow-speed dropoffs.

⑤ **Land under control.** As soon as both wheels are down on the ground, move your body forward and decide on your line for the rest of the descent.

See also
Off-road riding: trail jumping **pp.134–35** Off-road riding: adverse trail surfaces **pp.138–39**

Off-road riding: trail jumping

Jumping a mountain bike not only looks spectacular, it also feels spectacular. Some riders live to fly, launching themselves off improbable ramps, over deep gullies, and off dramatic, vertical walls. In fact, jumping is a sport in itself.

However, trail jumping is not purely for show. It is a skill that can be used again and again to avoid obstacles and allow uninterrupted progress along a trail. A well-timed jump can allow you to safely negotiate terrain that would otherwise force you to get off your bike and walk.

Trail jumping can be attempted in all kinds of situations, each one requiring slightly different techniques. The simplest method is to perform an exaggerated bunny-hop (*see* pp.128–29) from the top of a dropoff (*see* pp.132–33) that is too steep to negotiate slowly. Skill, technique, speed, and confidence are all important factors in ensuring a smooth take-off and landing.

Practicing your jumping skills is time well spent, but take time to build up your confidence. Never commit yourself to a jump until you have checked the takeoff and landing areas for tricky surfaces or obstacles that could impede your progress. If you know you will be doing a lot of jumps on a ride, or you have set out to practice these techniques, it is worth wearing some extra protective clothing. Knee, shin, and elbow pads should be added to your helmet and a tough pair of gloves to help protect you from injury.

Pro tips

- On a long jump, you can correct the position of the bike in flight with subtle changes of weight distribution. If the front wheel dips, move your body back over the saddle. If the rear wheel begins to drop too far, shift your weight forward, toward the handlebar.

- Keep the bike upright in midair until you reach the stage where you are very accomplished. Experienced riders carry out midair tricks and acrobatics, but even they have to land straight. If you land off-balance, you may lose control and crash.

Karl Hemsley Professional exhibition jumper

Applying jumping techniques | Skill rating ■■■■□

① **Check out the** takeoff and landing areas as you approach a dropoff. If you are unsure of anything, ride to the lip and look down the trail, rather than simply jumping into unknown territory.

② **Line up for takeoff** when you are satisfied with the trail. A steep dropoff requires a bit of speed, so do not approach tentatively. When you have almost reached the edge, crouch down over the handlebar.

③ **Take off.** As the front wheel hits the lip of the dropoff, pull up on the handlebar to lift it. The back wheel should just follow, so do not try to lift it, since this could cause the front wheel to drop.

Angle of wheel
Angle of ground

Flexing your body
Flex your upper body and arms to absorb shock.

④ **Move your weight** back to stop the front wheel from dropping too soon. An ideal landing is on both wheels together. Landing on the rear wheel first is acceptable, but coming down front first on a dropoff like this could cause you to crash.

⑤ **Landing successfully** depends on your having kept the bike upright in flight, and the handlebar straight. Absorb landing shocks with your arms and legs.

See also
Off-road riding: descending **pp.126–27** Downhill racing skills **pp.174–75**

Move your weight backward

Bend your arms and legs

Trail jumping demands confidence, agility, and robust equipment that can withstand the impact of landing.

Pull up on the handlebar

Once airborne, keep your body weight centered between the front and rear wheels to avoid landing front wheel first.

One big thrill you get from riding off-road is mastering all the different surface conditions that pass under your wheels during a ride. There are many types of off-road terrain, and the only way to become experienced at riding them all is to keep practicing and looking out for new challenges.

Take mud, for example. It comes in many varieties, from thick, bike-clogging clay, to wet, slimy, almost liquid mud that forms after a downpour during a period of hot weather. Though all could be described as mud, they require subtly different variations of the techniques outlined here to deal with them; only by experiencing each of the types will you be equipped to cope. The important thing when negotiating any adverse surface condition is to use your weight to help you balance and to assist with traction. This is true for many technical skills, and practicing each one of them increases your overall feeling for how your bike reacts in different conditions.

When riding over a stretch of tricky trail, keeping focused is crucial. Pick your line and visualize your way through it. This means taking the stretch as a whole—if you focus on just one part, such as a big boulder in a rocky stretch, you will probably hit it. If you concentrate on your line around it, you will be fine.

Pro tips

- Keep your body in the middle of the bike when riding over rocks and roots so that you can interact with both wheels.

- Try not to brake over rocks and roots, and pedal to keep your momentum. Also try using a higher gear than you normally would for the speed you are going, because the increased torque on each pedal will give you more control.

- Pick a line through to the end of a muddy section before you ride through it. This will prevent you from having to make corrections while you are actually negotiating the terrain.

Richard Barratt Former professional XC racer and coach

Negotiating adverse trail surfaces

Roots

Tackle roots in a straight line. Ride out of the saddle so that your bike can move up and down beneath you. Lift the front wheel over the biggest roots with a semi-bunny-hop.

Forest roads

Forest roads can get cut up, making sections difficult to ride. On a straight, treat them like sand and gravel. On corners, reduce speed and cross the loosest parts in a straight line.

Rocks

Rocks are best tackled out of the saddle. Pick a line where they are smaller, try not to turn too much, and use your shoulders as a counterbalance to control the bike.

Gravel/sand

If sections of gravel and sand are not too long, they just require a bit of speed. Hold the handlebar firmly, but do not fight it. Sit well back and keep pedaling.

Mud

Do not try any violent changes of direction. Keep pedaling, but in a lower gear than used for sand. Sit above the saddle so that you are light but maintain traction.

Snow

Snow is not as slippery as mud, so you can achieve reasonably good traction. Keep a light touch on the controls. As snow tends to ice up the rims, brake extra-early.

See also
Off-road riding: riding singletrack. **pp.118–19** Off-road riding: bunny-hopping **pp.128–29**

Health and fitness

Improving your level of fitness will undoubtedly increase your enjoyment of cycling. These training programs cover everything from warming up and cooling down to attaining an advanced level of fitness. They will add an extra dimension to your riding and leave your senses free to take in everything that is going on around you.

Improving your fitness

Preparing the body for an exercise program in order to improve your fitness is rather like building a house. First you lay firm foundations—in the body's case, a strong heart, efficient lungs, and a sound circulatory system (the network of vessels carrying blood and oxygen to the muscles)—and then you build layer upon layer of brickwork—in the body's case, increased fitness.

Knowing your limits

If you are over 40 years of age and have not trained or gotten regular exercise for some time, you should visit your doctor for a full checkup before embarking on any strenuous exercise program. This is particularly important if you have a history of cardiovascular problems or suffer from pins and needles, chest pain, dizziness, fainting, or any unexplained pain.

Building fitness

A cyclist can lay the foundations of his or her fitness by constant-pace, low- to medium-intensity riding. A more advanced level of fitness can be attained by performing shorter bouts of more strenuous training, which require more effort and improve the body's performance. It is possible to perform well on a bike, and become reasonably fit,

just by working at foundation level. Many top athletes spend most of their time working this way, using the higher training levels only sparingly.

Monitoring your fitness

To make training more productive and to encourage you to progress, you need a few essential items. A stopwatch is useful for timing your rides so that you can record your results week by week. A simple indicator of improving fitness is completing an established route in a faster time but expending approximately the same effort. A cycle computer that shows your speed fulfills the same function—some models also display your current, average, and maximum speed.

A heart-rate monitor (HRM) is a good way of quantifying your results, and is useful when you follow the training programs in this section (*see* pp.150–55). HRMs take the form of wrist- or handlebar-mounted units displaying heart-rate information that is transmitted from a chest-mounted sensor.

Working with training levels

A fitness training program can be structured on the basis of five levels of intensity of activity (*see* Using training levels, *opposite*), ranging from

Exercising on a turbo trainer

A turbo trainer consists of a stand and a resistance unit, and allows you to train indoors when the weather is bad. Secure your bike on the apparatus and begin pedaling. A trainer with variable resistance is particularly useful, as is one that displays distance covered, speed, and power output (measured in watts). Turbo trainers are also useful for advanced training, since there are no vehicles or corners to slow your pace.

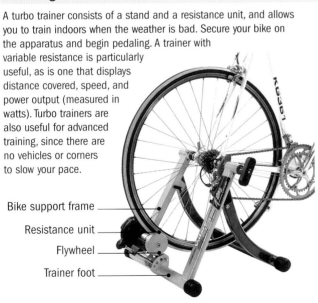

Bike support frame

Resistance unit

Flywheel

Trainer foot

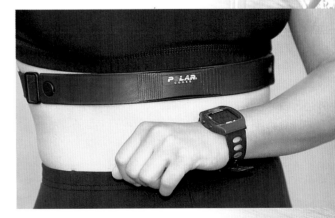

▲ **Using a heart-rate monitor**
A sensor mounted on a chest strap transmits information—such as current or average heart rate—to a display unit, in this case mounted on a wrist strap, so you can keep within your training level.

▶ **Timing yourself**
Keep records of how fast you complete a particular route. Timing yourself, combined with recording the amount of effort expended, allows you to assess your fitness level.

low-level intensity (active rest), to mid-level (endurance and utilization), and high-level intensity (threshold and capacity). These levels describe the target heart rate, which is measured as a percentage of your maximum heart rate (MHR), at which you must be working at each stage of training.

To measure your MHR, use a heart-rate monitor, or calculate your theoretical MHR by subtracting your age from 220. A 46-year-old, for example, has a theoretical MHR of 174 beats per minute (BPM). This method has been proven to be accurate to within three percent of the actual rate.

To work out your target heart rate for each of the different training zones, multiply your MHR by 0.6, 0.7, 0.75, 0.8, and 0.85 respectively. This will give you a precise BPM rate for each of the five training levels.

A talking index is also included in the table below. This shows how easy you should find it to talk when cycling at each level of exertion. With this less scientific method you can use the training schedules even without a heart-rate monitor.

Using training levels

Intensity	Target heart rate (% MHR)	Talking index
Active rest	60–70	Able to converse as normal
Endurance	70–75	Short breath needed after every sentence
Utilization	75–80	Deep breath needed after every sentence
Threshold	80–85	Deep breath needed after three or four words
Capacity	85 and over	Unable to speak

Active rest is the level of exercise you do the day after a hard session, to help your body to recover and rebuild.

Endurance is the level of exercise that develops and strengthens the heart muscle and stimulates the growth of blood capillaries, allowing more oxygen to be circulated to muscles throughout the body.

Utilization is the level of exercise at which muscles become more efficient at taking up and processing the oxygen they receive via the heart and circulatory system.

Threshold is the hardest level at which you can exercise constantly. The body's ability to reprocess lactic acid—a by-product of increasingly strenuous exercise—is just able to keep pace with its production.

Capacity is the hardest level at which you can exercise using oxygen (aerobically). Any more exertion and not enough oxygen will reach the muscles, which then operate without oxygen (anaerobically). Lactic acid is a by-product: it causes fatigue and pain, forcing you to slow down.

See also
Using a basic training program **pp.150–51** Using an intermediate training program **pp.152–53** Achieving advanced-level fitness **pp.154–55**

Warming up and cooling down

You should start every ride with a period during which you ease your body into cycling, and end by cooling down with gentle riding. If you are riding to improve fitness, your initial warm-up and finishing cool-down stretches are of great importance. Neither the warm-up or cool-down need to be complicated. Simply start riding slowly and build gradually to your training pace, and finish by pedaling in a low gear, followed by stretching.

Benefiting from a warm-up

The benefits of gradually easing yourself into exercise are numerous. Warming up helps you to "burn," or use, metabolized food components to release energy—rather than using the body's limited supplies of stored glucose (glycogen)—so that you can exercise for longer.

Muscles contract and the heart pumps blood around the body more efficiently with a raised body temperature. This increased efficiency of the circulatory system allows blood capillaries to dilate and more oxygen to reach the muscles, which produce less lactic acid. Warming up also stimulates the nervous system and aids smooth movements, which saves energy.

Warming up correctly

Before light exercise such as a recreational ride, warm up by riding gently to raise your heart rate and body temperature over a period of ten minutes. For a training session, exercise slowly to gradually reach your target heart rate (*see* pp.150–55). In each case, work gently until your muscles are moving well, and focus your mind on the exercise ahead.

▼ **Aiding performance**
Warming up thoroughly helps your body to perform at its optimum, and following a good cooling-down procedure speeds your body's recovery.

Stretching tips

● Never stretch cold muscles.

● Stretch gently; do not overstretch.

● If you feel any pain, do not stretch any farther.

● Stretch after every ride: it only needs to take about five minutes.

● Stretch between each weight exercise (*see* pp.146–147).

A warm-up is particularly important, and involves some stretching exercises, before a short-distance race (an hour or less). In this event, every second counts and your body must be prepared for working optimally. Using a heart-rate monitor, start slowly and build up speed steadily, riding until your heart rate is 80 percent of your maximum. Then stop and stretch thoroughly (*see below*). Start riding again, this time building up to 85 percent of your maximum heart rate and holding it there for five minutes. Follow this with three ten-second, flat-out sprints, with breaks of about two minutes' easy riding between each.

The timing of this warm-up is crucial. You need to have completed it just as you are about to start the race; otherwise, you will not be able to make the most of its benefits. The more experience you get of racing, the easier it will become to get the timing right, but you can also set aside training sessions for race simulations, practicing the warm-up procedure as part of the exercise.

Cooling down and stretching

To recover after a session, spend the last five to ten minutes of a ride bringing down your heart rate by pedaling in a lower gear.

Stretching after exercise helps to counteract the few ill effects that cycling may have on your body. Pulling on the handlebar may tighten the muscles in the chest and upper back, while pedaling may tighten the hamstring and lower back muscles.

Stretching should be done soon after a ride and in a warm place with no drafts. Do each stretch in a slow, controlled manner. Hold each stretch for at least ten seconds; do not strain your muscles.

Before performing the stretches below, start by stretching your quadriceps. Stand straight with your knees together, and put your left hand on a chair back for support. Bring your right heel up behind you and grab the foot with your right hand. Bend your left knee slightly and pull your right foot up toward your rear end. Hold for ten seconds. Release, and repeat with your left leg.

Stretching before and after exercise

Calf stretch
Stand up straight with your feet together, then step back about 3 ft (1 m) with your left foot. Bend your right leg forward slightly, keeping your left heel on the floor. You should feel a stretch in your left calf. Hold for a count of ten, then repeat with the other leg.

Hamstring stretch
With your leg straight, place your right foot on a step or low seat. Hold on to a wall or chair back to keep your balance. Bend forward, keeping your back straight, until you feel a stretch in your right hamstring. Hold for a count of ten, then repeat with your left leg.

Chest stretch
Stand up straight, feet hip-width apart, with your stomach muscles contracted. Clasp your hands behind your back and gently try to lift your arms upward slightly until you can feel a stretch in your chest muscles. Hold for a count of 20, then release.

Upper-back stretch
Stand as for the chest stretch (*see left*), but with your arms straight out in front of you and hands clasped. Slowly and gently try to push your hands farther away from you until you feel a stretch in your upper back. Hold for a count of 15, then release.

See also
Using an intermediate training program **pp.152–53** Achieving advanced-level fitness **pp.154–55**

Exercising off the bike

All the exercises featured here are specifically recommended for cycling training, and some mimic cycling positions or movements. The most appropriate time to do the weight-training exercises is before you start to prepare for a particular challenge on the bike. It is not advisable to do them on a day when you have an intense fitness-bike training session. Do the exercises in the order shown below, and complete each one before moving on to the next one. Repetitions (reps) are the number of times you do any given exercise; a set is a complete number of reps. Start with three sets of ten reps for each exercise. Then, for progression, increase the amount of weight you lift, or the number of reps.

Leg press

① **Position yourself** under the bar, with your feet as far apart as they would be on the pedals, knees bent close to 90 degrees, and your back straight.

② **Push upward**. Straighten your legs without locking the knees. Count to two as you go up and as you go down. A lifting belt will help support your lower back.

Chest press

① **Sit on the machine** with your back pressed against the support. Take hold of the bars, keeping your elbows level with the top of your chest.

② **Push forward** until your arms are straight. Do not arch your back. Return to the start position in a controlled way. Do not rest before the next push.

Leg extension

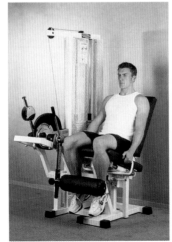 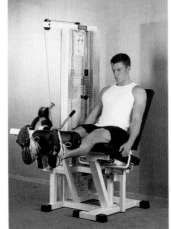

① **Hook your ankles** behind the pad in front of the machine. Keep your feet straight. Push your back well into the support and hold on to the machine's handles.

② **Straighten the legs** slowly. Hold the weight in that position for a count of one, then lower it, but do not let it touch the weight stack. Keep your rear end on the seat during the lift.

Leg curl

① **Sit with the back** of your ankles resting on the pad, which should touch each leg just above the Achilles' tendon. Press your back into the support and hold the machine's handles.

② **Slowly press** the weight down with your legs. Hold for a count of one when your legs form a 90-degree angle, then let the weight come back up in a slow, controlled movement.

How much weight you should lift is determined by how much you can lift just once. Familiarize yourself with how it feels to do each exercise correctly, then see how much weight you can lift by completing one repetition. Start training using 50 percent of that weight. When you can do three sets of ten reps, increase the weight or the number of reps.

Workout tips

- Consult a gym instructor before performing any exercise.
- To warm up, perform 20 reps of each exercise using light weights.
- Wear high-quality athletic shoes that provide good support.
- Wear suitable clothing that will keep your muscles warm.
- Make sure your technique is correct: never sacrifice technique in order to lift more weight, which might cause injury.
- Loosen up between each exercise by stretching (see pp.144–45).
- Cool down after a session on a turbo trainer (see pp.142–43) or exercise bike, pedaling for five to ten minutes at low resistance.

Seated row

1. **Sit in front of** the rowing machine with your legs braced against it, but knees slightly bent. Hold the bar with both hands. Do not lean forward.

2. **Slowly pull the** bar up to your lower chest, keeping your back straight at all times. Hold for a count of one, then lower the bar slowly.

Oblique abdominal crunch

1. **Lie on your back** on a soft but supportive surface, with knees bent, feet flat, and your lower back pressed into the floor. Rest your hands behind your ears on either side of your head.

2. **Raise your head** and shoulders off the floor and slowly tilt your left shoulder toward your right knee. Lower to the floor and repeat with right shoulder to left knee.

Power transfer ▶
Muscle strength developed in the gym means more pedal power on your bike, which in turn improves your capacity to climb and sprint at high intensity.

See also
Improving your fitness pp.142–43 Warming up and cooling down pp.144–45

Eating for maximum performance

The key to good nutrition is knowing what your body needs as fuel and when it is needed. In order to understand this fully, it helps to appreciate the properties of different food groups.

Carbohydrates

There are two types of carbohydrates: simple and complex. Both are broken down into glucose, which is used to generate energy in muscles. Complex carbohydrates go through a number of metabolic processes before energy is released at a slow, steady rate. This makes them ideal for activities such as cycling, which require a long-term supply of energy. Simple carbohydrates require less processing, so are a more immediate source of energy, but this immediacy results in highs of available energy, followed by lows as energy is quickly expended.

Proteins

The human digestive system breaks proteins down into amino acids, which are assimilated and used to repair body tissue and build new muscles. Every animal protein source contains all the amino acids the body needs, but some contain saturated fats. Vegetable proteins do not contain saturated fat, but a single source alone does not provide all the amino acids the body requires. Vegetarians must combine different proteins to meet the body's needs. Typical combinations include corn with beans or peas; rice with beans or peas; or lentils with bread.

Fats

There are "good" fats (unsaturated) and "bad" fats (saturated). Unsaturated fats are essential for vitamin absorption and are used as fuel, especially during sustained, low-level, aerobic effort. Saturated fats slow the metabolism, encourage the build-up of cholesterol, and are linked with high blood pressure and heart disease.

In general, good fats are liquid and bad fats are solid at room temperature. So olive oil is good, while the fat around meat is bad. However, some saturated fats are hidden—for example, in cookies, cakes, and pastries.

Vitamins and minerals

Vitamins and minerals are found in many different foods, and are required for various metabolic processes. They are often destroyed during cooking or storage, but a good supply can be ensured by consuming a wide variety of fresh foods.

Eating and drinking for energy

There are drinks and foods specially formulated for consumption before, during, and after exercise. Specialist advice can be obtained from a nutritionist, or, for particular dietary needs, a dietician.

◄ **Eating while riding**
Make sure you eat the right foods at the right time: for example, complex carbohydrates before a ride, simple carbohydrates during a ride, and a combination of carbohydrates and protein afterward.

On the day of a race, a hard ride, or a strenuous training session, carefully plan your food intake for the day. Before the ride, eat a combination of complex carbohydrates, such as cereals with skim milk, pasta, rice, a pre-race sports drink, or wholemeal sandwiches (which should include a protein source if you expect the ride to be arduous).

During the ride, eat a combination of simple and complex carbohydrates. These might include cakes and candies, sports drinks and bars, bananas, and wholemeal sandwiches.

Immediately after hard physical work, there is a 30-minute "window" during which the body's ability to process carbohydrates is accelerated, especially if the carbohydrate is combined with protein. So after you have finished doing hard exercise, consume carbohydrates and protein: a tuna or peanut butter sandwich, smoothies made with yogurt, or a recovery sports drink are all suitable.

Perhaps the most important aspect of fueling the body for performance is water consumption. Keep hydrated by drinking two to three quarts (liters) of water a day. Always carry water with you, and do not wait until you are thirsty before you drink, since this means you are already dehydrated.

▲ **Drinking on your bike**
When you are riding your bike, it is important to keep hydrated. If you lose even one percent of your body weight through dehydration, your performance will be negatively affected.

Eating for the Training, testing, and recovery program

The daily food plan provides a 132-lb (60-kg) woman or a 165-lb (75-kg) man with sufficient amounts of each dietary component to complete the Training, testing, and recovery program (see pp.150–51). This is calculated assuming that both men and women require 5 g of carbohydrate, 1 g of protein, and up to 1 g of fat per 2.2 lb (1 kg) of body weight per day, to exercise at this level. Note that although some foods have no fat listed, there are small traces of fats in most foods.

MEAL		FOOD OR DRINK	DIETARY COMPONENTS
BREAKFAST	Women	1¾ oz (50 g) granola	30 g carbohydrate, 5 g protein, 8 g fat
		1 cup (250 ml) skim milk	20 g carbohydrate, 10 g protein
		Two slices wholewheat bread or toast with olive-oil spread	25 g carbohydrate, 6 g fat
	Men	3 shredded wheat cereal biscuits	45 g carbohydrate, 1.5 g fat
		1 cup (250 ml) skim milk	20 g carbohydrate, 10 g protein
		Wholewheat roll with olive-oil spread	30 g carbohydrate, 6 g fat
MID-MORNING SNACK	Women	2 slices raisin bread	25 g carbohydrate
		7 oz (200 ml) orange juice	25 g carbohydrate
	Men	Bagel with cottage cheese	40 g carbohydrate, 10 g protein, 14 g fat
		7 oz (200 ml) orange juice	25 g carbohydrate
LUNCH	Women	5 oz (150 g) baked potato	45 g carbohydrate
		1¾ oz (50 g) green salad with 2 tsp (10 ml) olive-oil dressing	1 g carbohydrate, 10 g fat
		½ cup (125 ml) skim milk	10 g carbohydrate, 5 g protein
	Men	7 oz (200 g) baked potato	60 g carbohydrate
		4½ oz (135 g) baked beans	20 g carbohydrate, 10 g protein
		17 oz (500 ml) protein sports drink	30 g carbohydrate, 7.5 g protein
MID-AFTERNOON SNACK	Women	Banana	20 g carbohydrate
	Men	1 oz (30 g) chocolate	20 g carbohydrate, 10 g fat
		½ cup (125 ml) skim milk	10 g carbohydrate, 5 g protein
EVENING MEAL	Women	2½ oz (75 g) pasta with olive oil	50 g carbohydrates, 8 g fat
		5 oz (150 g) lean chicken	35 g protein, 5 g fat
		1¾ oz (50 g) salad with 2 tsp (10 ml) olive-oil-based dressing	1 g carbohydrate, 10 g fat
		12 oz (350 g) fresh fruit salad with 5 oz (150 g) low-fat yogurt	50 g carbohydrate, 5 g protein
	Men	2½ (75 g) rice	50 g carbohydrate
		5 oz (150 g) lean meat	40 g protein, 10 g fat
		1¾ oz (50 g) green salad with 2 tsp (10 ml) olive-oil dressing	1 g carbohydrate, 10 g fat
		3½ (100 g) sherbet	25 g carbohydrate

See also
Using an intermediate training program **pp.152–53** Achieving advanced-level fitness **pp.154–55**

Using a basic training program

The training programs described here and on pages 152–53 form a large part of a typical fitness schedule for all competitive cyclists, including professionals. The training schedules follow a theory of fitness improvement known as periodization, which means progressing through different training periods as you work toward an objective. The test and recovery schedule allows you to gauge your progress and rest your body.

Starting a training program

The Starter training schedule (*see opposite*) is for anyone new to cycling or progressive physical training. It is suitable for road- and mountain-bike training, since the fitness demands of each are similar. Mountain bikers must also practice specific off-road skills, so the Better Cycling techniques (*see* pp.112–39) should be practiced at race speed.

Progressing over time

Use the Training, testing, and recovery program in four-week blocks, following the Starter training schedule for three weeks, and in week four, the Test and recovery schedule. Progress by raising the intensity and duration of each block of training.

The value of training in blocks of this length and sequence is that the body can build strength and fitness over a three-week period and then have a well-earned week of rest and regeneration. Hard training sessions are easier to handle if you know that recovery is around the corner.

Testing and recovering

The test and recovery week is crucial to your progression. This is the time to gauge your level of fitness, while at the same time allowing your body to recover its impetus. Follow the instructions in

◀ **Improving fitness and technique**
Mountain bikers should do as many sessions as possible on their mountain bikes, and riding off-road, so that they can improve specific techniques at the same time as improving their fitness level.

the test carefully and record your results. You should see a steady improvement in performance as you complete each four-week block.

It is worth recording the time, intensity, and how your body has performed at the end of each session, not just after the test. Many top athletes keep extensive diaries, detailing every aspect of their training. Data such as your waking pulse each day, the times that different rides take, your weekly weight, and average pulse rates are well worth noting. Nothing is more inspiring than to see your progress mapped out in front of you.

Training, testing, and recovery program

Follow the Starter training schedule for 3 weeks, followed by the Test and recovery schedule for 1 week, then a second block of 3 weeks' training and a Test and recovery week. Follow the advice in the weekly progression box. In the second block of 3 weeks, increase the number of 1-minute fast pedaling bursts to a maximum of ten by week three. In the same period, lengthen the Sunday ride to a maximum of 2 hours.

Starter training schedule

DAY		Monday	Tuesday	Wednesday	Thursday	Friday	Saturday	Sunday
DURATION		Rest	45 minutes	1 hour	45 minutes	Rest	1 hour	1½ hours
TERRAIN	Road bike	Rest	Flat roads	Flat roads and rolling roads	Flat roads	Rest	Flat roads and rolling roads	Flat roads and hilly roads
	Mountain bike	Rest	Flat roads	Flat and rolling off-road trails	Flat roads	Rest	Flat and rolling off-road trails	Flat roads and hilly roads
INTENSITY (% Maximum Heart Rate)		Rest	70–75	70–75	70–75	Rest	70–75	70–80
INSTRUCTIONS		Rest	Ride at a constant pace, performing three 1-minute bursts of fast pedaling in a low gear while seated	Ride in higher gears and maintain a constant pace	Ride at a constant pace, performing three 1-minute bursts of fast pedaling in a low gear while seated	Rest	Ride in higher gears and maintain a constant pace	Ride at a steady effort on the flat, but stay in the saddle and raise your pace while climbing
WEEKLY PROGRESSION		Rest	Add 1 further minute of fast pedaling each week	Increase the ratio of rolling terrain to flat terrain	Add 1 further minute of fast pedaling each week	Rest	Increase the ratio of rolling terrain to flat terrain	Increase the ratio of hilly terrain to flat terrain

Test and recovery schedule

DAY		Monday	Tuesday	Wednesday	Thursday	Friday	Saturday	Sunday
DURATION		Rest	30 minutes	1 hour	30 minutes	Rest	1 hour	1½ hours
TERRAIN	Road bike	Rest	Flat roads	Flat 3-mile (5-km) road circuit	Flat roads	Rest	Flat roads	Hilly roads
	Mountain bike	Rest	Flat off-road trails	Rolling 2-mile (3-km) off-road circuit	Flat off-road trails	Rest	Flat off-road trails	Hilly off-road trails
INTENSITY (% Maximum Heart Rate)		Rest	60–70	70–80	60–70	Rest	70–80	70–75
INSTRUCTIONS		Rest	Ride at a steady pace, using low gears to aid recovery	Perform test	Ride at a steady pace, using low gears to aid recovery	Rest	Practice sprinting	Ride at a steady pace and stay in saddle on climbs

Test Warm up with 20 minutes' progressively harder riding, reaching high intensity. Start your stopwatch and heart-rate monitor and ride at the limit of your endurance for one lap of the circuit. Record your time and warm down with 20 minutes of low-intensity riding in a low gear.

Sprinting Warm up with 20 minutes' progressively harder riding, reaching high intensity. Sprint in a high gear for 10 seconds (20 seconds if you are on a mountain bike), recover for 5 minutes, and repeat twice. Warm down with 20 minutes of low-intensity riding in a low gear.

See also
Road riding: pedaling efficiently **pp.100–01** Off-road riding **pp.112–39**

If you have successfully completed two blocks of the Starter training schedule, with a test and recovery week after each block (eight weeks' training in total), or can comfortably complete a one-and-a-half-hour ride over hilly terrain, exercising for at least an hour at 75–80 percent MHR, you should be ready to progress to the Intermediate training schedule (*see opposite*).

This level of training allows you to build on your existing fitness. If you have a big race coming up, regularly riding at the levels prescribed here will allow you to build up great reserves of physical strength.

Raising your body's performance

The Intermediate training schedule is designed to improve your body's ability to use the increased amount of oxygen and fuel that your muscles will now receive due to your increased fitness level. The intensity of some of these sessions will also significantly increase muscle strength, and begin to raise your anaerobic threshold (*see pp.142–43*), which the Lactate- and Capacity-threshold training schedules (*see pp.154–55*) target specifically.

Each part of the schedule works on a particular area of fitness. Riding at 75–80 percent MHR actively increases your body's efficiency at processing oxygen and fuel. Staying seated on the climbs and concentrating on pedaling efficiency strengthens your legs and ensures that you use all your muscle fibers to utilize every part of your pedal revolution. Staying in the saddle also helps to toughen up the tendons, ready for the even harder training to come in the advanced schedules.

Progressing toward a challenge

To reach the peak of your fitness potential on a certain day (the day of a long-distance challenge, for example), calculate back from that day, and complete two three-week blocks of the Intermediate training schedule, with a test and recovery week after each. Follow this with two three-week blocks of each of the advanced schedules on pages 154–55, with a test and recovery week after each. This adds up to 24 weeks of training, so it is important to plan in advance. Once you have reached your peak, it need not mean the end of your progression. Pick another objective and establish another series of training blocks based on these schedules, just as you did the first time. The number of blocks you do depends on how far ahead your next challenge

◄ **Going it alone**
It is best to do most of your training alone. You achieve more and you train at the intensity that suits your level of fitness, not somebody else's.

Intermediate training schedule

Follow this schedule for 3 weeks, following the weekly progression specified. If you are coping easily, do not be tempted to do more than is advised here. If you are not progressing, repeat the schedule at the same intensity and duration. After 3 weeks, follow the recovery and test schedule of the Starter training schedule (see p.151).

In the second block of 3 weeks, increase the duration of high intensity work by 5 minutes a week. If you want to train for longer, increase the duration of low-intensity work. When returning to the schedule, increase the duration of high-intensity work as before, and the duration of low intensity work on Tuesday, Wednesday, and Saturday by 10 minutes a week.

DAY		Monday	Tuesday	Wednesday	Thursday	Friday	Saturday	Sunday
DURATION		Rest	1 hour	30 minutes	1 hour	45 minutes	1 hour	1½ hours
TERRAIN	Road bike	Rest	Rolling roads	Flat roads	Rolling roads	Flat roads	Rolling roads	Hilly roads
	Mountain bike	Rest	Rolling 2-mile (3-km) off-road circuit	Flat off-road trails	Rolling 2-mile (3-km) off-road circuit	Flat off-road trails	Rolling 2-mile (3-km) off-road circuit	Hilly off-road trails
INTENSITY (% Maximum Heart Rate)		Rest	70–80	60–70	70–80	60–70	70–80	70–80
INSTRUCTIONS		Rest	Ride at low intensity for 50 mins. Spend 10 minutes at high intensity on inclines. For mountain bikes, record the number of laps completed	Ride in low gears and concentrate on pedaling efficiency	Ride at low intensity for 55 min. Spend 5 minutes at high intensity on inclines. For mountain bikes, record the number of laps completed	Ride in low gears and concentrate on pedaling efficiency	Ride at low intensity for 50 min. Spend 10 minutes at high intensity on inclines. For mountain bikes, record the number of laps completed	Ride at a steady pace. For road riders, stay seated during climbs, and for mountain bikes, practice techniques in Better Cycling
WEEKLY PROGRESSION		Rest	Add 5 extra minutes at high intensity each week	Maintain the same intensity and duration each week	Add 5 extra minutes at high intensity each week	Maintain the same intensity and duration each week	Add 5 extra minutes at high intensity each week	Increase the length of your ride by 30 minutes each week

lies. With this new challenge, however, when you start on the intermediate schedule, you will be starting at a higher level of fitness, so you need to increase the duration of each session to build an even stronger foundation of fitness, and enable you to achieve much more from your training.

Most cycling events are held during the summer months, so, in a complete training program, much of this intermediate stage will be carried out during the winter and spring months. Late fall is a good time to ride less and spend more time building your muscles by weight training. One potential problem during winter training is bad weather, but you can still train with a turbo trainer (see p.142).

Any of the sessions in this schedule can be carried out using a turbo trainer. To increase the intensity of your work, simulate hills by increasing

the resistance setting or by using your gears. Specially designed props can be used to raise the front wheel to simulate the climbing position. A turbo trainer is an excellent training tool, since it is easy to control the intensity of the workout. Although it cannot compare to training outdoors, using a turbo trainer is preferable to cycling in poor weather or in the dark. If you find training indoors somewhat monotonous, play some music to help you maintain a good pedaling rhythm.

Riding in a group ▶

It is a good idea to ride with others now and again. This will provide an opportunity to establish your group riding skills. Sunday is a good day in the intermediate schedule for riding with company.

See also
Road riding: climbing pp.96–97 Off-road riding: climbing pp.124–25 Improving your fitness pp.142–43 Achieving advanced-level fitness pp.154–55

Before attempting these schedules, you should have completed the Intermediate training schedule (*see* pp.152–53) and be capable of a two-hour hard, hilly ride at 75–80 percent MHR.

Raising your lactate threshold

Your body's ability to transport oxygen to your muscles will now be vastly improved, making them function more efficiently. Further improvement is prevented, however, by lactic acid produced by the muscles during higher-intensity exercise. The body can only process and dispose of lactic acid up to a certain level of exercise, known as the lactate threshold. To raise this threshold you need to train at or near 80–85 percent MHR (*see below*).

Improving your capacity threshold

The capacity threshold schedule (*see right*) increases the body's ability to use oxygen during exercise. You can work harder than the intensities specified, but you risk exercising without oxygen (*see* pp.142–43), which leads to lactic acid build-up in the muscles.

The capacity threshold schedule includes racing practice in Tuesday's session, ideally with a group. Road riders can form a pace line, riding at high intensity when leading the line. This also provides an opportunity to hone group riding skills at near-race pace. Mountain bikers can follow the same session, or alternatively, follow Tuesday's session in the lactate threshold schedule, practicing cornering, climbing, and singletrack skills at race speed.

Overcoming your weaknesses

After completing two three-week blocks of each schedule, with a recovery and test week after each, you should have reached a high level of fitness and be ready for an advanced challenge, such as a race.

After a few races or long-distance challenges, completing different blocks of training for each new objective, turn your attention to your weak points. Identify which areas need improvement, and spend extra time practicing them. For example, you might be a strong climber, but lose out in head-to-head sprints. Concentrate on sprinting at high intensity.

Lactate threshold schedule

The schedule is performed in two blocks of 3 weeks, with a test and recovery week after each (*see* p.151). In the first block, follow the schedule as below. In the second block, increase the duration of high-intensity riding. However, Tuesday's session should progress to no more than 40 minutes of high-intensity riding, and in Thursday's session, you should progress to no more than eight 4-minute climbs (increase the duration of the session to fit them in). In subsequent blocks, train with greater precision—measure your actual MHR (*see footnote*) and use this figure to calculate intensities.

DAY		Monday	Tuesday	Wednesday	Thursday	Friday	Saturday	Sunday
DURATION		30 minutes	1 hour	30 minutes	1 hour	Rest	1 hour	2 hours
TERRAIN	Road bike	Flat roads	Flat roads and rolling roads	Flat roads	Hilly roads	Rest	Flat roads	Hilly roads
	Mountain bike	Flat off-road trails	Rolling 2-mile (3-km) off-road circuit	Flat off-road trails	Hilly off-road trails	Rest	Flat off-road trails	Hilly off-road trails
INTENSITY (% Maximum Heart Rate)		60–70	70–85	60–70	70–85	Rest	70–80	70–80
INSTRUCTIONS		Ride in low gears and maintain a constant pace	Ride at low intensity for 20 minutes, building to high intensity for 10 mins. Cool down at low intensity for 30 mins	Ride in low gears and maintain a constant pace	Ride at low intensity for 10 minutes, then climb a 4-minute hill, four times, at high intensity. Try to reach full intensity	Rest	Practice **sprinting** (*see* p.151)	Ride at a steady intensity; tackle inclines both in and out of the saddle
WEEKLY PROGRESSION		Maintain the same intensity and duration each week	Add 5 further min at high intensity each week	Maintain the same intensity and duration each week	Make one additional hill climb each week	Rest	Maintain the same intensity and duration each week	Add an extra 30 minutes to length of ride each week

Measuring your actual MHR On the same circuit that you use to perform the test (*see* p.151), warm up with 20 minutes of progressively harder riding, reaching high intensity. Start your heart-rate monitor (HRM) and ride at the limit of your endurance for one lap of the circuit, ending by climbing or sprinting as hard as possible until you cannot continue. Your HRM reading at this point is your actual MHR. Cool down with 20 minutes of low-intensity riding in a low gear.

Capacity threshold schedule

Perform two 3-week blocks with a recovery and test week after each. The 3-minute repeats on Thursday train your capacity to work with oxygen, and require precision—at 1 minute, your heart rate should reach 80% MHR, at 2 minutes, 85%, and at 3 minutes, just over 85%. Recover for 3 minutes between each repeat. In block two, increase the duration of each session, on Tuesday to a maximum of 2 hours, and on Sunday to a maximum of 4½ hours. In subsequent blocks, train with greater precision—measure your actual MHR (*see footnote*) and use this figure to calculate intensities.

DAY		Monday	Tuesday	Wednesday	Thursday	Friday	Saturday	Sunday
DURATION		30 minutes	1½ hours	30 minutes	1 hour	Rest	1 hour	3½ hours
TERRAIN	Road bike	Flat roads	Rolling or hilly roads	Flat roads	Rolling roads	Rest	Flat roads	Hilly roads
	Mountain bike	Flat off-road trails	Rolling or hilly off-road trails	Flat off-road trails	Rolling off-road trails	Rest	Flat off-road trails	Hilly off-road trails
INTENSITY (% Maximum Heart Rate)		60–70	70–85	60–70	70–85	Rest	70–80	70–85
INSTRUCTIONS		Ride in low gears and maintain a constant pace	If possible, ride in a group, at medium intensity for 70 min, with short bursts at high intensity totaling 20 minutes	Ride in low gears and maintain a constant pace	Ride at low intensity for 20 mins. Do three 3-minute high intensity repeats. Cool down with 20 mins at low intensity	Rest	Practice **sprinting** (*see* p.151)	Ride at a steady pace, building to higher intensity for climbs. Tackle inclines both in and out of the saddle
WEEKLY PROGRESSION		Maintain the same intensity and duration each week	Add 15 minutes to your ride each week	Maintain the same intensity and duration each week	Add one 3-minute repeat each week to a maximum of five	Rest	Maintain the same intensity and duration each week	Add 15 minutes to your ride each week

Measuring your actual MHR On the same circuit that you use to perform the test (*see* p.151), warm up with 20 minutes of progressively harder riding, reaching high intensity. Start your heart-rate monitor (HRM) and ride at the limit of your endurance for one lap of the circuit, ending by climbing or sprinting as hard as possible until you cannot continue. Your HRM reading at this point is your actual MHR. Cool down with 20 minutes of low-intensity riding in a low gear.

▲ Using a trainer
A personal trainer will give you expert guidance and motivation, and provide you with new impetus to raise your performance.

◀ Making training specific
Set specific goals to overcome your weaknesses. If your time-trialing is letting you down, train on your time-trial bike.

See also
Improving your fitness **pp.142–43** Using a basic training program **pp.150–51** Using an intermediate training program **pp.152–53**

Competitive cycling

As a cyclist you can test yourself in a variety of ways. You can take on a personal challenge such as perfecting a freestyle BMX jump, choose to race against others, or enter events in which your riding skills are assessed. This insight into the world of competitive cycling profiles its various disciplines and outlines the skills that are needed to take part.

Competing on the road

Road racing for beginners is done in a group on a closed circuit or on the open road, generally over distances of 30–50 miles (50–80 km) with around 60 competitors, more on a closed circuit. The winner is the first rider over the line. Most races are one-day events, but some last several days. You do not have to be a member of a cycling club to road race, but you will probably need to apply for a racing license. Use the Internet, cycling press, and bike shops to check for races that are held locally and nationally to suit different racing abilities.

Gaining racing experience

Before you start racing, follow the training schedules on pages 150–53. Make sure your bike is in good running order (*see* pp.178–223), paying particular attention to your brakes and gears.

The best way to gain experience of road racing is to join a cycling club that has races as part of its regular activities. If you wish to race professionally or represent your country, clubs offer the best opportunities for meeting qualified coaches, and provide a good introduction to the sport. Clubs can be found through cycling associations and the Internet (*see* pp.228–31).

To gain experience of riding in a group, mass-participation charity rides such as the London-to-Brighton event in the UK and Ride for the Roses

Long-distance road racing

For the ultimate long-distance challenge, it is hard to beat the Race Across America (RAAM)—some 3,000 miles (4,800 km) coast to coast. There are no stage towns in between, so it is up to competitors when they rest. The course—and hence the time taken to complete the ride—changes each year. The race requires a rigorous training program and a substantial financial investment, since each rider must have a motorized backup team. Race Across America is open to individuals, teams of up to four, and tandems, and competing is not beyond the reach of a group of committed individuals.

◀ Preparing to race

Once you have decided which race or challenge is for you, prepare yourself by working on your fitness. Joining a local club will give you access to other cyclists who will be eager to help you progress.

in the US are good events to enter. Although they are not officially races, these rides often have a competitive element.

A race that is fast becoming one of the ultimate challenges is the Etape du Tour. Regularly attracting more than 8,000 entries, the race takes place on the roads of a stage of the Tour de France.

Racing competitively

Road racing is governed by various national bodies throughout the world, which are controlled by the International Cycling Union (UCI). Races are held for beginners and experts of all ages.

For racers between the ages of 18 and 40, riders are normally organized by ability into categories (commonly called "cats"), ranging from Elite (mainly professionals) through First, Second, Third, and Fourth categories. Most races are conducted in ability groups—for example, First and Second category, or Third and Fourth. As an entry-level

rider over age 18, you would be in the Fourth category. By earning points from getting into the top five places in a race, you will gain promotion into the Third category.

The top riders in the world race in the Elite category, and the best of those are contracted to professional teams. Riders under 18 and over 40 compete within their age groups.

If you just want to try racing once, find a local league in your area and choose a race. You will need to ask the organizers about a "day" license.

Choosing a challenge

The Etape du Tour, the Paris-Roubaix cyclo-sportif, the Gran Fondos in Italy, and American races such as the Tour of the Scioto River Valley are all events in which competitors start together and there is an overall winner, as well as those in age-group classifications. There are also long-distance rides that can be ridden alone or as a group. Famous routes—such as Land's End to John o'Groats in the UK, and the Vancouver-to-San Francisco trail in Canada and the US—can be ridden at any time of year.

▼ Experiencing riding in a group

Mass-participation rides, such as England's London-to-Brighton charity event, allow new cyclists who would like to try road racing to experience riding in a large group.

▼ Racing in the Etape du Tour

The Etape du Tour is held on a stage of the Tour de France, and is open to amateurs. You can enter on the Internet, with a form found in cycling magazines, or via specialist tour companies.

See also
Using an intermediate training program **pp.152–53** Achieving advanced-level fitness **pp.154–55** Directory **pp.228–31**

Road racing skills

The key to road racing is the ability to ride at high speed in a group. Competitors start the race together and quickly form a pack (a group of riders), which is the base around which all road races evolve. During a race, riders will try to keep up with the pack, maintain their position in it, break away from it in an attack, and launch a sprint for the finish line.

Riding in the pack

One of the most useful skills a road rider can develop is the ability to keep a good position in the pack. A racer riding in the slipstream of a cyclist at the edge of the pack uses roughly 33 percent less energy than a racer who is not slipstreaming another rider. In the middle of the pack, the amount of energy saved is even greater, but there you are hemmed in by other riders and cannot follow if someone attacks.

You must gain maximum shelter, yet give yourself space to move out of the pack to follow another rider's potentially race-winning move or to launch one yourself. To do this, place yourself in the front quarter of the pack, toward its edge, and on the leeward side. This is not easy, since at any time there may be riders dropping back from the

front or moving forward, and the pack will constantly bunch and stretch in response to attacks, wind, and road width.

Using your position in the pack

You must be confident and comfortable on your bike, so ensure that you are in the correct riding position (*see* pp.86–87). To keep your place in the pack, be observant. Focus on a point midway between the shoulders of the rider in front of you, and use this to gauge your distance. You will also be able to see what is in front of the pack, such as hills, corners, or narrow roads. Plan your movements for the rest of the race based on this information.

Once you are settled in the pack, consider making an attack. This requires an element of surprise. The best position to attack from is four or five places behind the leader. If you attack from the front or from too far back, other riders will see what you are doing and follow. Once you are away, some strong riders might catch you, but you can use this to your advantage by forming a pace line (a line of riders who cooperate to keep the main pack behind by taking turns leading, or pacemaking). One rider sets

▼ **Tackling hills**
If you are not a strong climber, try to move forward in the pack by the time you reach the bottom of a hill. You can then afford to lose some ground during the climb, yet retain your original position.

▼ **Sprinting for the line**
Many races end in a sprint for the finish line. Time your effort carefully and take advantage of any shelter offered by your rivals for as long as possible, but be careful to avoid being boxed in by them.

Riding in the wind
If the wind is blowing side- or head-on, road racers gradually take up positions in an echelon formation.

the pace while the others follow, then the leading rider moves over, the next takes his place, and the first rider tucks in at the back.

Making the wind work for you

When riding in a pace line, wind direction is important. Riders shelter from the wind behind the cyclist in front. And when moving back from the front, riders shield the incoming leader by cycling on the windward side of the road. For protection from a side wind, riders move into the echelon formation (*see below*).

The wind is useful when making attacks. If you are not a good sprinter and you are in a large pack, you can reduce competition by making frequent attacks to eliminate good sprinters. If you are a good climber, attack near the top of a hill when other riders are easing off. If the wind blows from the left, for instance, attack to the right of the pack. This way, no one can find a favorable spot behind you.

If the race is likely to be decided by a sprint, wind direction is all-important. In a head wind, shelter with other riders as long as you dare and sprint late. For a downhill sprint or in a tail wind, begin earlier.

Echelon riding in the wind

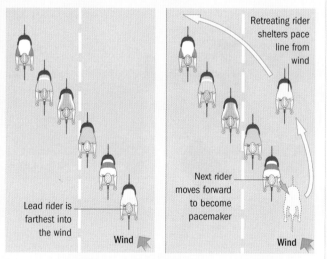

Retreating rider shelters pace line from wind

Next rider moves forward to become pacemaker

Lead rider is farthest into the wind

Wind

Wind

In a side wind, riders fan out across the road in an echelon formation (*above left*). The front rider shelters those behind from the effects of the wind, and the following riders adjust their position to gain the most shelter. Gauge how sheltered you are by listening to the sound of the air rushing past your ears: the point of maximum shelter is where this is quietest. When dropping back (*above right*), the outgoing leader rides on the windward side to give shelter to the incoming leader.

See also
Road riding: adjusting your position **pp.86–87**

Triathlon racing is made up of three sports—swimming, cycling, and running—each forming a separate leg of a race. Amateur races are held on roads open to traffic; professional races are held on closed roads. There are four standard distances: the Sprint (750-m swim, 20-km cycle, and 5-km run), the Olympic (1.5-km swim, 40-km cycle, and 10-km run), the Half Ironman (1.9-km swim, 90-km cycle, and 21-km run) and the Ironman (3.8-km swim, 180-km cycle, and 42-km run).

Practicing the water-to-bike transition

Between the first leg of the race, swimming, and the second, cycling, you may experience disorientation and other physical difficulties. After spending between ten minutes and over an hour exercising mostly with your arms, you must then stand up, find your bike, and exercise mostly with your legs.

During a race, to prepare your legs for pedaling in the cycling leg, you can use breast-stroke for the last few yards of the swim, since this exercises your legs harder. However, this will lose you time—it is better to kick harder in the freestyle stroke.

Problems during the transition from swim to bike can be minimized by pre-event preparation. Familiarize yourself with the transition area, usually

Triathlon tactics

Goal	Tactic
To take advantage of strong cycling skills in the cycling leg of a triathlon.	Conserve your energy, and do not cycle as fast as you can. Your pace might be matched by others going their fastest, but you will have energy left for the run ahead.
To adapt a normal road-racing bike for the best riding position in a triathlon.	Fit a clip-on tribar (see pp.56–57); move the seat forward so that, in the fore and aft position check (see pp.86–87), your knee is slightly in front of the pedal spindle.
To race in triathlons despite a weakness in swimming.	Consider a long-distance Half Ironman or Ironman triathlon, since the swimming leg takes up a much smaller proportion of the race (1.9- or 3.8-km swim, 90- or 180-km cycle, 21- or 42-km run) than a standard Olympic-distance event (1.5-km swim, 40-km cycle, and 10-km run).

a series of bike racks on flat ground close to the swim. To find your bike quickly, note where you have left it by memorizing landmarks beyond it. Practice putting your shoes and helmet on, and if you are cold after the swim, put on extra clothing.

Making the most of the bike leg

Once on the bike, ride steadily and assess the conditions. Is the road slippery? What is the traffic like? Are there many riders nearby? Considering these things helps to focus your attention. During this phase use lower gears than usual, especially if

◀ **Riding steadily**
When you are settled, concentrate on pedaling efficiently. Pick the best line through corners and be as aerodynamic as possible. The bike leg also offers an ideal opportunity to drink to rehydrate yourself, and to eat to build up energy levels for the ride and run to come.

◀◀ **Preparing to run**
Use lower gears and stretch the leg muscles in the last mile (2 km) of the ride to prepare your legs for running. Practice transitions in training to get your body used to the changeovers. For short triathlons, practice riding and running without socks so that you can save time by not putting any on.

it is cold. Change gear as soon as you exceed or drop below 85 95 rpm, which is the optimum pedal revolution rate for most people.

Most importantly, use a heart-rate monitor to make sure you do not exceed your lactate threshold range (*see* pp.142–43 and pp.154–55). This is particularly important in long-distance races. In a Sprint triathlon, you can exceed the threshold once or twice, but in a longer triathlon you should spend most of the race well below it.

Preparing for the second transition

In the last few miles of the ride, you need to prepare your body for running. Many competitors find this transition more difficult than the first. As before, practice the procedure of removing cycling clothing and donning running shoes, and familiarize yourself with the layout of the area.

Cycling does not use the hamstring muscles as much as running does, so you must stretch these muscles in preparation while you are still on the

bike. Do this by leveling your pedals and standing up on a flat or downhill section, and straightening both legs to stretch out your hamstrings.

Dealing with drafters

If someone drafts you (shelters in your slipstream) on the bike leg, go on as if they were not there. If someone wants to cheat, it is difficult to stop them. It can be frustrating, however, especially if their tactics go unnoticed by the marshals.

One way of discouraging drafting is by passing strongly. Ease off as you approach a rider, take deep breaths, and relax. Then, pass as close to them as you are permitted. Your brief rest will mean you have a little strength in reserve. Maintain an increased effort until you are 15 to 20 yards in front, then return to your normal pace. Passing in this way conveys that you are going too fast to follow.

See also

The triathlon bike **pp.56–57** Road riding: adjusting position **pp.86–87**
Improving your fitness **pp.142–43** Achieving advanced-level fitness **pp.154–55**

▼ **Following rules on drafting**
Triathlon rules specify how far behind a rider you must follow if you are overtaken, and how close you can pass when you overtake. This is policed by motorcycle-mounted marshals, who are known as "draftbusters."

Competing on the track

There are many different kinds of track races, but they broadly divide into sprint and endurance races, held on elliptical tracks with banked corners of up to 45 degrees. Riders compete in categories defined by ability and age, and World Championships are held in different countries each year.

Competing in sprint events

The purest, most exhilarating test of speed is the match sprint. Two riders race head-to-head over three laps in a knockout contest. The two fastest riders meet in the final.

Much of the time, the riders play a waiting game, watching for the inattention of another so that they can launch an attack. This leads to thrilling battles for the line. There is often physical contact between riders, and collisions are common, so confidence is as important as physical strength. Other sprinting races include the one-kilometer individual time trial and the Keirin, another race with frequent crashes that only the bravest win.

In team sprinting, two teams of three riders start together at opposite points of the track. In each team, the first rider leads for one lap while the other two riders follow. The first then swings up the banking out of the way and the second takes

▼ Competing in a velodrome

In recent years, the Master's Track Championships, for men and women over age 30, have been held at the velodrome in Manchester, England. Athletes from all over the world compete in this event.

◀ Keeping a low profile

Riders need to adopt an aerodynamic position, as well as wear aerodynamic clothing, in pursuit racing, which is really a time trial on the track.

over for lap two. Rider three then completes the third and final lap alone, and the last rider's time counts for the team—the fastest time wins.

Racing in endurance events

In pursuit racing, men race over a distance of 4,000 meters and women over 3,000 meters. Two riders compete against each other, starting at 12 o'clock and six o'clock on the elliptical track. If one catches the other, the race is won. This rarely happens, however, so the winner is the rider with the fastest time for the distance. Pursuit racing requires speed, pace judgment, and the ability to ride very close to your limit, without exceeding it and therefore having to slow down.

The team pursuit is based on the same principle. Each rider in a team of four sets the pace for a half or full lap, depending on the track size; the others ride in the leader's slipstream. When the leader's turn is over, he or she swings up the banking, the next rider takes over the lead, and the first joins at the back. Fast, strong riders with a flair for longer scratch or points races are good at team pursuits.

In a points race, riders race in a group over a set number of laps but compete for points at the end of every five- or ten-lap section. The rider with the

Track racing disciplines

Discipline	Description
Match sprint	Two riders race each other for three laps of the track
Time trial	Solo race against the clock. Men ride for 1,000 m, women for 500 m
Pursuit	Riders, or teams, start on opposite sides of the track and race for 4 000 m; first over the line wins
Points race	Riders race for points every few laps; most points wins
Scratch race	Several riders race for a set distance; first over line wins

most points wins, but if one or more riders lap the field, it is they who then contest first place. This kind of race suits fast riders who recover quickly.

The Madison is a points race for teams of two riders. Rider one races while rider two rides on the outside of the track, waiting his turn. Every few laps the riders change over, rider two racing while rider one rests. This makes for fast, spectacular races.

Starting out in track racing

Locate a track in your region and make inquiries. Some tracks organize leagues in which you can ride in all the above disciplines to find the one for you.

Track riding can be useful even if you do not want to specialize in this field. The speed skills you gain are invaluable for road racing, and indoor tracks are useful for training during bad weather.

▼ **Record-breaking cycling**
Chris Boardman was a world and Olympic pursuit champion on the track. Here he is in the process of setting the world one hour record at the velodrome in Manchester in 2001.

▼ **Watching out for an attack**
The match sprint is often a game of tactical cat-and-mouse. The rider in second place has the advantage of surprise, and the leader must constantly look over their shoulder to watch out for an attacking move.

See also
The track bike **pp.54–55** Track racing skills **pp.166–67**

Track racing skills

The skills needed to race on the track are similar for each discipline. Holding the line at the bottom of the track in pursuiting, while centrifugal forces are trying to push you upward, is similar to the skill needed to accelerate away from a chasing group of riders in a scratch race (*see* pp.164–65). Sprinters often launch their moves from the top of the track banking, using gravity to increase their speed. This is also a good way of attacking in points races.

Familiarizing yourself with the track

If you are new to track racing, your first goal should be to feel comfortable riding on any part of the track. Once you have confidence—and this might take time—everything else should fall into place. A bike track may seem daunting at first. Indoor tracks are up to 275 yd (250 m) around and have 45-degree bankings, often more than 20 ft (6 m) high. Bankings may be intimidating, but they are there to stop you from flying off at the end of the straight while guiding you around into the next one.

The only way to build your confidence in riding on a track is to spend as much time as you can riding in a track environment. Many tracks run introductory courses and, where they exist, they are usually required for new riders. You will learn how to move up and down the bankings in a line of riders, and the basics of track etiquette, such as looking over your shoulder before you change direction, and indicating before you maneuver with a quick flick of the elbow.

Learning track skills

To join a group of riders already circling the track, ride down the banking and join directly behind the rear wheel of the last rider. This is an art you will develop over time. You must ride up the banking only as far as you need to, which depends on your speed and the length of the line of riders. Only with experience will you be able to get this right. Study team pursuit riders—the accomplished ones can execute this maneuver perfectly.

Sprinters tend to attack each other by riding high, then plunging down the banking into the straight. Often they do this by moving diagonally, causing their rivals to back off a fraction to avoid a collision. There is a fine line in track cycling between tactics and unsportmanlike riding.

If you want to become a sprinter, you must also be very good at riding slowly. In a two-rider sprint, the rider in second place has the element of surprise. Sprinters often vie for this spot by riding slowly, sometimes coming to a complete stop as they balance their bikes against the slope of the track.

▼ **Attacking from the banking**
Launching attacks from the top of the banking is a tactic that occurs in all kinds of track racing. Here, a group rides around the outside of the track, waiting and watching to see who will make the next move.

▼ **Finishing first in a match sprint**
Once the tactical finessing is over, match sprinting becomes a battle for the line. Sprinters need total bike control and the ability to ride on all parts of the track at any speed.

Making the all-important start

In some championship events, starts are made from a machine that clamps the rear wheel, releasing it when a signal is given. Start with your pedals in the ten-to-four position, the ten-to pedal highest on the track. Your first pedal turn is crucial, and all your strength must go straight into the pedal. To get away powerfully in a straight line, pull equally on both sides of the handlebar, press down on the pedals, and try not to rock or sway. Concentrate on each pedal revolution, and stay out of the saddle until you have achieved an optimum number of revolutions.

Sit down smoothly and focus for the rest of the ride. These may seem like small details, but kilometer time trials are often won by a thousandth of a second.

Bear in mind the angle of your head when riding on the track. Always keep your head at 90 degrees to horizontal, not to the track, which varies in angle. This tricks your brain into believing that you are riding on the flat and prevents you from losing your balance. Monitor your shoulder and neck muscles; do not let tension build up.

See also
The track bike **pp.54–55** Competing on the track **pp.164–65**

▼ **Changing position**
Riders in team pursuiting are adept at using track bankings to change their position in a line. They are able to drop down to within half an inch (1 cm) of the rider ahead of them.

Moving from the front of a line

Rider turns back down the banking

Rider joins the back of the line

Line continues around the track

Leader climbs the banking

Use the banking to move from the front of the line. First, take a quick look over your right shoulder as you approach the banking to make sure no one is overtaking you. Flick out your right elbow and, as you enter the banking, continue in a straight line. This will take you up the banking. Let the line of riders pass below you on the track, then aim your bike back down the banking, joining the other riders at the rear of the line.

Competing off-road

Away from the restrictions of paved roads, mountain bikers seek the challenge of off-road terrain. There are many ways of doing this, from following marked trails to racing in cross-country or downhill races, or even competing in multi-day endurance and orienteering events.

Riding noncompetitively

Mountain-bike magazines often include pullout route guides, which grade the severity of marked trails and give information about transportation, accommodation, and local facilities.

Many regions in the world actively encourage mountain bikers, maintaining trails of varying degrees of difficulty. Les Gets in France, Boulder, Colorado, and Todtnau in Germany's Black Forest, for example, all have good facilities.

Racing as an amateur

National organizations and the cycling press are good sources of race information, and as with road racing, there are many events held for amateurs. In France, the organizers of the Paris–Roubaix road race hold a separate race for amateurs on parts of the course the road professionals use, on the same weekend.

Some events amount to mountain-biking festivals, such as the Roc d'Azur in France, which includes races, demonstrations, and a trade show.

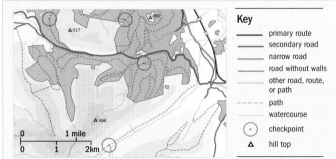

Bicycle orienteering

Key

— primary route
— secondary road
— narrow road
— road without walls
⋯ other road, route, or path
-- path
— watercourse
⊙ checkpoint
△ hill top

Physical endeavor, map-reading, and trailcraft are the key elements of Enduro and Trailquest events. The Polaris Challenge in the UK (*above*) consists of a series of two-day events that require contestants to navigate their way around various checkpoints and camp overnight. The Adventure Challenge in the Czech Republic and the Chequamegon Fat Tire Festival in Wisconsin are two similar events.

The Cheddar Challenge in England offers similar activities and attractions, as does the festival at the Rockies resort of Telluride, Colorado.

In the UK, you can ride a mountain bike in most cyclo-cross races except the National Championships, National Series, and one or two traditional events. Endurance events, such as the Welsh 100, a 100-km

▲ **Competing in extreme weather**
The Iditabike race is named after the annual sled-dog race that follows the snowy Iditarod trail, which runs from Nome to Anchorage in Alaska. Riders race in extreme winter conditions.

(60-mile) race in mid-Wales, are increasing in popularity. Six-, 12-, and 24-hour races are also becoming popular throughout the world.

In the downhill Megavalanche event held at Alpe d'Huez in the French Alps, competitors of all ages and abilities ride one spectacular glacier course.

Mountain biking also has its own multi-stage races. Australia's Crocodile Trophy is one of the most famous and is run over two courses: the Classic, 930 miles (1,500 km) in 12 stages, and the Light, 330 miles (532 km) in five stages.

Adventure racing is a mixture of running, trekking, climbing, kayaking, mountain biking, and swimming. The annual, multi-day Eco Challenge is an international competition for mixed teams, each of which must include at least one woman. Many mountain-bike challenges of this kind have sprung up in recent years, and some organizers have been criticized for staging events in ecologically vulnerable areas. Be aware of such issues, and take care to ride in an environmentally sensitive way.

Racing as a professional

National cycling associations oversee a calendar of mountain-bike events run by clubs, associations, and promoters. There are World Championships and World Series, too, for both cross-country and downhill disciplines. Riders compete in categories of age and ability similar to those in road competitions. The junior and under-23 categories tend to share their World Championships with Elite mountain bike riders, although in separate races. The Masters (over-30s, divided into five-year age bands) have separate World Championships.

Joining organizations and taking part in official races are the only ways for young cross-country mountain bikers to work toward Olympic or World-Championship ambitions. Coaching is vital to development, so they should seek out clubs with specialist mountain-bike sections and mountain-bike coaches.

See also
The race-level cross-country mountain bike pp.60–61

▼ **Riding over rough ground**
The two-day Paris-Roubaix race in France is notorious for its cobbled course. This, of course, makes it an even more desirable challenge for mountain bikers.

Cross-country racing skills

Fitness, good bike-handling skills, and mental resolve are the key to competing in a cross-country race. Starting well and maintaining your energy level are important, while tips and techniques can be learned to give you an edge over the opposition.

Making the right start

You must be in shape to start at high speed, so make sure you train sufficiently (*see* pp.152–55). Racers line up in rows across the width of the trail, but the course often narrows soon after the start. If you do not start well, you may have a frustrating wait at the first bottleneck as riders ahead of you file through. Once the course widens again, you will have to ride faster than the leaders to catch them.

Starting technique also involves choosing the correct line. Avoid areas of soft ground, and make sure the place you start from gives a good line into the first corner. The inside line is not always the best, due to rocks, roots, and even the number of competitors aiming for the same line. Watch where the best riders position themselves and stay close by.

▼ **Crossing water**
Cross-country racing involves riding over all kinds of terrain, including shallow streams. If crossing a long stretch of water, pedal constantly in a low gear, or you will quickly come to a halt.

Maintaining energy

Physiologically, riding at the limit of your endurance for the duration of a race is not possible, so once you are underway, expend energy only as it is needed. Over a typical course, you will need bursts of power as you climb hills or cross tough terrain, but less energy for descents or narrow singletrack.

Push yourself, but not too hard. Even if you started badly, you will overtake riders who have overestimated their strength. Imagine your energy as a solid block that is chipped away by every effort you make. You need to finish the race just as the last bit of the block is used.

Maximizing your chances

If you can, study the circuit before the race so that you can choose appropriate tire types and pressures. Narrow tires and high pressure suit dry courses, while knobbled tires and lower pressure suit mud. Try to memorize the course, so that you can visualize stretches as you approach them and anticipate opportunities to pass.

Avoid dropping behind slow riders along a narrow stretch. Riding with riders of a similar standard, as in a road-race pace line (*see* pp.160–61), can be of benefit. When you want to leave them, however—

Cross-country racing equipment

The rules of cross-country racing forbid any outside assistance during a race, so you must be prepared to carry out repairs yourself. Include the following essential items:

- Multi-tool
- Chain-link extractor
- Spare inner tube
- Tire levers
- Inflater (pump or gas cartridge)
- Saddlebag for stowage

perhaps in a move to win the race—take advantage of your strengths. If you are a strong climber, attack on a hill; if you are a fast descender, use a downhill trail. Maintain your effort on the next stretch to prevent other riders from catching up with you.

Do not be reluctant to dismount and carry your bike over obstacles or across an off-camber slope, even uphill; it might be quicker in the long run. Try carrying in lap one, then use the technique to gain time in a later lap. Practice until it becomes second nature. Conversely, "bunny-hopping" over obstacles (*see* pp.128–31), especially toward the end of a race where others dismount, can gain you ground. Make sure you have enough energy in reserve.

Race course designers try to take in as many differents surfaces as possible, from rocks and roots to sand and mud. Adverse weather conditions can also change a course completely, so make sure you train on different surfaces in all conditions.

◄ **Carrying your bike**
If you decide to carry your bike for a stretch, allow sufficient time to dismount in a smooth movement to avoid muscle strain.

▶ **Working together**
Riding in a small group, with each rider taking a turn at the front, can gain valuable time. However, use the terrain and your skills to leave the group behind as the finish approaches.

▶▶ **Balancing your weight**
When attacking uphill, do not move your body weight too far forward, but stay evenly balanced between the wheels. This delivers maximum traction to your tires.

See also
Off-road riding: bunny-hopping **pp.128–31** Using an intermediate training program **pp.152–53** Achieving advanced-level fitness **pp.154–55**

Endurance racing skills

Endurance racing is divided into many categories, the largest and simplest division being team or solo challenges. How well suited you are to one or the other is partly a matter of personality. In order to succeed in team events, the group has to be considered by all to be more important than the individuals within it. Some people find this easier to cope with than others. Consider carefully whether a team or individual challenge would be a better match with your personality.

Orienteering on bicycles

One of the most straightforward team challenges is bicycle orienteering, such as the Trailquest and Polaris events in England. This usually involves teams of two. Some events require an overnight stop, and you are required to carry camping equipment with you. Map reading and compass skills are essential, as is a good knowledge of outdoor survival.

By far the most valuable skill to acquire and practice in order to succeed at bike orienteering is the ability to interpret what you see on a map into a three-dimensional picture of your location. This will enable you to keep track of where you are, and to monitor your progress as you pass features that you have noted from studying the map.

▼ **Navigating outdoors**
Map-reading and compass skills are essential for endurance events, as is a good knowledge of outdoor life and survival techniques. Make sure at least one member of the team can map-read confidently.

◀ **Being determined**
To take part in solo endurance events, you must be not only physically fit, but also mentally prepared. The power of the mind can be the key to success.

Riding other challenges

Other exciting team challenges are long-distance and adventure racing. The ultimate long-distance challenge is the 24-hour race. Teams and individuals may take part, team members taking turns riding while the others rest. In adventure races, all members of the team must cover the whole course.

In both events, team members must take advantage of their strengths and recognize their weaknesses. In a long-distance race, if one rider is stronger than the others, he or she should do longer stints of racing. In adventure races, some team members will be physically stronger than other members and able to carry more equipment; others might be chosen for their map-reading skills.

It is important that all team members get along well, understand their responsibilities, and practice together regularly.

Preparing for the event

A solo 24-hour event needs a lot of preparation. Try to put in long training rides of up to eight hours, and do at least two all-night rides, so that you know that you can do it in the race. That knowledge is invaluable; many endurance sportspeople agree that the line between success

▼ Negotiating obstacles

You must be prepared to negotiate any obstacle the organizers include in the course of an adventure race. Part of the attraction and the challenge is the ingenuity you will have to use to complete the course.

Endurance racing equipment
Endurance races take place over long distances, often at night. Be sure you are self-sufficient, and carry the following basic items: • Spare inner tube, tire levers, chain tool, inflater • Head torch	• Powerful bike lights • Helmet with peak for sunsets and sunrises • Cycling backpack with bladder drinking system • Tent and sleeping bag for multi-day events

and failure is often in the mind. Stubbornness and confidence in your own ability are assets that can be called upon in times of difficulty. Practice everything needed for the event repeatedly to build your confidence. You will then avoid finding yourself in an unfamiliar situation with reason to doubt your ability to cope.

Many events involve riding over rough terrain at night. To allow your eyes to adapt to the dark, train at night-time with powerful off-road lights. When racing at night, ride with extra care.

Training your mind

The importance of mental preparation is recognized by athletes and coaches in all sports. Many professional cyclists practice visualization techniques, such as picturing themselves riding a perfect race. Some also spend time in the off-season doing different sports with their teammates—for example, rock climbing—to build team spirit and trust in each other.

The following mental techniques will help you to complete an endurance event. Constantly monitor your physical state. Not only will this help you to meet nutritional and hydration needs, but it will also help you to focus on your immediate surroundings, rather than dwelling on what is to come.

Do not think too far ahead. Concentrate only on the part of the course that you are currently riding. This leaves little room in your mind for worrying about the distance left to travel.

Imagine how bad you will feel if you give up. This is especially pertinent in a team race, when you have a responsibility to your teammates. If this is not enough, imagine someone you respect is watching, and think about their disappointment if you fail.

See also
Basic touring **pp.38–39** Off-road touring **pp.42–43** Competing off-road **pp.168–69**

Downhill racing skills

To be good at downhill racing you need physical strength, good bike-handling skills, confidence, and a good eye for a racing line. These qualities can be nurtured through training. It may look as though some riders glide down steep, rock-strewn descents with ease, but acquiring such skill takes hard work.

To gain physical strength, start with some basic exercises (*see* pp.146–47), and consider a program devised by a qualified trainer. Add to this with on-the-bike fitness and downhill technique training.

Starting well

The outcome of a downhill race can be decided by a split second, so the start is very important. Practice finding the ideal starting gear, pedal smoothly, and perfect a smooth change into higher gears to build up speed (*see* pp.114–15). The start is not unlike the track start (*see* p.167).

Find out as much as you can about the course before the race. Ride and walk each section, study the jumps, and look at the entrance and exit of corners. Memorize everything. By the time you reach the start, you should have a map of the course in your head. This will enable you to focus your attention on, anticipate, and react in good time to the features of the course as they come up.

◀ **Reducing time in the air**
Time in the air is lost time. Inevitably, you will have to jump parts of the course, but do the minimum to clear the obstacle. Keep your body low, stretched, and as flat as you can—this will reduce flying time.

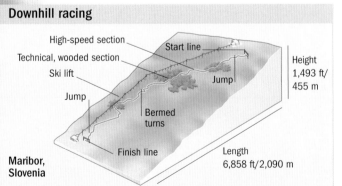

Downhill racing

High-speed section
Technical, wooded section
Ski lift
Jump
Start line
Jump
Height 1,493 ft/ 455 m
Bermed turns
Finish line
Length 6,858 ft/2,090 m

Maribor, Slovenia

The illustration above shows the course of a round of the UCI Downhill World Cup series. It combines fast, straight runs and jumps with berms and twisting technical sections typical of a downhill course. Several changes of gradient are designed to test the competitors' fitness as well as their cycling skills. Men and women compete on the same course.

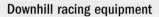

Downhill racing equipment

Downhill racing is a fast and extremely physical discipline. The same can be said for BSX and Four Cross, which have even greater potential for crashes than Downhill. In order to ride safely, you must have the proper equipment. Look for full-face helmets that offer good protection to the back of your head and neck, and lightweight body armor that will not cause you to overheat. Below are some of the first items you should put on your shopping list (they should not be viewed as additional extras):

- Full-face helmet
- Full-body armor
- Downhill gloves
- Goggles
- Downhill-specific shoes or boots

Full-face helmet

Body armor

Learning to jump

Cornering quickly is a key part of succeeding at downhilling, so riders carry speed through corners by steadying themselves with their feet. Some riders use flat pedals to permit free movement of the feet. To jump, the foot is pressed backward on the pedals and flicked up to raise the rear of the bike in a bunny-hop. This requires practice and good timing.

▼ **Competing in Bicycle Four Cross**
In Bicycle Four Cross (4X) races, four riders compete at the same time on a downhill course, created with plenty of berms and jumps. Speed and aggression are vital, and heat winners go through to the final.

Controlling your body

To execute turns at maximum speed, you have to develop a feel for how much to lean the bike, and how to control it with shifts in your body position. Mountain bikers and road riders shift their body weight over the outside pedal while cornering. A downhiller needs to exaggerate body shifts to maximize speed through corners.

You will spend a lot of your time out of the saddle in a downhill race. This is the only way to let the bike move beneath you to absorb bumps in the trail. This puts a strain on the legs, arms, and shoulders, so make exercises to strengthen them an important part of your training. On-the-bike training will condition the legs.

Conquering fear

If you push yourself to the limit—and you will have to if you want to win—crashes are inevitable. You may be caught out by something that you did not spot when you surveyed the course, or you may take a corner too fast. As long as you are wearing sufficient body armor and a good full-face helmet, it is unlikely that you will get hurt. But if the prospect of crashing worries you excessively, downhill racing is probably not for you.

▼ **Downhilling in the extreme**
In the dual slalom, two riders race head to head on separate tracks of the same course laid out down a hillside and complete with berms, jumps, and corners. Again, heat winners progress to the final.

See also
Off-road riding: braking and changing gears **pp.88–89** Exercising off the bike **pp.146–47** Track racing skills **pp.166–67**

Extreme riding

Extreme riding includes a number of disciplines, and each requires specialist skills and equipment. Freestyle and racing Bicycle Motocross (BMX) are the longest established, but Trials and Bicycle Four Cross (4X) are all gaining in popularity.

Discovering BMX racing and freestyle

BMX racing has its own National and World Championships. Riders are classified according to the kind of bike they ride—20-inch or Cruiser, referring to wheel size—and by age. The age rules cater to the vast range of people who compete, so check with national cycling federations or individual tracks for full details.

Races are short and fast and require good bike-handling skills. At a time when many traditional sports fail to capture the imagination of young people, BMX is a superb energy outlet, and the skills learned on the track are useful for all forms of cycling.

Visit a race meeting at a local track to find out about rules, race categories, and events. Many tracks are community-based, and depend on volunteers and family members, with parents often refereeing.

Extreme riding disciplines

Discipline	Description
BMX racing	Short, fast races that require skilled bike handling
Freestyle BMX	Points are awarded for the execution of stunts
4X	Similar to BMX racing, but uses downhill courses, four riders race together; winner goes to next round
Trials	Balance- and obstacle-based competitions in which points are deducted for mistakes

Freestyle BMX tests the execution of tricks and jumps of varying degrees of difficulty. Like skateboarding and freestyle skiing, it appeals to riders who do tricks for their own sake. Freestyle BMX also forms the basis for street riding, where riders use street fixtures, such as curbs and benches, to do tricks. In competitions such as the X-Games, held all over the world, riders compete against each other and show off their skills.

Racing Bicycle Four Cross

Bicycle Four Cross—known as Bicycle Super Cross (BSX) in the UK—is one of the newest disciplines in cycling. Courses are similar to BMX courses but

▼ **Making a good start**
BMX races start from a gate at the top of a slope. Up to eight riders race against each other at any one time; if there are more than eight competitors, heats take place to decide who goes through to a final.

▼ **Riding in close contact**
Bicycle Four Cross riders need to have skills from both BMX and Downhill disciplines. They have to cope with berms and jumps, and at the same time race in close proximity to each other.

run downhill. They contain bermed corners and jumps, and lend themselves to even faster racing than BMX courses.

Four riders descend the course simultaneously, using features of the terrain to steal a lead over their competitors. Races are often part of Downhill competitions, and both require the same combination of fast riding, good bike-handling skills, and confidence. Both disciplines are governed by the International Cycling Union (UCI).

The start of a 4X race is all-important, since it provides a chance to pick the best line. Passing is possible on bermed corners by positioning yourself inside the line of the leader and moving up the bank of the berm—known as a "T-bone."

Riding Trials

Trial riding involves hopping the bike onto and over a variety of obstacles, using techniques such as the track stand and bunny-hop (see p.112–13 and pp.128–31). Penalties are assessed for putting a foot down, so riders must have good balance and complete control over their bikes. The winner is the rider who accrues the fewest penalties. However, competing is not the only form of trial riding, and many riders devote their time to perfecting maneuvers and inventing new ones.

◀ **Overcoming obstacles**
Trials competitors negotiate natural or man-made obstacles by using a combination of delicately balanced pedaling and huge athletic jumps.

▲ **Jumping off the walls**
Freestyle BMX competitions are often held on half-pipe (semi-circular) ramps. Riders use the steep walls to launch into dramatic twists and somersaults.

See also
Off-road riding: improving your balance pp.112–13   Off-road riding: bunny-hopping pp.128–31

Maintaining
your bike

6

Regular maintenance of your bike means increased safety for you and an extended life span for your bike and its components. The following step-by-step sequences show you how to maintain and repair every aspect of your bike, with invaluable tips and techniques provided to ensure that the jobs are completed as efficiently as possible.

Tools and workshop principles

Regularly maintaining your bicycle and being able to carry out essential repairs will enable you to keep the bike at peak performance. There are, however, some general principles about working with bikes that should be followed.

The first is that bikes, especially lightweight ones, need a delicate touch. If you are used to working on cars, then you must use less force when dealing with your bike. Nuts and bolts only need to be tight; do not overtighten them or they will strip. If in doubt, you can buy torque gauges that accurately measure the correct level of tightness on a bike's nuts and bolts. Recommended torque settings are included in component manufacturers' instructions. Keep all the instructions that come with your bike, tools, and the components you buy.

Bikes often have different material interfaces, such as an aluminum seat pin in a steel frame. With one or two exceptions, you must always apply grease or some other antiseize barrier between the two materials. Finally, buy the best-quality tools you can. Cheap tools will bend and become chipped, making it impossible to carry out some of these maintenance jobs properly. They could even damage the components you work on.

Essential tools

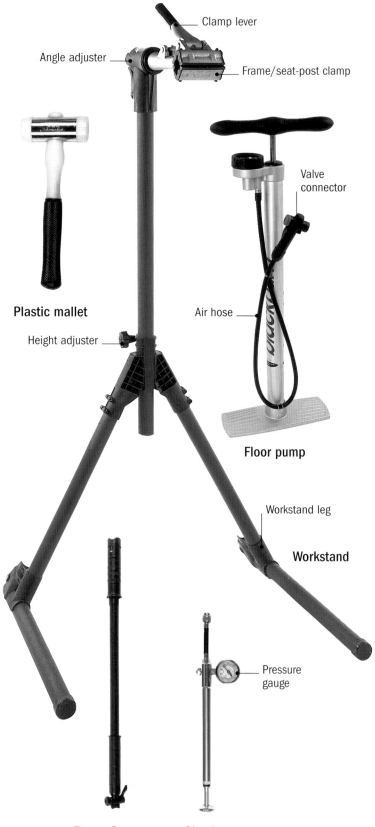

Plastic mallet

Clamp lever

Angle adjuster

Frame/seat-post clamp

Valve connector

Height adjuster

Air hose

Floor pump

Workstand leg

Workstand

Pressure gauge

Frame-fit pump   Shock pump

Workshop tips

- Keep your tools clean.
- Never leave your tools outside; they will rust.
- Use a specific toolbox for your bike tools, preferably one with compartments. Separating wrenches, Allen wrenches, and specialty equipment means your tools are always at hand.
- When working on your bike, make sure the area is well lit.
- Keep one dry rag and one soaked in degreaser, for cleaning components, close to hand. Use another one to wipe your hands.
- Buy a box of disposable mechanic's gloves, since some products, such as spray oils, can be unpleasant on your hands.
- Remember the order in which things come apart. Put them down in that order—it will make reassembly easier.
- Put a little grease on your fingers to help pick up nuts and bolts.
- After removing a nut and bolt from something, screw the nut a couple of turns onto the bolt before you put them both down. This makes them easier to find should they be dropped.

Screw handle

Chain tool

Chain

Chain whip

Crank puller

Socket

Crank-bolt remover

Headset wrench

Handle

Multi-tool

Allen wrenches available in sizes of 2–10mm

Cone wrenches available in sizes of 13–18mm

Needle-nosed pliers

Spring

Cable cutters

Advanced toolbox

MEASURING DEVICE AND CHAIN LINK EXTRACTOR

A measuring device (*right*) is a quick and useful way to check on chain wear. Link extractors are essential for taking off old chains and fitting new ones. Since replacing a chain is an important piece of maintenance, a link extractor should be part of your advanced toolbox. As with all tools, buy a good-quality, strong model.

CASSETTE REMOVER AND CHAIN WHIP

An appropriate cassette remover (*below*) is needed for the type of cassette fitted to your bike. A chain whip is also worthwhile to stop the cassette from turning while its lockring is taken off with the remover. Special tools to turn the remover can be bought, though a good adjustable wrench will suffice, as long as the remover is locked in place with the quick-release.

CABLE PULLER

A cable puller (*below*) grabs cables and pulls while the cable is secured to a component with its cable fixing clamp. Though not essential, it can be helpful, since it is sometimes difficult to get the right amount of tension in a cable just by pulling it.

SPOKE KEY

A spoke key (*below, top*) is essential for anyone wanting to true a wheel and replace broken spokes. So is a spoke ruler (*below, bottom*) with which a spoke's length and gauge can be measured. However, unless you have experience at doing this, let a bike shop true your wheels or replace any broken spokes. To learn how to replace spokes, or even build your own wheels, look on the Internet, or buy a book on the subject.

BENCH VISE

Though it is by no means essential, a bench vise (*below*) can be very useful, especially when something is difficult to remove. It is also handy when replacing cartridge bearings. Make sure the vise is bolted securely to a workbench, or something similar, to keep it steady. It is a good idea to use blocks of wood between the jaws of the vise and any object being held, since bike components are made from light materials that scratch easily and could be damaged by the vise. Do not overtighten the jaws.

Cleaning your bike

Cleaning not only keeps your bike looking good, it also helps to keep everything in working order. The various moving parts of a bike are efficient and also quite delicate, and many are exposed to the elements. Regular cleaning removes the grit and dirt that sticks to the components, helping to maintain their efficiency and prolong their life.

A few basic cleaning accessories will make the job easier—a selection of stiff brushes, a bucket, two big sponges, and a few cloths are the minimum you will need. Using a bike stand is helpful for turning the pedals while the bike is stationary and reaching inaccessible areas of the frame, but hanging it up by hooking its saddle over a clothesline, or something similar, also works.

If the bike is particularly muddy, the dirt needs to be removed before any other jobs are carried out. The best way to do this is to hang up the bike, then use a garden hose or pressure washer to force the mud off. Keep the hubs and cranks turning forward, because bearing seals are designed to work when the bike is moving. While cleaning the bike, keep in mind the safety checks outlined on pages 184–85. Pay attention to the frame—with the wheels out, parts you would not normally be able to see now become visible. Check for cracks, especially under the fork crown and around the bottom bracket. When scrubbing the tires, look out for cuts and remove anything lodged in the tread.

If you take up racing, a clean bike will boost your confidence, and it can have an adverse effect on rivals who may not have prepared as well as you. Many of the world's top cyclists prepare their bikes with meticulous attention to detail.

Cleaning equipment

- Plastic bucket
- Sponges
- Degreaser
- Hard-bristled brushes
- Cassette scraper
- Cloth

Hard-bristled brushes

Bucket and sponge

Removing dirt and oil

1 **Remove both wheels** from the bike and either put the frame in a stand or hang it up. Then place a chain holder—a device that keeps the chain tight while the rear wheel is out of the bike—in the rear dropout. It is important that the chain is able to run freely on this so that it can be cleaned thoroughly.

Cleaning the cassette
Before pouring away the water, use a brush to clean the cassette, working the bristles between the cogs.

5 **Use the cassette scraper** to gouge out any debris that has accumulated between the cogs. Then apply degreaser to the chain and spray some on to the cassette. Use plenty, making sure that it gets into the spaces between the cogs. Allow a few minutes for the degreaser to work.

Working soap in
Use a sponge to work soap into intricate parts of the bike, such as between the brake arms and the pads.

② **Apply a** degreaser to remove any old oil and grit. Spray on to the crankset, front and rear derailleurs, and the chain, covering each link.

③ **Use a sponge** to apply hot, soapy water over the drivetrain. Wrap it around the chain, turn the pedals, and run the chain through the sponge.

④ **Take another sponge,** and apply plenty of soapy water to the rest of the bike. Different-sized hard-bristled brushes will also be effective here, especially when combined with the soapy water being worked into the places that are hard to reach. Then rinse off with clean water and dry the bike with a clean cloth.

⑥ **Use a bigger brush** to clean the rest of the wheel, including the tires, and work the bristles in between the spokes and around the hub. Then rinse with clean water and dry everything with a cloth. Once you have replaced the wheels, sparingly apply a light oil to the chain and moving parts of the front and rear derailleurs.

Workshop tips

- Use diesel fuel as an alternative degreasing agent. It is cheap and effective, and can be applied to drivetrain parts with a 1-in (2.5-cm) paintbrush. Never use gasoline—it is dangerous and will dry out the equipment. Diesel and other good degreasers leave an oily residue behind after they have been washed off, which is an ideal condition for the bike to be left in.

- Always clean from the top of the bike, working downward so dirt does not get washed into parts that have already been cleaned.

Troubleshooting

Problem	Solution
After riding in bad weather it is difficult to clean off mud from the dirty bike.	Spray the bike all over with cooking oil or bike polish before going out. When the bike is cleaned, the degreaser will cut through this oil and lift off the dirt with it.
Difficult to clean hard-to-reach places on the bike.	Use a bottle brush with a flexible wire handle.
An accumulation of dirt between the spoke heads on the hubs.	Use a toothbrush to scrub between them. Remove the cassette from time to time and thoroughly clean behind it.

See also
Making routine safety checks pp.184–85

Making routine safety checks

Before going out on your bike, even for a short ride, you should get into the habit of running through a few basic checks. By doing this, you will minimize the chances that mechanical failure will cause you to have an accident.

Step locator

These checks, which apply equally to road and mountain bikes, take just a couple of minutes, but will help you avoid the majority of accidents caused by equipment failures: brakes that cease to work, a loose handlebar, a tire blowout, slipping gears, or a part coming off. They also help to keep you familiar with the maintenance needs of your bike. For example, does it need cleaning when you get back? Are the brake cables rubbing any paintwork? How long before the tires need replacing?

Safety checks help you manage your bike, allowing you to replace parts in good time or carry out some non-urgent maintenance work. It is time well spent.

Making frame checks

1 **Inspect the frame of your bike** every now and then, since there is always a chance that metal can be fatigued. First, run a finger around the area underneath the down tube where it joins the head tube. If there is a ripple in the tube's surface, this is a sign that the tube is fatigued and could break.

Making pre-ride checks

Checking for movement
Try to twist the bar upward to ensure that there is no rotational movement.

1 **Hold the front wheel** firmly between your knees and try to turn the handlebar from side to side. If there is any movement at all, check both the stem and steerer bolts and tighten if necessary.

Testing the front brake
Apply the front brake; if you feel any movement in the steerer assembly, then the headset needs tightening.

2 **Simultaneously apply** the front and rear brakes fully and push the bike forward. If you have to pull the levers back to the bars before the bike stops, the travel needs adjusting, or the pads need replacing.

Examining the tire
Pay attention to the tire walls, since they are thin and susceptible to blowouts.

3 **Slowly spin** the wheels and check for cuts, splits, or bulges on the tires. Cuts may blow soon; bulges almost certainly will. If you find a bulge, or are in any doubt, replace the tire. Check the tire pressure.

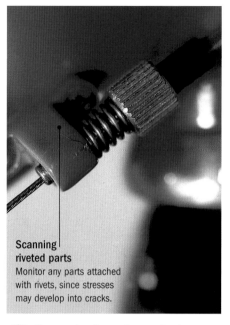

Scanning
riveted parts
Monitor any parts attached
with rivets, since stresses
may develop into cracks.

Checking
the slot
Look at the slot;
it breaks the
seat tube's
integrity, so
stress can
cause a split.

2   **Check around the** area where the chainstay bridge is brazed to the chainstays, particularly on a steel frame. Cracks may form here because the heat of the brazing process can weaken the metal.

3   **On an aluminum frame** check anything that is riveted to the frame, such as cable guides or front derailleur hangers. These are potential weak areas on the frame where cracks can develop.

4   **Examine the slot** under the seat-post binder bolt, since it can crack on any frame. To reduce the chances of this happening, never fit a seat post that does not exactly match the tube's inside diameter.

4   **Finally, run through** the gears and check that they are properly adjusted. There is nothing more distracting than gears that will not shift properly after a change. When this happens, it is only natural to look down, which is a potentially dangerous situation. If the gears are adjusted and the chain is still jumping, check for a stiff link.

Workshop tips

- Get into the habit of periodically going over your bike to check all nuts and bolts for tightness, not just before going out for a ride. It does not have to take long, and a couple of wrenches and a multi-tool are all the tools needed.

- Give the wrench just the right amount of torque when tightening bolts, and be careful not to overtighten nuts and bolts. They need to be tight, but if too much force is used, there is a chance that a bolt could weaken, or even shear off. You will soon get a feel for what is right as your experience builds.

Troubleshooting

Problem	Solution
Looking at the bike from the front, the back wheel is not in line with the front. The frame might be out of alignment.	Take the bike to a shop and get it checked.
When the rear wheel is placed into the frame, it does not immediately sit square in the dropout. The rear of the frame may be out of line, which is a surprisingly common problem.	Take the bike to a shop, where it should be easy for them to put the frame straight.
On checking the rims, there is crack around a spoke nipple or deep scoring on the braking surface.	The rim needs replacing.

See also

Adjusting a front and a rear derailleur **pp.190–91** Replacing a chain **pp.192–93** Adjusting brakes **pp.198–207**

Replacing road bike cables

To maintain your shifters, it is essential to keep an eye on the brake and gear cables and replace them when worn. They should be replaced at intervals depending on how much you ride; from every year for a bike that is used for short journeys two or three times a week, to at least every two months for a bike in heavy use.

Although gear cable replacement on both STI and Ergo systems is fairly simple, the mechanisms inside each shifter are delicate and complex. The way each system shifts gear is different, so both methods of fitting a gear cable are illustrated. However, since both systems operate the brakes in a similar way, only Shimano brake cable replacement is shown; the Campagnolo's construction is essentially the same. Consult a bike shop if anything goes wrong.

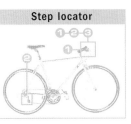

Step locator

Shifters

Campagnolo Ergoshift

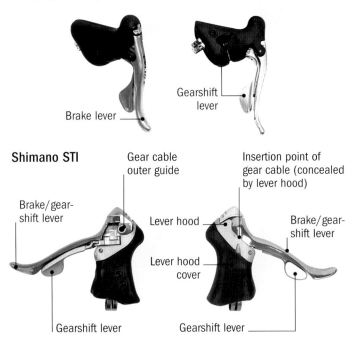

Gearshift lever

Brake lever

Shimano STI

Gear cable outer guide

Insertion point of gear cable (concealed by lever hood)

Brake/gear-shift lever

Lever hood

Brake/gear-shift lever

Lever hood cover

Gearshift lever

Gearshift lever

Toolbox

- Needle-nosed pliers
- 5mm Allen wrench
- Cable cutters

Replacing a brake cable

Locating the hole
The hole where the nipple seats is located inside the lever hood.

Remove the old brake cable by grabbing the cable nipple with needle-nosed pliers. Lubricate the new one with light grease and insert it into the hole where the nipple seats. Look for it coming out of the back of the brake hood and pull it through. Once the nipple is seated, thread the cable through the housing and attach to the brakes.

Replacing a Campagnolo gear cable

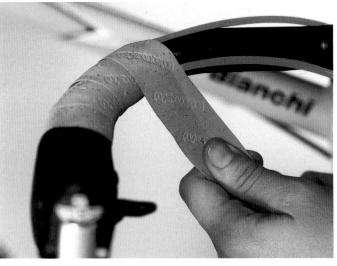

1 **Remove the handlebar tape** if you are replacing either the brake or gear cable on Campagnolo shifters, since both cable outers run under the tape. Carefully unwind the old tape from the center of the handlebar to just below the shifter and leave it hanging from there while you carry out any work. When replacing or fitting new tape, start at the bottom of the handlebar and tightly wind the tape upward, covering at least half of one wind with the next. Secure at the top of the handlebar with electrical tape.

Replacing a Shimano gear cable

1 **Place the gearshift** in the smallest cog for the rear shifter and the smallest chainring position for the front shifter. Insert a new lubricated cable into the hole on the outer side of the brake lever and pull back the brake lever to reveal this hole. Ease the cable through and insert into the cable housing.

2 **Pull the gear cable** through precut lengths of housing. For the rear derailleur, use one length from the shifter to the cable guide on the down tube, and another from the guide on the right-hand chainstay to the rear derailleur's barrel adjuster. Once through, pull the cable through the barrel adjuster and cable clamp bolt. Then tighten.

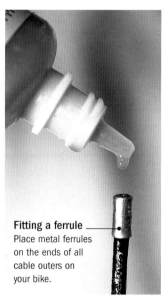

Fitting a ferrule
Place metal ferrules on the ends of all cable outers on your bike.

2 **Put the rear** shifter in the smallest cog and the front shifter in the smallest ring. Grease the cable; push it through the hole under the hood cover. Pull through and insert into the housing. Then follow Step 2 for Replacing a Shimano Gear Cable.

3 **As well as** putting grease on the cables, dribble oil into the cable outers, which should be cut to fit between the components and cable guides. Cut outers to allow cable to run freely inside; too short constricts and too long increases friction.

Workshop tips

- Always cut cable with specially designed cable cutters.
- Once a cable is clamped to any component, cut off the excess and crimp a cable end to the cable. A cable end stops the ends from fraying and can be bought in bike shops.
- Note that both brake and gear cables are taped to the handlebar in the Campagnolo system, whereas just the brakes are taped in the Shimano system. Use electrical tape to secure these to the handlebar before covering with handlebar tape.

Troubleshooting

Problem	Solution
When operating the lever to shift to a smaller chainring or cog, nothing happens. Caused by dirt in the cable outers or lack of lubrication.	Strip down and renew outers. If fairly new, flush out with degreaser and dribble some oil down the insides. Clean/grease the cables. Reassemble.
On an Ergo shifter, the lever that shifts to a larger chainring will not move when you try to change gear.	Can happen on older shifters. Lift the lever that shifts to smaller chainrings, then operate the stuck lever.
After carrying out all the above, the gearshift still will not make the change, or is sluggish in doing so. Caused by grit or dirt in the shifter mechanism.	Flush out the mechanism with degreaser, then spray some fine spray lubricant inside it. Protect the handlebar tape while doing this.

See also
Road riding: braking and changing gears pp.88–89   Adjusting a front and a rear derailleur pp.190–91

Replacing hybrid and mountain bike cables

In one form or another, Rapidfire and Grip Shift systems are used on almost every new mountain bike. Like road STI and Ergo systems, they are designed for convenience and safety, enabling you to change gears with minimum effort while never having your hands too far from the brake levers. Unlike STI and Ergo systems, though, Grip Shift and most Rapidfire systems are not attached to brake levers, so you can fit levers from different manufacturers.

Fitting a new brake cable is the same whatever system you use. First pull the brake lever toward the handlebar to reveal a cradle where the brake cable nipple sits in the lever. Remove the old cable, replace it with a new one, and insert the end into the barrel adjuster from inside the lever body. Pull the cable through precut lengths of cable housing and attach to the brakes.

Step locator

Gearshift units

Grip Shift gearshift unit

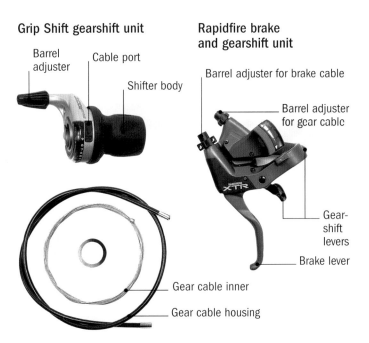

Barrel adjuster

Cable port

Shifter body

Gear cable inner

Gear cable housing

Rapidfire brake and gearshift unit

Barrel adjuster for brake cable

Barrel adjuster for gear cable

Gear-shift levers

Brake lever

Toolbox

- Needle-nosed pliers • Cable cutters
- 5mm Allen wrench • Cable pullers (optional)

Replacing a Rapidfire gear cable

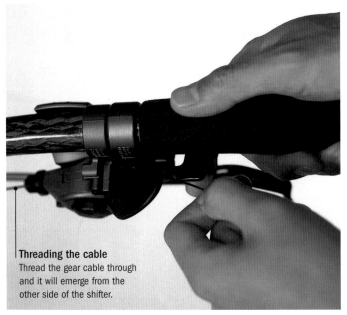

Threading the cable
Thread the gear cable through and it will emerge from the other side of the shifter.

1 **Having removed** the old cable with needle-nosed pliers, put the rear shifter in the smallest cog position to fit a new cable and the front one in the smallest chainring position if you are replacing that cable. Insert the end of the lubricated new cable into the hole where the cable nipple sits inside the shifter.

Replacing a Grip Shift gear cable

Sliding the port
Slide the cable port forward before you lift it.

1 **Shift into the smallest** cog and chainring. The place where the gear cable fits on a Grip Shift system has a cover over it called the cable port. Lift the port to reveal the old cable and remove it with needle-nosed pliers. Spray a small amount of manufacturer-approved light oil into the mechanism.

Adding a ferrule
Fit a ferrule to the ends of all cable outers, ensuring it fits into the frame's cable guides.

② **Push the cable** through until its end shows through the barrel adjuster on the outside of the shifter body, then thread it through the first length of pre-cut and lubricated cable outer.

③ **Cut the cable** and cable outers with cable cutters. Dribble a drop of oil down each length of cable outer, which should be cut sufficiently long to allow the cable to travel freely inside. Feed the cable through.

④ **Thread the cable** through the barrel adjuster on the rear mech, pull hard, and tighten the cable clamp. With the front mech, insert the cable into the clamp and tighten. Cut off any excess cable.

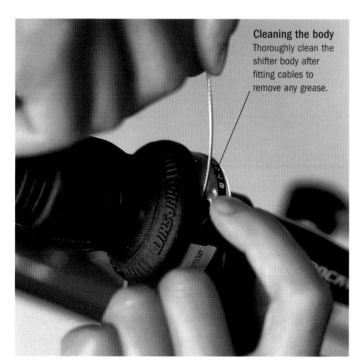

Cleaning the body
Thoroughly clean the shifter body after fitting cables to remove any grease.

② **Grease the new cable** before you insert it into the Grip Shift and push it until the end reveals itself at the other side of the shifter. Then thread the cable through the various outers and secure to either the front or rear mech as in Step 4 for Replacing a Rapidfire Gear Cable. Replace the cable port.

Workshop tips

● Spray a little oil into the Rapidfire or Grip Shift mechanisms now and again, but do not use too much. Be careful not to get oil near the handlebar grips because if it gets underneath the grips they will move when you grip them tightly.

● Take care to cut the right length of cable outer. Too little causes tight corners for the inner cable to get around, increasing friction. Also, if the section of outer from the shifters to the first cable guides on the bike frame is too short it will restrict the steering.

Troubleshooting

Problem	Solution
Changes to smaller sprockets and chainrings are slow on both systems. Caused by grit and dirt in the cable outers.	Strip down and replace cable outers and inners. If fairly new, clean cables with degreaser. Lubricate cable outers, grease cable inners, and reassemble.
After cleaning or replacing the cable outers, Grip Shifts are still sluggish. Caused by the surfaces between the grip and the shifter being dry.	Peel the grip back and carefully lubricate the surface of the shifter where it touches the grip. Make sure you do not get any oil under the grip.
After cleaning or replacing the cable outers, Rapidfires are still sluggish. Caused by grit and dirt in the Rapidfire mechanism.	Flush out with degreaser and spray fine oil into the Rapidfire mechanism.

See also
Off-road riding: braking and changing gear **pp.114–15** Adjusting a front and a rear mech **pp.190–91**

Adjusting a front and a rear derailleur

Gears are changed by a component that essentially derails the chain from one cog or chainring to another. The rear derailleur works the cog set, while the front derailleur works the chainring. The derailleurs only work well if the distance they travel is adjusted so that they cannot push the chain too far—for example, into the spokes of the back wheel.

Indexed shifting systems depend on the front and rear derailleurs starting their travel from a point in line with the smallest chainring or cog. Travel is controlled by adjusters on each of the derailleurs, and finding the optimum setup is straightforward.

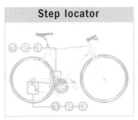
Step locator

Derailleurs

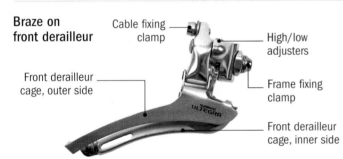

Braze on front derailleur

Cable fixing clamp

High/low adjusters

Front derailleur cage, outer side

Frame fixing clamp

Front derailleur cage, inner side

Elements of a standard cage rear derailleur

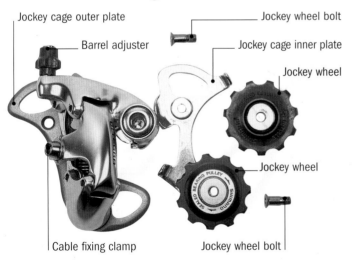

Jockey cage outer plate

Jockey wheel bolt

Barrel adjuster

Jockey cage inner plate

Jockey wheel

Jockey wheel

Cable fixing clamp

Jockey wheel bolt

Toolbox

- Needle-nosed pliers ● Cable cutters
- 5mm Allen wrench ● Screwdriver

Adjusting a front derailleur

Setting the position
Before starting to make any adjustments, shift the chain into the largest cog and the smallest chainring.

1 **Undo the cable fixing clamp** until the cable is free. Look for the low gear adjuster (usually marked "L") and screw it in or out until the inner side of the front derailleur cage is 1/16 in (2 mm) from the chain.

Adjusting a rear derailleur

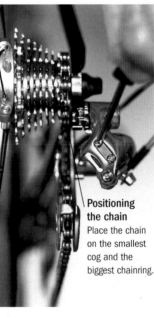

Positioning the chain
Place the chain on the smallest cog and the biggest chainring.

Shifting across
Shift the chain over to the biggest cog and the biggest chainring.

1 **Undo the** derailleur cable fixing clamp. Use the high adjuster to align the jockey wheels with the smallest cog. Rotate the pedals and keep adjusting until the chain runs smoothly. Re-clamp cable.

2 **With your fingers**, push the rear derailleur toward the spokes. If the rear derailleur moves beyond the largest cog, screw in the low adjuster until the rear derailleur stops at the largest cog.

Relocating the chain
Shift the chain across so that it is now in the smallest cog and the largest chainring.

② **Once the inner side** of the front derailleur cage is aligned with the chain, pull the gear cable through the cable clamp and tighten the cable clamp bolt. Cut off any excess cable with your cable cutters, and crimp on a cable end.

③ **Screw in the high adjuster** (usually marked "H") to bring the outer side of the front derailleur cage to $\frac{1}{16}$ in (2 mm) from the chain. If you shift into the outer ring and the chain will not move all the way across onto it, unscrew the higher adjuster to allow more travel.

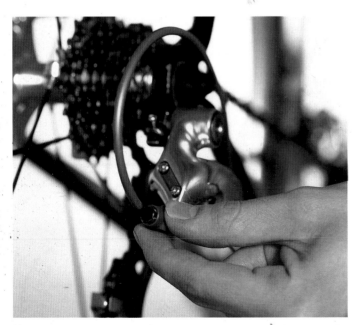

③ **Run through all the gears** with the rear shifter one at a time. If you shift and the chain does not make it onto the next cog, there is not enough tension in the cable running to the rear derailleur. To increase this, screw the barrel adjuster on the rear derailleur outward with your fingers. Conversely, if the chain goes over the next cog after one click of the shifter, there is too much cable tension and the barrel adjuster must be screwed inward to reduce it.

Workshop tips

- Ensure that the outer part of the front derailleur cage is not more than $\frac{1}{16}$ in (2 mm) above the outer chainring, and is absolutely parallel with it. If it is not, undo the cable fixing clamp and the bolt that attaches the front derailleur to the frame, then move it until it is in exactly the right place.

- Pay particular attention to the guide where the cables pass under the bottom bracket. It gets exposed to everything thrown up from the road, so keep it really clean and well-lubricated.

Troubleshooting

Problem	Solution
Some time after fitting a new rear gear cable, the chain goes on to the next cog when shifting but "chatters" because it is not snug on the cog. Caused by the cable stretching.	Follow Step 3 for Adjusting a Rear Derailleur again.
Cable stretching persists, or the gear still "chatters". The rear derailleur hanger on the frame is bent.	Straightening rear derailleur hanger requires special tools; consult a bike shop.
Shifting to a smaller cog, the rear derailleur does not take the chain all the way on, but the gear shifts if the derailleur is pulled by hand. Caused by grit getting into a cable housing, or lubrication drying up.	Remove cable from housing. Wipe with degreaser. Apply degreaser into housing to flush out debris. Lubricate and reassemble.

See also
Road riding: braking and changing gears pp.88–89 Replacing road bike cables pp.186–87

Replacing a chain

Chains must be kept clean and well lubricated, and periodically replaced. As well as being inefficient, a dirty, dry, or worn chain soon wears out the rest of the drivetrain, and you could have to replace the whole system. This is an expensive exercise, so care and regular chain replacement makes sense.

The three main types of chain found on a modern bike require different installation methods, so it is very important to recognize which one you have on your bike. The images below will help you to identify it, but the manufacturer's name is also stamped on to each link, and a good bike shop will be able to advise on what chain works best with your shifting system.

For example, Campagnolo ten-speed systems only work with their own ten-speed chain and used to have a slightly different method of joining than the others. Nowadays, though, they can all be removed and joined with a good-quality link-extractor tool.

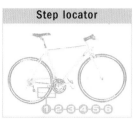

Step locator

Chain types

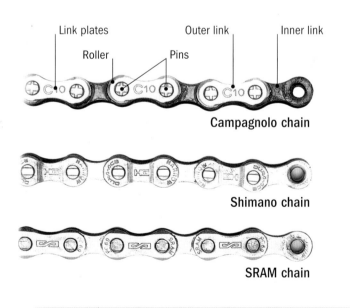

Link plates   Outer link   Inner link
Roller   Pins

Campagnolo chain

Shimano chain

SRAM chain

Toolbox

- Needle-nosed pliers (Shimano only)
- Chain link extractor ● Chain measuring tool (optional)

Checking and replacing a chain

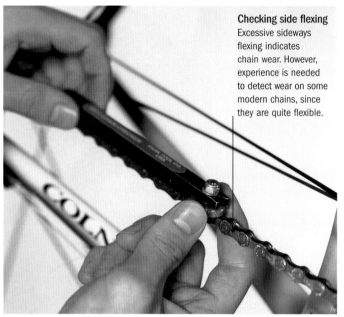

Checking side flexing
Excessive sideways flexing indicates chain wear. However, experience is needed to detect wear on some modern chains, since they are quite flexible.

1 **Measure the length of the chain**—this is the most effective way of checking whether a chain is worn. You can buy a chain measuring tool to do this, such as the one shown here. However, as a guide, 24 links should measure 12 in (308 mm). If the chain length exceeds this, it is worn and should be replaced as soon as possible.

Driving the pin through
Make sure the joining pin is completely through both link plates.

4 **Your new chain** will incorporate a link with its pin pushed out. This is called the joining link. Remove extra links from the end opposite this one, so that there is an inner link showing. Then close the chain by pushing the joining pin through the joining link and the inner link of the other end of the chain with your link extractor.

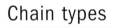

② **First remove the old chain**. To do this, shift to the smallest chainring and smallest cog so that the chain is slack. Then, using the link extractor, push the pin out of one of the links until the chain breaks. If you want to reuse the same chain, do not push the pin fully through the inside of the outer plate.

③ **Thread the chain** around the biggest chainring and the smallest cog and through the jockey wheels of the rear derailleur so that you can reduce the new chain to the correct length for your bike (check manufacturer's instructions). Then pull the ends of the chain together until there is a little tension in the jockey wheels.

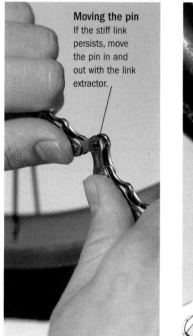

Moving the pin
If the stiff link persists, move the pin in and out with the link extractor.

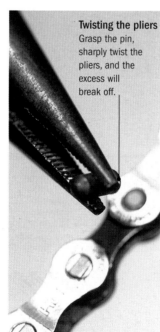

Twisting the pliers
Grasp the pin, sharply twist the pliers, and the excess will break off.

Workshop tips

- Make sure there are no stiff links in the chain before adjusting the rear derailleur if the chain is jumping—backpedal and check the chain as it goes through the jockey wheels. If it jumps every time a particular part of the chain goes through, a stiff link is the problem, which can be solved by following Step 5.

- Do not push the pin all the way through the inside link plate if you want to reuse an SRAM/Sachs or Campagnolo nine-speed chain—you need this pin in the plate to rejoin the chain.

⑤ **Joining the chain** can compress the plates of the joining link, creating a "stiff" link. To rectify this, flex the link and exert a little sideways pressure.

⑥ **The joining pin** on a Shimano chain is extra-long, so after the chain is joined, the excess must be broken off with needle-nosed pliers.

Troubleshooting

Problem	Solution
On rough surfaces the chain repeatedly slaps the bike's chainstays. The chain is too long.	Refer to Step 3 and see if there is sufficient tension in the chain. Remove links as necessary.
After fitting a new chain, "chainsuck" occurs—that is, the chain sticks to the chainring and gets sucked up between the chainring and chainstay. The original lubricant some manufacturers put on their chains is heavy, causing it to stick to the chainring.	Degrease the chain and put lighter lubricant on it.
The chain is jumping on all the cogs.	The chain is worn out and needs to be replaced.

See also
Cleaning your bike pp.182–83

Removing a crankset, a cassette, and a block

A cassette or freewheel block and a crankset are the transmission components that determine the gear ratios on a bike. If cycling in a mountainous region, you might want to fit a smaller chainring or a cassette with larger cogs to give you lower gears.

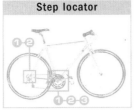

Cassettes, blocks, and chainrings (which along with the cranks make up a crankset) get worn and need replacing from time to time, so it is useful to know how to remove these components. A good starting point is recognizing what parts are on your bike so that the right tools can be used for the job. The manufacturer's name is usually stamped on each component, but a bike shop can help you identify them and provide the correct tools.

Elements of a crankset

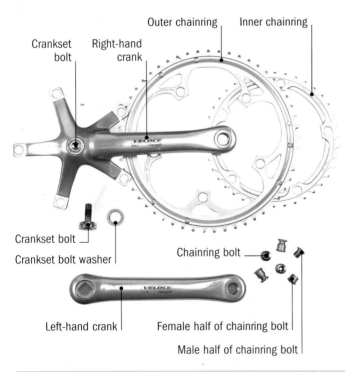

Outer chainring | Inner chainring

Crankset bolt | Right-hand crank

Crankset bolt

Crankset bolt washer

Chainring bolt

Left-hand crank | Female half of chainring bolt

Male half of chainring bolt

Toolbox

- Cassette remover ● Block remover
- Wrench to fit either ● Chain whip (cassettes only)
- 8mm Allen wrench or socket wrench ● Crank extractor
- 5mm Allen wrench ● Chainring bolt wrench

Removing a cassette

① **Remove the wheel's** quick-release skewer. Insert the remover into the teeth of the lockring, which holds the cassette on the wheel. Replace the skewer, using it to secure the cassette remover in the lockring. Do not overtighten. Wrap the chain whip around one of the larger cogs and push down on each tool to unscrew the locknut.

Removing a crankset

Removing axle bolts
Use a socket wrench to detach hexagonal crankset bolts.

① **To remove the crankset,** first remove the bolt holding it on to the bottom bracket axle. There are two types of bolt: one has a hexagonal head, the other incorporates an Allen wrench head. Whichever one is on your crankset, remove it with the appropriate tool. Note that a few cranksets have self-removing Allen bolts that take the crankset off as you unscrew.

Removing a block

② **Remove the skewer** and take off the cassette, keeping the remover in the lockring. Some cassettes have cogs that are bolted or pinned together, but some do not, so hold the cassette carefully until you find out which type you have. What is left on the hub is the cassette body, which contains the freewheel mechanism.

Follow the first part of Step 1 for Removing a Cassette so that the block remover is locked into the block by the rear wheel skewer. Each block screws on to the hub in the direction you pedal, so remove it by pushing the handle of the remover—or wrench, if the block remover has no handle—in the opposite direction.

② **If the crankset** has not come off, screw the correct crank extractor into the threads where the bolt has just been removed. When it is firmly in, turn the handle of the crank extractor clockwise.

Workshop tips

- Check the crankset after it has been installed, since it can work loose, and sometimes a well-tightened crankset bolt will need a quarter-turn with an Allen wrench soon after. Always check it after your first ride, and get into the habit of doing this anyway.
- While it is a good idea to put a bit of grease on the threads before you screw the block back on the hub, cranksets must be a dry fit on to the bottom bracket axle; degrease both parts before you refit.
- Do not get any grease on the threads of the cassette lockring.

Troubleshooting

Problem	Solution
A new chain jumps on one or more of the cogs. Caused by one or more of the cogs being worn.	Some cassettes allow you to replace single cogs; others need to have the whole cassette replaced. This is the same for blocks.
The chain sits badly on the chainring, with a gap between the chain and the teeth. Caused by a worn chainring.	Replace the chainring and the chain.
The chain keeps rubbing on the inner or outer part of the front derailleur cage. Could be caused by a bent chainring.	Take the chainring off. Lay it on a flat surface. Mark any part that does not touch the surface. Reassemble, then use an adjustable wrench to bend the marked part back in line.

③ **To remove a chainring,** use a 5mm Allen wrench on one side and a chainring bolt wrench to hold the bolt on the other. This can be done without taking the crankset off the axle, but it is easier if you do.

See also
Cleaning your bike pp.182–83   Replacing a chain pp.192–93

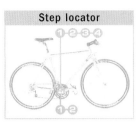

Step locator

There are two types of bottom brackets: cartridge and open bearing. Most new bikes are equipped with the cartridge type, which has sealed bearings and requires very little maintenance. Open-bearing bottom brackets do not have very strong seals and regularly require disassembling to have their parts cleaned and regreased, or even replaced. Cartridge-bearing bottom brackets can also wear out, so it is worth knowing how to remove and replace them.

To check for wear on either type of bottom bracket, take hold of a crank and try to push it toward your bike. If there is any side-to-side play, the bottom bracket needs attention or (if it is a cartridge-bearing bottom bracket) replacement.

Bottom brackets

Elements of an open-bearing bottom bracket

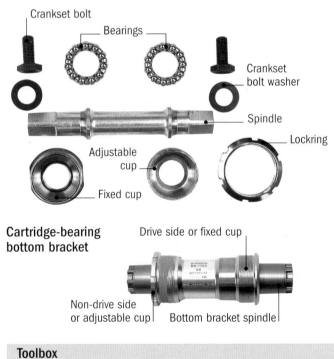

Crankset bolt

Bearings

Crankset bolt washer

Spindle

Lockring

Adjustable cup

Fixed cup

Cartridge-bearing bottom bracket

Drive side or fixed cup

Non-drive side or adjustable cup

Bottom bracket spindle

Toolbox

Open-bearing bottom bracket
- Lockring spanner ● Pin spanner ● Fixed cup box spanner

Cartridge-bearing bottom bracket
- Cartridge bottom bracket remover ● Open-end wrench

An open-bearing bottom bracket

1 **First remove both cranks** by following Steps 1 and 2 from Removing a Crankset (*see* pp.194–95). Then use a lockring spanner to remove the lockring on the non-drive (adjustable cup) side of the bike. Turn the spanner counterclockwise. Ensure that the hook of the spanner is correctly located in one of the notches around the lockring. You need to use a fair amount of force, so be careful.

A cartridge-bearing bottom bracket

1 **Follow Steps 1 and 2**, Removing a Crankset (*see* pp.194–95). Insert a remover into the non-drive side of the bottom bracket. Remove the adjustable cup with an open-end wrench on the flats of the tool, turning counterclockwise. Free the bottom bracket by repeating on the drive side, turning clockwise (counterclockwise on an Italian part).

Cleaning the bearings
Use a rag and degreaser to clean the bearings, spindle, and seal.

2 **Insert a pin** spanner into two of the holes on the adjustable cup, turn counterclockwise, and remove the adjustable cup. Take out the bottom bracket spindle and check inside the bottom bracket for a plastic seal, which needs to be removed.

3 **Remove the fixed cup** on the drive side of the bike by using a fixed cup box spanner on its two flats and turning clockwise. For Italian-made brackets—identified by "36 x 1" stamped on the fixed cup—the spanner is turned counterclockwise.

4 **Clean and examine** the two cups when they are off. If their surfaces are pitted, or the seal is split, replace the cups. To reassemble, follow the steps above in reverse, tightening the fixed cup all the way before assembling the rest.

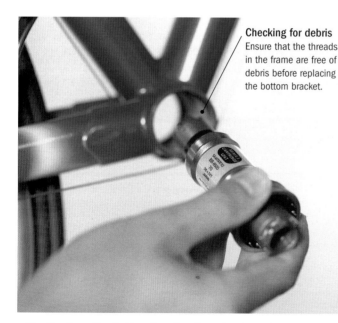

Checking for debris
Ensure that the threads in the frame are free of debris before replacing the bottom bracket.

2 **Replace the bottom bracket** from the drive (fixed cup) side of the bike using the remover tool. When the drive side of the bottom bracket is almost in position, attach the adjustable cup part of the way from the non-drive side. Then fully tighten the drive side, followed by the non-drive side.

Workshop tips

- Take your bike to a shop if the cartridge bottom bracket is proving difficult to remove. The shop will have special tools for this.

- Smear some grease on a non-Italian cartridge-bearing bottom bracket when replacing it, and also apply some to the threads. It will then be easier to remove next time. Do the same on the threads of the cup on an open-bearing bottom bracket.

Troubleshooting

Problem	Solution
There is a persistent creaking from the bottom bracket. Caused by dry threads in the bottom bracket cups.	Remove the bottom bracket and put grease on the cup threads. On the drive side of Italian versions, cover the threads with plumber's tape.
The fixed cup of an Italian open-bearing bottom bracket repeatedly comes undone.	There may be no other option but to refit the cup with a locking compound on the threads.
The cups of any bottom bracket keep coming loose. Caused by damage to the threads in the bottom bracket shell (part of the frame).	Remove the bottom bracket and take the frame to a bike shop. Ask them to run a thread-cutting tool through the shell. If this does not work, buy a threadless bottom bracket.

See also
Removing a crankset, a cassette, and a block **pp.194–95**

Adjusting a caliper brake

Dual-pivot caliper brakes are used on most modern road bikes and some hybrids. These brakes give better and more progressive stopping power than the single-pivot calipers found on older bikes. It is also much easier to keep the brake pads of dual-pivot calipers an equal distance from each side of the wheels.

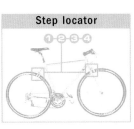

Step locator

Maintaining calipers involves regularly checking brake travel, alignment of the pads on the wheel rims, brake pad wear, and whether both pads are touching the rim simultaneously. Nowadays, most caliper brakes on new bikes are made by either Shimano or Campagnolo. Fortunately, except for one difference, the way they work is very similar, so all maintenance jobs on both systems can be tackled in the same way. Calipers are fairly simple braking systems, so if your bike is equipped with calipers from another manufacturer, the steps outlined here can be easily adapted.

Elements of a caliper brake

Caliper arm

Caliper return spring

Caliper arm

Cable fixing bolt

Caliper arm

Center fixing bolt

Caliper return spring

Centering adjuster screw

Quick release

Brake shoe

Brake shoe bolt

Travel adjuster, spring, and washer

Pad retaining bolt

Washers

Brake pad

Toolbox

- Full set of Allen wrenches
- Needle-nosed pliers
- Phillips screwdriver

Setting up a caliper brake

1 **Periodically check** for pad wear. If the pads are wearing down toward half their original depth, they must be replaced. Undo the Allen wrench pad retainer and push the pad out. If the pad and shoe are one complete piece, replace the whole unit, releasing the old pad and installing the new one with a 5mm Allen wrench.

4 **Adjust the brake travel** if you have to pull the brake lever back a long way toward the handlebar before the wheel stops moving. Undo the cable fixing bolt and squeeze the sides of the caliper until the pads nearly touch the rim. The brake cable will then move through the fixing bolt. Tighten the bolt and release the caliper.

② **The brake pads** must be directly in line with the braking surface of the wheel rim. If they are not, release the 5mm Allen bolt on the pad and line the pad up with the braking surface. Note pad wear at this point; if the pads have been set too low, a lip will have formed on them and the pad will have to be replaced.

③ **Pull the brake on** with the brake lever and check to see if both pads come in contact with the braking surface simultaneously. If they do not, an adjustment screw on the side of the caliper can be used to get both sides working together. This process is called "centering" the brakes.

Using quick-release mechanisms

Releasing the pads
Press the small button at the side of the Campagnolo brake lever to move the caliper away from the rim.

Campagnolo and Shimano have different systems for releasing the pads from the rim; this is necessary when adjusted pads are so close to the rim that it is impossible to remove the wheel. Shimano brakes have a small lever on the cable fixing bolt; lift it and the caliper moves away. Tighten the mechanism after replacing the wheel.

Workshop tips

● Put a drop of oil on the caliper return spring and at the pivot point every so often. This keeps everything working smoothly. Only use oil from a can so that you can direct it accurately, and remove the wheel first so that you do not get any on the tires or rims.

● Test the brakes—how far they travel before they are fully on is a matter of preference. For example, riders with small hands might like a little longer travel. Many professional riders have rear brake travel set farther than front, to avoid locking the back wheel.

Troubleshooting

Problem	Solution
The caliper will not release fully after application. Caused by lack of lubrication, or foreign matter inside the brake housings.	Clean, lubricate, and refit all inners and housings. Replace anything that is worn.
Brake travel increases during a ride. Caused by pad wear, cable stretching, or a loose cable fixing bolt.	Make sure the cable fixing bolt is tight and use the travel adjuster on the caliper to take up the extra travel.
When climbing very steep hills, the back wheel keeps catching on the brake pads. Caused by the wheel flexing under the force of pedaling. Can be a problem with light wheels.	Flip the quick-release partway to "off" before the climb. This will increase the distance between the pads and the rim for the climb. Do not forget to do it up for the descent.

See also
Road riding: braking and changing gears **pp.88–89** Making routine safety checks **pp.184–85**

Adjusting a V-brake

The V-brake is standard equipment on most current mountain and hybrid bikes. The V-brake's long arms—compared with those of a cantilever brake—provide a high leverage ratio, meaning that the bike stops firmly. This type of brake is also easy to maintain.

Step locator

Braking conditions will vary greatly when you ride off-road, and your brakes must be set up perfectly to cope, allowing you to apply the right amount of stopping power in every situation. This means regular adjustment, both at home and out on the trail. Follow the manufacturer's instructions; or, alternatively, the steps on these pages can be applied to all models of V-brakes.

Adjustment is best performed with the tire and inner tube off the wheel, allowing you to work without the tire obscuring your view. As well as removing the tire and tube, first release the brake tension by unhooking the cable from its cradle.

Elements of a V-brake

Cradle — Cable guide tube — Cable fixing bolt

Pad retaining spring clip

V-brake arm

Washer

Washer

Brake-pad fixing nut

Brake pad

Brake shoe — Spacers — Pivot bolt

Pivot bolt washer

Toolbox

- 5mm Allen wrench • Phillips screwdriver
- Cable puller

Setting up a V-brake

Check the fit Fit the stopper pin into the correct hole on the brake boss.

① **Check that the stopper pin** on each brake arm is seated in the same hole on the brake boss. If not, remove the pivot bolt, slide the brake arm off the boss, and put the pin in the correct hole. Next, press the brake arms together—if they are not vertical when the pads touch the rim, the spacers need rearranging on either side of the pad.

④ **Tighten or loosen** the spring-tension screw on each brake arm so that, when the brake lever is applied, both arms move an equal distance before the pad touches the rim. Ideally, the tension on each screw will be even, since there should be an equal number of spacers on either side of the brake arm.

Loosening the bolt
Use an Allen wrench to loosen the brake-pad fixing bolt.

Undoing the bolt
Use an Allen wrench to undo the cable fixing bolt.

② **Undo the brake-pad** fixing bolt, remove the pad, and swap the spacers around. Then check the pads. When pressed against the rim, they should hit the middle of the rim with the surface of the pad flat-on. They should also be horizontally parallel with the rim. Make sure the pads are doing this before tightening the fixing bolt.

③ **Retension the brake**s by placing the cable back in its cradle, and check the distance between each brake pad and the rim. There should be a $\frac{1}{32}$-in (1-mm) gap between the two. Undo the cable fixing bolt and pull the cable through until this is achieved. Tighten the cable fixing bolt.

Turning the adjuster
Screw the barrel adjuster to fine-tune the brakes by altering brake travel.

⑤ **Unscrew the barrel adjuster** on the brake lever to tighten up the brakes and make them feel more responsive. Screwing the adjuster outward reduces brake travel, resulting in firmer braking. This technique is quick and easy to perform, and is especially useful for riding in the wet, when brake pads can wear down rapidly.

Workshop tips

- Unscrew the barrel adjusters by two full turns before setting up the V-brakes. This provides the option of screwing the adjusters back in if the pads rub against the rim.

- Keep an eye on brake-pad wear. If in doubt, always replace them, since a wet ride in gritty conditions can reduce a worn brake pad down to nothing very quickly.

- Check to see if a wheel is buckled; adjusting the brakes is futile if it is. The wheel needs to be straightened in a process known as "truing." This procedure is best done by a bike shop.

Troubleshooting

Problem	Solution
Brake pads grab when applied to the rim, with the pads biting unevenly during each wheel revolution. Caused by residue on the rim.	Clean the rim with a cloth soaked in denatured alcohol.
A scraping noise is heard when the brakes are applied and the pads hit the rim. Caused by grit in the brake pads.	Unhook the cable from the cradle and remove grit with a screwdriver.
On a new bike or after installing new cables, the brake lever must be pulled hard before the pads hit the rim. The brake cable is stretching.	Follow Step 3 to take in excess cable travel.

See also
Off-road riding: braking and changing gears pp.114–15　Making routine safety checks　pp.184–85

Adjusting a cantilever brake

Cantilever brakes used to be installed on all mountain bikes, though the majority of bikes now come with the recently developed V-brakes, which are easier to adjust.

Step locator
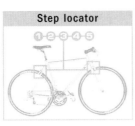

Cantilever brakes can still be found on cyclo-cross and touring bikes because they allow more clearance—for bigger tires—than calipers. V-brakes are not used on these bikes because they do not work well with the brake levers that are found on dropped handlebars.

Cantilever brakes are applied by the pull of a central brake cable, which is transferred to each side of the cantilever by a straddle wire. This direct central pull means that none of the force required to apply the brakes is dissipated. As a result, the braking power of cantilever brakes is excellent. It also means that, once correctly adjusted, each brake pad hits the wheel rim at exactly the same time.

Elements of a cantilever brake

Straddle wire

Spacer

Brake shoe

Brake pad

Pad-retaining spring clip

Cantilever arm

Cable clamp bolt

Allen nut washer

Brake pad Allen nut

Cantilever arm

Spring tension screw

Pivot bolt

Pivot bolt washer

Toolbox

- 5mm Allen wrench
- Grease • Grease gun (optional)

Setting up a cantilever brake

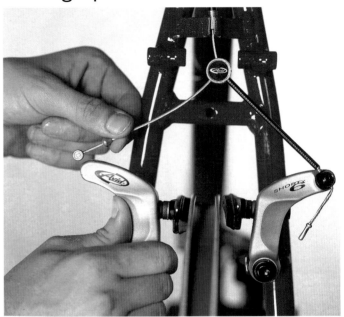

① Occasionally lubricate the frame bosses the brakes are bolted to, in order to keep cantilever brakes working smoothly. First disconnect the straddle wire by pushing the relevant cantilever arm toward the wheel with one hand, while unhooking the nipple on the straddle with the other hand.

Check the distance
Ensure that the front of the pad is closer to the rim than the rear.

1 mm

2 mm

④ To achieve "toe-in," loosen the Allen bolt that holds the pad to the cantilever's arm, and adjust the pad to get it in line with the rim. A good tip for achieving the correct angle with the rim is to place an emery board between the rear of the pad and rim, apply the brakes, then tighten the Allen bolt.

Applying grease
Use light grease on the bosses, not heavy-duty industrial grease

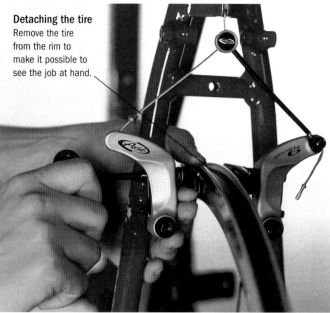

Detaching the tire
Remove the tire from the rim to make it possible to see the job at hand.

② **Undo the pivot bolts** that attach the cantilever arms to the frame bosses and remove the arms. Clean the exposed bosses with a cloth soaked in degreaser, then lubricate with a light grease. Once this has been done, bolt both arms back on to the bosses, making sure the stopper pins are inserted into the same hole on each boss.

③ **Line up the pads** horizontally with the braking surface of the rim and ensure that they fit flush to it, so that when they touch the rim, all of their surface area is being used. The pads on cantilever brakes must also be angled to the rim so that the front edge touches the rim first when the brakes are applied ("toe-in").

⑤ **To adjust brake travel,** undo the brake cable clamp on the other cantilever arm and pull the cable through the clamp while squeezing both arms of the brake in order to bring the pads close to the wheel rim. When the brake pads on either side are each ½₂ in (1 mm) from the rim, tighten the cable clamp.

Workshop tips

● Use a cable pulling tool if you find that adjusting cantilevers for travel is proving to be a difficult job. Available from bike shops, the tool works by grabbing the brake cable and pulling it through against the cantilever arm, thereby squeezing both sides of the cantilever together.

● Adjust the spring tension screw—a small adjuster found on most cantilever brake arms—to make sure that each brake pad is touching the wheel rim at the same time.

Troubleshooting

Problem	Solution
One or both of the cantilever arms will not return when the brake lever is released. Caused by foreign matter either in the brake inner cables or on the brake bosses.	Strip down, clean, and lubricate all cables. If the problem persists, clean the bosses (Steps 1 and 2). On a new bike, it could be paint on a boss; remove with a mildly abrasive material.
The brakes squeal when applied. Caused by residue on the rim. Can also be caused by the pads coming into contact with the rim flatly.	Clean the rim with denatured alcohol. Adjust the angle (Steps 3 and 4).
On inspecting the pads, a ridge is visible on them. Caused by the brake pads being set too low.	File the ridge flat, if it is not too large. Adjust by following Steps 3 and 4.

Adjusting a cable disc brake

Though usually heavier than cantilever or V-brakes, disc brakes have one major advantage over their lighter counterparts: their perform- ance is not affected by the

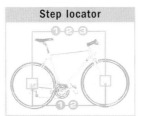

Step locator

elements. While the stopping power of cantilever and V-brakes is greatly diminished in the wet, discs will provide the same response every time they are used. This consistency is maintained even if the wheel or rim is slightly damaged.

The two types of disc brakes are cable-controlled and hydraulic. Cable discs need more maintenance than the hydraulic variety, and although recent advances have helped their performance to almost rival hydraulic systems, they still suffer a slight loss in brake modulation. They are, however, much cheaper. Cable disc brakes use standard brake cables and do not require a special brake lever. As a result, good-quality items can be bought for half the price of hydraulic systems.

Elements of a cable disc brake

Pad retaining spring   Brake pad   Hub

Spring clip

Pad retaining bolt

Washer

Caliper fixing bolt

Caliper

Barrel adjuster

Spacer

Brake lever

Brake lever reach adjuster

Barrel adjuster

Rotor

Rotor fixing bolt

Toolbox

- Allen wrench multi-tool ● Needle-nosed pliers
- Cable pullers (optional)

Adjusting cable travel

1 **Loosen the cable clamp** bolt on the caliper and pull through enough cable, with pliers or a cable-pulling tool, so that any slack in the cable is taken up. Tighten the clamp bolt. This will reduce the travel on the brakes and is a necessary adjustment if the brake levers need to be pulled a long way before the brakes work.

Replacing pads

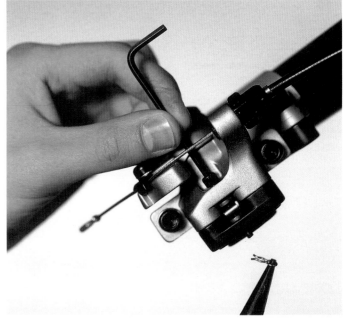

1 **If the brakes are still not** working effectively after taking up cable slack, the pads are worn and need replacing. Remove the spring clip and loosen the pad-retaining bolt that holds them in the caliper. Needle-nosed pliers are ideal for removing spring clips, but take care not to damage the clips. The pads should now drop out.

2 **Use the barrel adjuster**—found just above the point where the cable housing seats on the caliper body—to fine-tune the brake travel. If a new cable is needed, loosen the fixing clamp to get the old one off, then follow Steps 1 and 2 with the new cable. Lubricate the new cable before it is fitted.

3 **Align the callipers with** the rotors. Some brakes incorporate bolts that allow this adjustment; undo them, align the caliper so that each side of it is parallel with the rotor, and then tighten. Brakes without this adjustment facility can be aligned by using spacers to pack out the caliper fixing bolts.

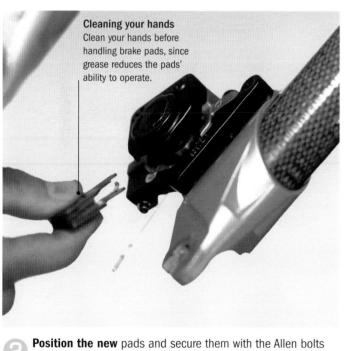

Cleaning your hands
Clean your hands before handling brake pads, since grease reduces the pads' ability to operate.

2 **Position the new** pads and secure them with the Allen bolts and the spring clips. Only use replacement pads that are specific to the manufacturer of brakes fitted on the bike. Pads with different compounds might be worth investigating if you want to alter the performance of your brakes.

Workshop tips

- Never be tempted to clean rotors with car brake cleaners—car brake discs are often made of cast iron, so the cleaner contains oil, which will drastically reduce the effectiveness of your brakes.
- Remove the wheels when lubricating your bike; no matter how careful you are, oil could get on the discs.
- Fit only the best brake cables to the mechanical discs. This makes good sense with all types of brakes.

Troubleshooting

Problem	Solution
On a new bike, or after fitting a new brake cable, brake performance diminishes during a ride. Caused by the cable stretching.	Pull more cable through as in Steps 1 and 2 of Adjusting cable travel.
The brake will not release, or it is hard to apply. Caused by dirt and grit inside the cable outers.	Replace cable and housing. If new, strip, flush housing with degreaser, clean cable, lubricate, and reassemble.
Brake performance fades toward the end of a cross-country race or a demanding ride. Caused by pad wear.	Pads can wear out very quickly. Always start a race or demanding ride in wet weather with new pads. Roughen the surface of the pads with sandpaper beforehand.

See also
Off-road riding: braking and changing gears **pp.114–15** Making routine safety checks **pp.184–85**

Bleeding a hydraulic disc brake

Hydraulic disc systems are virtually maintenance-free, so brake cables will not seize if you have left your bike for a day or two following a muddy ride. The main

Step locator
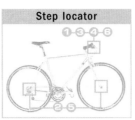

maintenance jobs for hydraulic discs are keeping the rotors clean, replacing the brake pads, and very occasionally bleeding the system if performance falls off. However, bleeding should only be carried out when absolutely necessary; the best-performing hydraulic systems are those that have never been bled.

A workstand is especially helpful when bleeding the brakes, since you need the bike held securely at a level that you are comfortable working at. DOT brake fluids are corrosive, so protect any surfaces you are working over with newspaper. At the start, place a spacer in the brake caliper once the wheel has been removed. These are usually supplied by the brake manufacturer but can be mislaid. If this is the case, use a piece of cardboard instead.

Draining and replacing brake fluid

Removing the grips
Remove grips from the handlebar to prevent them from being splashed.

① **Remove the wheels** from the bike to reduce the chance of any brake fluid getting on the brake rotors, and place a spacer in the caliper between the brake pads. Take off the brake fluid reservoir cover on the brake lever with an Allen wrench. Be careful not to get any of the brake fluid on your hands.

Elements of a hydraulic disc brake

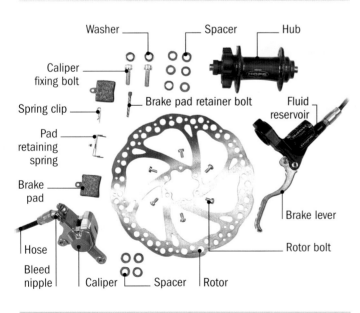

Washer — Spacer — Hub

Caliper fixing bolt

Spring clip

Brake pad retainer bolt — Fluid reservoir

Pad retaining spring

Brake pad

Brake lever

Rotor bolt

Hose

Bleed nipple — Caliper — Spacer — Rotor

Toolbox

- Allen wrench multi-tool ● Needle-nosed pliers
- 10mm wrench ● Length of clear hose

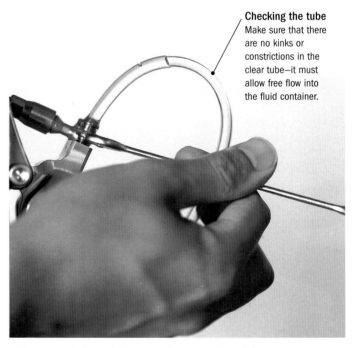

Checking the tube
Make sure that there are no kinks or constrictions in the clear tube—it must allow free flow into the fluid container.

⑤ **Repeat Step 4,** filling up the reservoir until there are no more air bubbles flowing through the clear tube. The step will probably have to be repeated four or five times before the bubbles completely disappear. Once the tube is bubble-free and the reservoir is full, close the bleed nipple.

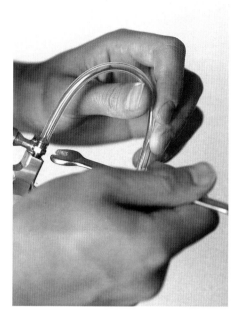

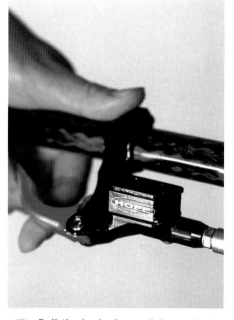

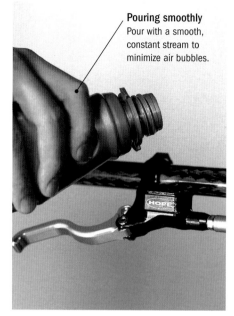

Pouring smoothly
Pour with a smooth, constant stream to minimize air bubbles.

② **Using a 10mm wrench,** open the bleed nipple and slide one end of a short length of clear tube onto it. The other end should go into a plastic container big enough to collect the old brake fluid.

③ **Pull the brake lever** all the way back to the handlebar to remove some brake fluid. Tighten the bleed nipple. Now make sure that all tools are at hand, since the next steps require you to be organized.

④ **Check that the bike** is level. Open the bleed nipple and fill the reservoir with brake fluid. Squeeze the brake lever all the way to the handlebar and hold it there. Close the bleed nipple.

⑥ **Replace the reservoir cover.** Be careful not to displace any brake fluid as you do. Refit your wheels and pump the brake lever a few times to center the brake pads. Go for a flat test ride. If your brakes are not performing as they should, there is probably still air in the system. Repeat Step 4, and make sure everything is tight.

Workshop tips

- Keep the manufacturer's instructions that came with either the bike or the brakes. Note which fluid—mineral oil or DOT 4—your system uses and ensure that you replace it with the same fluid. As a rule, DOT 4 oils perform best, but they are not biodegradable and are very corrosive.
- Remember that immediately after use, the bike's rotors are likely to be extremely hot. Keep this in mind if a wheel needs to be removed because of a puncture.

Troubleshooting

Problem	Solution
Despite maintaining the brakes and trying different pad compounds, they are not working well. Caused by the braking surfaces being too smooth.	Roughen the braking surfaces with sandpaper; rub pads diagonally in one direction top to bottom and rotors diagonally in the opposite direction.
The brake pads are wearing unevenly. Caused by the pads not hitting the rotor absolutely flat.	Adjust if the brake has the capacity to do this. See Step 3 of Adjusting Cable Travel (p.205).
The brakes need to be pumped before they will work. Caused by a loss of brake fluid.	There is a leak somewhere. Investigate to see where it is coming from. If it is not obvious what has happened, take the bike to a bike shop.

See also
Off-road riding: braking and changing gear **pp.114–15** Adjusting a cable disc brake **pp.204–05**

Repairing a puncture

Mending a puncture and replacing an inner tube are two of the maintenance jobs that you will probably become most familiar with.

Carry a spare inner tube whenever you are out on your bike, only taking a repair kit as a backup in case you get a second puncture. The reason is that there are few things more frustrating than trying to get a repair patch to stick in the pouring rain. Even on dry days, it is easier to simply replace the tube and pack the old one away. Once home, you can repair the tube in comfort; this one can then be your new spare.

Follow the steps carefully, carrying out each one thoroughly. If you hurry, you will miss something, and there is a chance that the repair will not work.

Step locator

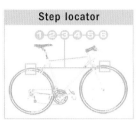

Elements of a wheel

Tire   Inner tube   Hub   Spoke   Rim

Toolbox

- Tire levers • Crayon • Sandpaper
- Patch adhesive • Repair patches • Chalk

Mending a punctured inner tube

1 **Take the wheel** out of the bike, place one tire lever under the tire bead, and lift it off the rim. Hook this lever around one of the spokes. Near the hooked lever, insert another lever under the tire and push it forward, running around the whole circumference of the rim to remove one side of the tire. Remove the tube from the rim.

5 **Thoroughly check the inside** of the tire for anything that may be sticking into it before refitting a new or repaired inner tube. To do this, take the tire off the wheel, turn it inside out, and look and feel for anything that should not be there. If something is found, remove it by pulling it from the outside of the tire.

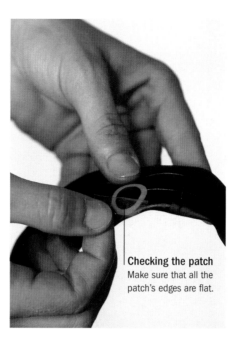

Applying adhesive
Cover an area slightly larger than the patch that will be applied.

Checking the patch
Make sure that all the patch's edges are flat.

Scraping chalk
Use sandpaper to scrape dust from the chalk.

2 **Inflate the tube** enough to hear air escaping from the puncture. When you have located it, mark the hole with crayon, let out any air, and spread a thin layer of adhesive over and around the hole.

3 **Allow a few minutes** for the adhesive to become tacky—it should change from clear to slightly opaque. Peel the foil off the back of the patch and press it firmly on to the adhesive for at least one minute.

4 **Dust some chalk** from the repair kit over the patch to prevent any excess adhesive from sticking to the inside of the tire. Leave the tube for a few minutes to make sure the adhesive has dried.

Examining the tire
Make sure the tire has not trapped the tube underneath it before fully inflating the tube by pinching the tire together and looking around the whole circumference of the wheel.

6 **Put one side** of the tire fully back on to the rim. Then slightly inflate the tube, insert the valve into the rim, and work the tube back inside the tire. To get the other side of the tire in place, push the valve upward, then lift the section of tire next to the tube over the rim. Pull the valve into place and work the tire back around the rim.

Workshop tips

- Do not use metal tire levers, since they damage the rims and can easily nip tubes.

- Immerse the tube in a bowl of water, section by section, if no air can be heard escaping when the inflated tube is placed by your ear. A stream of bubbles will locate the puncture.

- Roughen the area on the tube around the puncture with sandpaper before applying adhesive. This provides a better surface for the adhesive to hold on to.

Troubleshooting

Problem	Solution
Frequent impact punctures (which happen when your tire hits an object). Caused by the inner tube sticking to the tire wall.	Sprinkle talcum powder all over the tube and put some inside the tire.
Punctures on the underside of the inner tube. Caused by rough edges on the rim.	Make sure the rim tape is renewed regularly. File down anything found sticking up from the rim.
Frequent blowouts around the valve. Caused by an incompatible valve hole in the rim, or rough edges on the hole.	Make sure thin Presta valves are not being put though wide Shrader holes. Always fit the knurled lock to a valve. File down any sharp edges around the hole (using a fine file).

See also
Making routine safety checks pp.184–85

Servicing an open-bearing hub

Like bottom brackets, hubs come in either open-bearing or cartridge types. Open-bearing hubs require far more maintenance than the cartridge variety, since their bearings need regular inspection, cleaning, and regreasing. Consequently, being able to strip them down for a service is a useful skill to have.

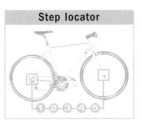

Step locator

The following steps cover removing an axle and freehub, and regreasing and retightening the bearings. They can be applied to a Shimano front or rear hub, and a Campagnolo front hub, but servicing a Campagnolo rear hub requires special tools, so it is best left to a bike shop. Before tackling the steps, remove the cassette or block (*see* pp.194-95).

Elements of an open-bearing hub (rear)

Locknut — Spacer — Drive-side cone

Allen bolt

Freehub body — Axle

Ball bearings — Non-drive-side cone

Hub body

Quick release — Locknut

Toolbox

- 15mm and 16mm cone wrenches (Shimano)
- 12mm and 13mm cone wrenches (Campagnolo)
- Grease • Grease gun (optional) • Adjustable wrench
- Allen wrench multi-tool • 8mm or 10mm Allen wrench

Overhauling an open-bearing hub

1 **First remove the locknut.** Hold the non-drive-side cone with a cone wrench while removing the nut from the drive side. Some locknuts can be removed with an ordinary wrench, some with an Allen key. Once the locknut is off, while still holding the non-drive-side cone, use the other cone wrench to remove the drive-side cone.

4 **Take out all the ball bearings** from each side and clean them with degreaser. Replace any that are pitted or have flat spots on their surface. Insert a layer of grease into each groove where the ball bearings sit (race), then put the ball bearings back into each race, pressing each bearing down firmly so that the grease holds it in place.

2 **Pull out the axle** from the non-drive side, being careful not to dislodge any ball bearings as you do so. Now clean the cones and axle and inspect them for damage. Check to see if the axle is bent by rolling it on a flat surface to look for any irregular motion. Damaged cones or bent axles need to be replaced immediately.

3 **Insert an Allen wrench into** the 8 or 10mm Allen bolt located in the center of the freehub that holds the freehub body on the axle, and turn it counterclockwise to remove the freehub. Sometimes it can take quite a bit of force to loosen this bolt, so use an Allen wrench with a long handle for extra leverage.

5 **Fit the new hub body,** or cleaned old one, by reversing Step 3. Reinsert the axle from the non-drive side. Tighten the drive cone up to the bearings and check that the axle spins freely with minimal play. Lock this cone into position with its locknut. Finally, with the cone wrenches, check that the non-drive cone is tight against its locknut.

Workshop tips

- Note where any rubber seals are located when taking off the cones, and put them back in the same place.
- Use an upturned jar lid as a vessel for cleaning bearings.
- Apply a small amount of grease to the end of your finger to help pick up each bearing when putting it back into the hub.
- A small amount of play in the axle is permissible.

Troubleshooting

Problem	Solution
There is a lot of side-to-side movement on the cassette, or the chain has engaged a gear but the bike does not go forward when pedaling. Caused by the freewheel body being worn out.	Follow the above steps to replace it.
When spinning a wheel, a crunching noise is heard coming from the hub. Caused by bearings being dry or grit getting into them, or by cones being tight.	Slacken off the cones. If this does not cure the noise, remove the axle, clean, and regrease.
When spinning the axle, it moves up and down as well as around, or it is stiff at one point and there is play at another. Caused by the axle being bent.	Strip down the hub and replace the axle.

See also

Making routine safety checks pp.184–85 Removing a crankset, a cassette, and a block pp.194–95

Servicing a cartridge hub

Cartridge hubs can be a blessing to a cyclist. Since their bearings are sealed units, they require minimal maintenance because there is little opportunity for water

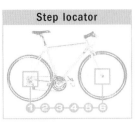
Step locator

and dirt to get inside them. However, the bearings do wear out eventually, and when they do, replacing them is a job that requires a number of special tools and a certain amount of confidence, because the process requires several sharp blows with a hammer. As long as the advice on these pages is followed and no tools other than the recommended ones are used, there is no chance of damaging the bike. But if, for example, bearings are removed with a screwdriver instead of a drift, or an ordinary hammer is used instead of a plastic one, the hub could be damaged beyond repair.

For illustrative purposes, the following steps are shown on a hub that has not been built into a wheel. You will be dealing with the hub in the wheel, but the job should still be tackled in exactly the same way. These steps can also be used to replace a broken axle, which is quite rare, but can happen if you are unprepared and hit a pothole in the road, or take a big impact off-road.

Elements of a cartridge hub (front)

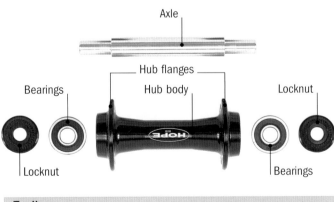

Axle

Hub flanges

Bearings   Hub body   Locknut

Locknut   Bearings

Toolbox

● Allen wrench multi-tool ● Plastic mallet ● Vise ● Drifts suitable for make of hub (check manufacturer's instructions)

Overhauling a cartridge hub

Replacing the seal
Make sure the grooves on the seals snap back into place when you refit them, or the seals will not work.

① **First remove the seals** from each side of the hub axle. Some seals are retained by a locknut that is secured with a set screw, while others just require prying off. Whatever the retaining method, remember how they look in situ and where they fit; they will need to be put back in exactly the same position.

⑤ **Push the second** bearing onto the axle, then place the drift on to a flat surface such as the flat portion of the vise. If you are not using a vise, place a piece of thick metal on the work surface, or even the floor—whatever you are hitting down onto must be solid. Lay the second bearing on it and tap the axle fully into the bearing.

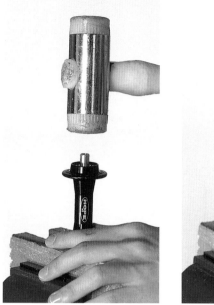

② Rest the hub flange on two blocks held in a vise. Tap the axle down with a plastic mallet, then drive it through the upper bearing with a drift.

③ The axle comes out with a bearing still on it. Lay this bearing on the blocks and drive the axle through. Then "drift" the other bearing out of the hub body.

④ To insert the first new cartridge bearing, align the bearing square to the hub, and drive it home with the drift. Although it can sometimes take a bit of force to knock the old bearings out, it should not take too much force to position the new ones in place, so you only have to knock them in gently.

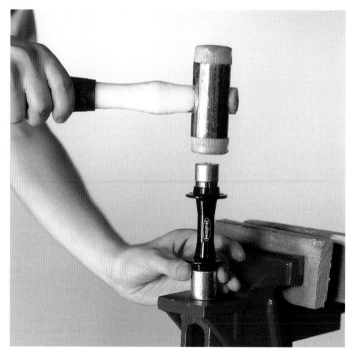

⑥ Lower the hub down on to the axle, making sure that the axle is through the middle of the bearing that has already been fixed inside the hub. Then, using the drifts, tap the hub down so that the axle goes all the way into the bearing. Finish off by replacing all the seals and spacers, and securing the locknuts on to the axle.

Workshop tips

- Spray a penetrating fluid into the bearings if you are having trouble removing them, coating the inside walls of the hub body. Leave to soak for a while before trying again.
- A collapsible workbench is a suitable alternative if a well-secured vise is not available.
- Inspect seals regularly; any that are split should be replaced.
- When the axle is free of bearings, roll it along a flat surface; if it wobbles at all, it is bent and needs replacing.

Troubleshooting

Problem	Solution
There is side-to-side movement on either wheel, or the hub makes a dry, cracking sound when the wheel is rotated. Caused by worn bearings.	Replace the bearings.
The bearings need to be replaced, but you need to know their size before the job is carried out so that new ones are ready to fit.	Consult a bike shop or call the manufacturer or distributor for the contact number of your nearest supplier.
There is difficulty removing the quick release from a hub. Either the quick release or the hub axle is bent.	Insert a straight quick-release into the axle. If you have difficulty doing so, the axle is bent.

See also
Making routine safety checks pp.184–85 Removing a crankset, a cassette, and a block pp.194–95

Adjusting a handlebar, a stem, and a headset

There are two types of headsets on modern bikes: threadless headsets, which are sometimes called A-headsets, and threaded headsets. For both types, it is essential to know how to disassemble and reassemble the handlebar and stem in order to adjust the headset and to service the bearings inside it.

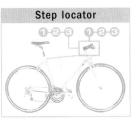

Step locator

The bearings inside all headsets act in the same way, in that they are of the cup-and-cone type found on all bikes. Just like those in open-bearing hubs, headset bearings and their cups—and the surfaces in the frame—must be checked for wear. While it is relatively easy to service a headset, installing a new one requires specialized tools and is a job for a bike shop. Fortunately, a new headset is rarely needed if the original one is regularly maintained.

Elements of headsets

Threadless headset

Allen bolt

Expander wedge

Stem cap

Top cup

Top race

Bottom cup

Fork crown race

The parts of the upper race fit above the frame's head tube in the order shown.

The parts of the lower race fit below the frame's head tube in the order shown.

Threaded headset

Locknut

Spacer

Top cup

Top race

Bottom cup

Fork crown race

Toolbox

Threadless headset
- Allen wrench multi-tool

Threaded headset
- 6mm Allen wrench ● Plastic hammer
- 30mm headset wrench ● 32mm headset wrench

Adjusting your handlebar

Upper race

Lower race

1 **Loosen the** stem to realign the handlebar if it is not in line with the front wheel on a threadless headset. On an A-headstem, first undo the Allen bolt in the stem cap. Then undo the clamp bolts on the side of the stem. The stem should now move easily.

Adjusting a stem and a headset

1 **The stems in** threaded headsets are secured by wedges which, when drawn upward by the expander bolt, jam the stem in the steerer. To remove them, first loosen the expander bolt in the center of the stem—this should stand proud of the stem after a few turns.

2 **Using a plastic hammer,** hit the expander bolt down firmly toward the stem. This should dislodge the wedge that is holding the stem inside the fork's steerer and will then free it up. The stem can now be removed if required.

Once the stem is free, center the handlebar by standing astride the front wheel and looking directly down on the stem. Sometimes the handlebar needs to be recentered after a fall. Also check that it has not been bent inward. If it has, pull the bar straight using a metal tube as a lever.

Tighten the stem cap bolt, but only enough to prevent play in the A-headset—overtightening will prevent the steering from being free. To check for play, apply the front brake and push on the bar—there should be no movement in the headset. If no movement is felt and the steering is free, tighten the stem clamp bolts.

Use two headset wrenches to adjust the headset. First adjust the top cup on to the top bearings sufficiently to prevent play in the headset. Then hold the top cup in place with one wrench while tightening the locknut down onto it with the other. Just as the locknut touches the top cup, hold the locknut with the wrench and tighten the top cup back to it. This means turning the wrench that has been holding the top cup counterclockwise for just a small part of a turn.

Workshop tips

- Always smear some grease around the steerer in the case of an A-headset stem, or on the quill inside the steerer on a threaded headset stem when reassembling. This prevents them from seizing and can stop them from creaking. With a carbon steerer, only use antiseize compounds recommended for that material.

- Clean and regrease the bottom bearings. This will require removing the fork from the head tube, so disconnect the brakes as well.

- Two types of adjusters fit in the stem caps of A-headstems: one tightens on to a wedge, the other on to a star washer. Never use the washer type on forks with a carbon-fiber steerer; they will damage the forks and the steerer could snap.

Troubleshooting

Problem	Solution
When applying the front brake, the headset moves. Caused by a loose headset.	Follow the steps for Adjusting a Stem and a Headset.
When turning the handlebar, the steering feels notchy or the headset creaks. Caused by the headset being too tight.	Loosen off and then tighten. If the problem persists, the bearings may be damaged, and they will have to be inspected, following the steps outlined for Adjusting a Stem and a Headset.
A creaking sound is heard when pulling on the handlebar. Somewhere a metal interface is dry.	Remove the stem and apply grease to the quill or around the steerer. Could also be the bar/stem interface; remove the bar and grease where the stem holds them. Reassemble.

See also
Road riding: adjusting position pp.86–87   Off-road riding: adjusting position pp.110–11

Maintaining pedals

There are many different pedals available on the market today. Most of the selection featured here are clipless pedals, which use a system in which the foot is clipped to the pedal by a mechanism that engages a cleat fixed to the sole of the shoe. Having your foot held in this position allows power to be applied to the pedals throughout an entire revolution because you can pull up as well as push down. With all these pedals, the foot is easily freed from the cleat with a simple sideways flick of the heel, so that your foot cannot become trapped in the pedal.

Step locator

Some pedals require a degree of maintenance, and most can be adjusted to suit a rider's particular requirements. These adjustments include the facility to alter the amount of pressure needed to detach your foot from the pedal; commuters might want to be able to release their foot easily, while racers will prefer the increased security of a tighter binding. The amount your foot can pivot while pedaling is another factor to consider—less strain is placed on your knees if your foot can pivot than if the foot is held rigid.

Elements of a pedal

Pedal spindle

Retaining nut

Inner bearing

Outer bearing

Inner retaining nut

Washer

Dust cap

Toolbox

- 15mm bike wrench
- Allen wrench multi-tool

Lubricating pedal threads

① **Smear some grease** on to the pedal spindle threads whenever removing pedals or installing new ones. Spindles are usually made from steel, and a chemical reaction with the alloy cranks can cause the two components to fuse together. The grease prevents this.

② **Remove pedals with** a pedal wrench or Allen wrench inserted into a hexagonal hole central to the spindle, and replace them the same way. Left and right pedals have different threads, so they both screw on in the direction you pedal. Each is marked to avoid confusion.

Workshop tips

- Try not to overtighten the pedals on to the cranks; otherwise, the fragile alloy threads on the cranks could be damaged.
- Spin the pedals regularly to check whether they oscillate up and down. If they do, a spindle is bent and must be replaced.

Troubleshooting

Problem	Solution
The pedals creak when pressure is applied. Caused by the threads in the crank being dry.	Take the pedal off, grease the threads, and put it back. If the problem persist, the pedals may need new bearings. Consult a bike shop.
The pedals start to feel loose on the spindles. Their bearings are probably worn.	Take the bike to a shop to have new bearings installed.
You have difficulty getting your feet out of the pedals. Caused by the release tension being too tight or a small stone jammed in the cleat or under the back plate of the pedal.	Loosen the release tension. Check the cleats regularly and keep them clean. Replace when worn.

Types of pedals

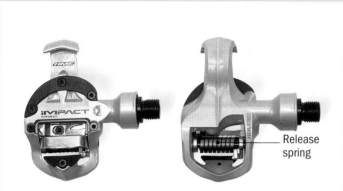

Release spring

Release bar
Spindle cover
Release bar
Spindle
Inner bearing

Time road pedal

These pedals offer a range of movement that can be adjusted to suit the requirements of individual riders. In order to keep them well maintained, they should be scrubbed regularly with degreaser, washed, and their moving parts lightly oiled.

Time off-road pedal

One of the simplest pedals available. Two bars, one of which is spring-loaded, keep the cleat on the shoe in place. There is very little to maintain. Excellent at dispersing mud; every time the cleat engages, it squeezes any dirt from the surface of the pedal.

Pivot adjuster

Release tension adjuster

Release tension adjuster

Look road pedal

These pedals are based on ski-binding technology. An Allen adjusting bolt alters the degree to which the foot can pivot when pedaling. The yellow switch on the pedal's back plate determines the release tension of the pedal. This pedal is easy to maintain.

Shimano off-road pedal

This was the first off-road clipless pedal. Open to the elements, it requires occasional replacement of its working parts. Some are easy to replace, but others are best left to a bike shop. Regularly clean with degreaser and soap and water. Lubricate with a thick lubricant.

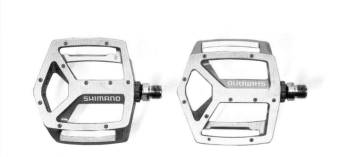

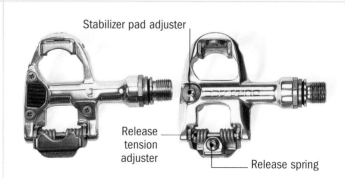

Stabilizer pad adjuster

Release tension adjuster

Release spring

Shimano BMX pedal

These pedals are similar to the type found on many off-road/commuting bikes. Since they do not require special shoes, they are ideal for those who ride in ordinary shoes or sneakers. Check the spindles for straightness and keep the pedals clean.

Shimano road pedal

These are relatively lightweight pedals. Like Shimano's off-road example, it has its workings exposed, so these areas must be cleaned and lubricated regularly. The pedals' movement can be adjusted, as can their release tension.

See also
Road riding: adjusting position pp.86–87 Off-road riding: adjusting position pp.110–11

Adjusting suspension forks

A suspension fork works by a slider on the fork leg moving up and down the stanchion. The fork's legs respond to the contours of the surface they are traveling over and give a smooth ride over lumps and bumps you would otherwise have trouble negotiating when venturing off-road with your bike.

To absorb shock, a fork has a suspension medium of either a chamber of air (air/oil) or a metal spring (coil/oil). Both compress with each bump they hit, then rebound. The speed at which all this happens (the damping) is controlled in all but the most basic forks—and a few advanced ones that use air—by an oil bath or cartridge located in one of the stanchions.

Generally, air/oil systems have the least amount of travel, but are light, so can be found on cross-country bikes. Coil/oil systems have far greater travel and possess superior adjustment facilities, so are more suitable for rough trail riding and downhilling.

Step locator

Suspension forks

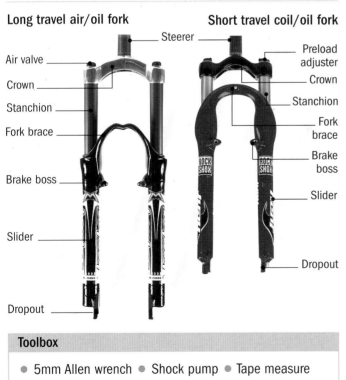

Long travel air/oil fork

- Air valve
- Crown
- Stanchion
- Fork brace
- Brake boss
- Slider
- Dropout
- Steerer

Short travel coil/oil fork

- Preload adjuster
- Crown
- Stanchion
- Fork brace
- Brake boss
- Slider
- Dropout

Toolbox

- 5mm Allen wrench • Shock pump • Tape measure
- Phillips screwdriver

Setting sag

Pulling the tie-wrap
Make sure the tie-wrap is pulled very tight around the stanchion.

1 **The amount a fork** depresses when sitting on a bike is called the sag. For a fork to work optimally, the sag should be about 25 percent of its available travel, though cross-country racers often prefer less, and downhillers more. Put a tie-wrap around the stanchion of the unloaded fork next to the top of the slider.

4 **Increase the air** in the chamber if the proportion of available travel is more than 25 percent. With a coil/oil system, increase the spring preload (usually a dial at the top of the fork leg), or even install stronger springs. If the proportion is less, release some air, reduce the preload, or use lighter springs.

Measuring the distance
Use a metal tape measure to get an accurate reading of the tie-wrap to slider distance.

② **Sit on the bike wearing** your normal cycling clothes. Place both feet on the pedals, and if you do not have someone to hold you upright on the bike, lean your elbow against a wall. The slider will travel up the stanchion, pushing the tie-wrap up with it.

③ **Get off the bike** and carefully measure the distance between the tie-wrap and the top of the slider. Calculate this measurement as a proportion of the fork's available travel. If the distance is 25 mm on an 80 mm fork, the proportion is 32 percent.

Adjusting advanced systems

Tuning on the move
Make damping adjustments while riding the bike on some types of fork.

Some more expensive forks allow the level of damping in the fork to be adjusted. The adjusters for these are commonly found in the bottom of one of the fork legs. Since damping controls the speed of the fork's action, the ideal setting is for the forks to absorb a hit and then rebound to a neutral position, ready for the next one.

Workshop tips

- Keep the suspension fork spotlessly clean. After each ride, it is a good idea to give the exposed stanchions a wipe.

- Keep any seals clean and renew them regularly; they keep the dirt out and the air and oil (if your fork has an open bath damping mechanism) in.

- Alter damping characteristics by replacing the oil in the fork with one of a different viscosity.

- Tighten leaking air valves with a Shrader valve key.

Troubleshooting

Problem	Solution
The air/oil fork regularly reaches the limit of travel. Caused by too little air in the chamber.	Pump more air in.
There is a slow falling off in the performance of the fork. Caused by the fork being overdue for a full service.	The more sophisticated the fork is, the more it is recommended that the service is carried out by a qualified technician. A good bike shop should be able to advise.
The front wheel judders when taking a corner. Caused by the rebound being set too fast.	Problems like this can be due to poor initial adjustment. Use the adjuster to reduce the speed of the fork.

See also
Tuning and maintaining suspension forks pp.220–21 Adjusting rear suspension pp.222–23

Tuning and maintaining suspension forks

There are a number of ways of tuning suspension forks. The characteristics of an air/oil fork can be altered by changing its oil, and those of a spring/oil fork by replacing its oil and springs. Stronger springs can be used if the fork is regularly reaching its limit of travel on the terrain, or is simply reacting too much to the surface. If, on the other hand, the fork is only working on bigger bumps and is not activated by smaller ones, the springs can be replaced with a softer type.

Step locator

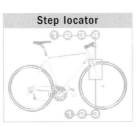

The oil in the fork can also be changed to one of a different viscosity. This alters the resistance encountered by the damping rod inside the fork as it plunges through the oil, thus keeping the fork in tune with the terrain. Changing to a more viscous oil will help if the fork is responding too quickly to the ground or judders under braking. Oil should also be changed regularly to maintain the fork, since it may become dirty and impair performance.

Replacing oil (air/oil fork)

Shrader valve

1 **Remove the cap** from the top of the stanchion that does not have the Shrader air valve positioned on it. This whole procedure can be carried out with the fork still in the bike; it has only been taken out here for illustrative purposes. However, it is useful if you can enlist someone to help you.

Inside a coil/oil suspension fork

Fork crown — Steerer

Stanchion —

— Fork brace

Seals —

— Coil spring

Coil spring —

— Brake bosses

Slider —

— Damping mechanism

Dropouts —

Toolbox

- 5mm Allen wrench ● Wrench
- Phillips screwdriver

Replacing springs (coil/oil fork)

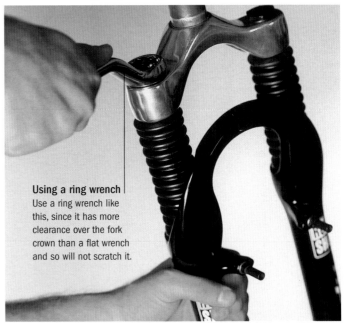

Using a ring wrench
Use a ring wrench like this, since it has more clearance over the fork crown than a flat wrench and so will not scratch it.

1 **Remove the cap** that retains the springs inside the stanchion. On the model illustrated, the springs are located near the top of the stanchion, so the spring can simply be lifted out with your finger. Other forks have springs in the bottom of the stanchion; with these, further retainers may have to be removed before they can be accessed.

Pour the old oil out into a plastic cup. This fork has an open bath damping system, where the damping rod moves up and down an open oil bath, and this oil also lubricates the rest of the system.

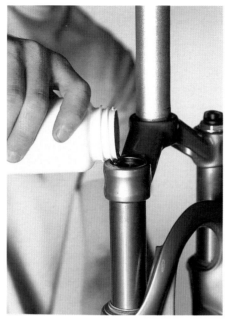

Make sure that the fork legs are held absolutely vertical. Carefully pour new oil into the stanchion until it is full, and replace the cap. Place a bowl under the fork to catch any spillage.

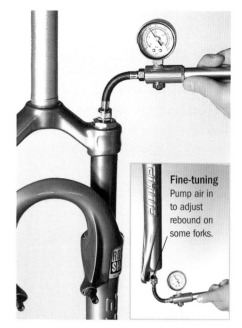

Fine-tuning
Pump air in to adjust rebound on some forks.

If the oil has been replaced with one of a different viscosity, sag will have to be reset. Follow the steps on pages 218–19 to do this and let out or pump in air to obtain the ideal sag.

Once the old spring is out, replace it with the new one, and reassemble. Some forks have springs in each leg, so perform Steps 1 and 2 on both.

Refitting the nut
Refit the nut carefully, since threads in alloy fork crowns are fragile.

Set the sag on the fork again once the new springs have been fitted. You can use the preload adjusters to dial in the sag.

Workshop tips

- Always pour oil from a narrow-necked container or use a funnel to make sure that none is spilled.
- Do not let any oil drip on to the brakes.
- Use a special shock pump on an air/oil fork to ensure that sufficient air pressure is forced into it. A standard bike pump will not be able to do this.

Troubleshooting

Problem	Solution
The ring of dirt normally seen on a stanchion after a ride is no longer visible. Caused by the seals being worn out.	Dirt is now getting into the fork. Replace the seals.
The nut on the fork stanchion cap is "rounded" while trying to remove or tighten it.	Buy a new nut. Then file two new flats on the old one and use a good adjustable wrench to remove it. Do not force it. If this does not work, take it to a bike shop.
On a course with steep but smooth descents, the rear wheel lifts during braking. Caused by the front of the bike diving under braking.	Increase the stiffness of the suspension with more preload or more air.

See also
Adjusting suspension forks pp.218–19 Adjusting rear suspension pp.222–23

Adjusting rear suspension

High-quality full-suspension bikes marry a suspension fork to a rear shock absorber, which allows the back wheel to adjust to the bumps. The way the rear shock does this depends on which application it was designed for. Just as with suspension forks, there are a few general tasks that need to be undertaken to ensure that a full-suspension bike is working well and maintaining consistent efficiency.

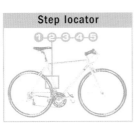

Step locator

The air/oil and coil/oil combinations found in suspension forks are also the two types of shock absorber available. A full-suspension bike has to be set up for sag like its fork-only counterpart—with the front adjusted at the same time as the rear—and then, if the shock absorber has the facility, adjusting rebound needs to be carried out. There may be other facilities on the shock, such as "lockout," and it is wise to familiarize yourself with these.

Pay attention to the frame mounts to which the shock absorber is attached; add checking these to the frame damage checks suggested earlier in this section. And be aware of the various bushings and pivots that allow the rear wheel to move, since they may also require periodic care and attention.

Rear suspension unit

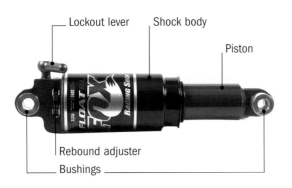

Lockout lever | Shock body

Piston

Rebound adjuster

Bushings

Toolbox

- 5mm Allen wrench
- Phillips screwdriver

Adjusting sag

Shock mounting bolt

Customizing the setting
Try different settings to get a custom fit, since a comfortable sag is unique to an individual.

Shock mounting bolt

① With the bike unloaded, measure the center-to-center distance between the shock mounting bolts. Sit on the bike and get someone to measure this distance again. Calculate the second measurement as a proportion of the first; it should be somewhere in the region of one-quarter to one-third.

④ Undo the quick-release lever to alter the total amount of travel available, ranging from 3½ to 4½ in (90 to 115 mm). This can be particularly useful at the start of a descent, where increased speeds will mean bigger impacts from any obstacles on the trail; the increased travel will help to absorb them.

2 **Let air out or pump** it in as needed on an air/oil shock absorber. Then take the second measurement again. Keep doing this until it falls where you want it to within the range recommended. On a coil/oil shock absorber, increase or decrease the preload to achieve this. Remember that the recommendation is only a guide.

Turning the adjuster
Set the damping so that the suspension reacts quickly to impacts, but does not overreact.

3 **Once you are** used to riding a suspension bike, the rebound adjuster can be used—if your bike has one—to fine-tune the damping speed. On an air/oil shock the adjuster is turned, with instructions on the shock informing users which way to turn. But do not set it too fast—it can upset the handling of the bike.

Override facility
Even when locked out, the suspension still reacts to big impacts.

5 **Some shocks** incorporate a lockout mechanism; it is the small blue lever on the illustrated unit. Across flat ground, up a smooth climb, or on the road, the mechanism can be used to temporarily prevent the suspension from working and absorbing the power being put into pedaling.

Workshop tips

- Bushings inside the frame mountings allow the bike's rear triangle, and the shock absorber, to pivot freely. Some bushings require regular lubrication with a grease that will not be washed out by water. Others do not require lubrication. Always follow the manufacturer's instructions or get advice from a specialist.
- Get the shock unit regularly serviced by a suspension specialist, a recommendation for anything but the most basic shock unit.
- Keep the shock unit clean, preferably wiping it down when you return after every ride.

Troubleshooting

Problem	Solution
The coil shock keeps reaching its limit of travel. Caused by too light a spring for the rider's weight or type of terrain being ridden over.	Fit a heavier spring.
After picking the bike up off the ground, a sharp clunk is heard coming from the shock unit.	The alloy bushings that fit between the shock and the frame mount are worn and need replacing.
The shock makes a squishing noise when it is operating. Caused by air getting in with the oil.	It is time for a service.

See also
Adjusting suspension forks pp.218–19 Tuning and maintaining suspension forks pp.220–21

Glossary

Terms set in *italics* within individual entries are defined under their own headings within the glossary.

A

AEROBIC EXERCISE Exercise that is within the body's capacity to supply adequate oxygen to working muscles.

AERODYNAMICS The interaction between traveling objects and the air through which they travel.

ALLOY A mixture of metals. In bike manufacture, steel can be mixed with metals such as chromium, molybdenum, and manganese to alter its characteristics and tailor it to its purpose. The same can be done with aluminum and titanium.

ANAEROBIC EXERCISE Exercise that is at a level in excess of the body's ability to supply oxygen to the muscles.

ANATOMIC Any cycling component designed to better accommodate the shape of the human body, such as the anatomic saddle and handlebar.

APEX (OF A CORNER) The middle point of a corner.

ATTACK An acceleration made by a competitor in a race in an attempt to leave the *bunch* behind.

B

BEAD The strengthened bottom edge of each tire *sidewall* that holds the tire on the rim when the tire is inflated.

BEARING A mechanism, usually consisting of ball bearings and circular channels, or "races," that allows two metal surfaces to move freely while in contact.

BERM A natural or man-made bank that runs around the outside of a corner and enables a cyclist to take the corner faster by riding on it.

BICYCLE FOUR CROSS (4X) Four riders compete together in heats in a knockout competition, the fastest of them progressing to a final. They start together from a start gate and race a course similar to a *BMX* course but with bigger jumps. Most courses are downhill, but some are flat. Also called *BSX* (Bicycle Super Cross).

BLOCK *Cogs* fitted to a *freewheel*.

BMX (Bicycle Motocross) Competitors race on single-speed bikes, either 20-inch-wheel or 24-inch-wheel (Cruiser) bikes, competing in two subdisciplines, *BMX freestyle* and *BMX racing*.

BMX FREESTYLE The performance of acrobatic tricks on a *BMX* bike; split into two subdisciplines: aerial for tricks performed in midair, and flatland for those done on the ground.

BMX RACING Competitors race *BMX* bikes in heats on a dirt course of jumps and *bermed* corners. The fastest racers in the heats progress to a final.

BOSS Threaded metal fixture on a bicycle frame to which an item such as a bottle cage or a pannier rack can be attached.

BOTTLENECK Describes a point in a race where the course narrows, resulting in a *pack* of riders having to slow down so that they can get through it without colliding.

BOTTOM BRACKET Rotating unit that connects the *cranks* on either side of the bottom bracket shell to each other.

BRAKE-LEVER HOOD The body in which the brake lever sits, connecting it to the handlebar.

BRAKE TRAVEL The distance the brake lever moves before the brake pads engage the braking surface on the rim or hub of a wheel.

BREAK, OR BREAKAWAY One or more cyclists in a race who accelerate away from the *bunch*.

BREATHABLE FABRIC A material with ventilation that prevents excess body heat from building up and allows some of the body's perspiration to escape as vapor.

BSX (Bicycle Super Cross) The name given in the UK to *Bicycle Four Cross*.

BUNCH The biggest group of cyclists in any race; also called a *pack* or *peloton*.

BUNNY-HOPPING The act of jumping a bike over an obstacle.

C

CABLE END CAP A small cylinder of soft metal that is closed at one end and fits over the cut ends of cables to prevent them from fraying.

CADENCE The rate at which full *revolutions* of the bike's pedals are made. Usually measured in revolutions per minute (RPM).

CAMBER The angle of a cross-section of road or *trail*. Commonly found on *bermed* corners (cambered on the outside of the turn), off-camber corners (cambered on the inside of the turn), and off-camber slopes (cambered across the trail in the direction of a downward slope).

CARBON FIBER Carbon filaments hardened by resin. In cycle manufacture, filaments are woven and formed into tubes, or used to form a monocoque (single-piece) shape.

CASSETTE A collection of *cogs* that fit on the rear wheel's *freehub*.

CHAINRING A toothed ring attached to the *cranks* that drives the chain and, in turn, the *cogs* and the rear wheel of a bicycle.

CHAINSTAY The frame tube joining the *bottom bracket* shell and rear dropout.

CHROMOLY An alloy of steel, chromium, and molybdenum, used as a frame material.

CIRCUIT RACE A road race that takes place over several laps of a circuit.

CLASSICS A number of Europe's oldest single-day road races are referred to as the Classics. The five biggest Classics are Milan–Sanremo, Tour of Flanders, Paris–Roubaix,

Liege–Bastogne–Liege, and the Tour of Lombardy.

CLEAT A plastic or metal plate that fits to the sole of a cycling shoe and engages into a *clipless pedal* to hold the foot on the pedal.

CLIPLESS PEDAL A pedal that has a mechanism to engage the *cleat* on the sole of a cycling shoe and hold it securely in place. Called clipless because they replaced pedals that had *toe clips* and *straps*.

CLUNKER BIKE An American term for a heavy bike with fat tires, once popular with newspaper deliverers, and adapted by enthusiasts as the first mountain bikes.

COBBLESTONES, OR COBBLES An irregular road surface of flat bricks, paving slabs, or rough or round stones.

COG A toothed wheel that is turned by the chain. Combined with other cogs, it forms a *cassette* or *block*.

COOL DOWN A period of easy riding and stretching at the end of a training session or hard ride that allows the body's recovery process to begin.

CRANK The lever that joins the pedals to the *chainrings* and transfers energy from the rider's legs into the *drivetrain* of the bike.

CRANKSET The assembly of *chainrings* and *cranks*.

CROSS-COUNTRY A mountain-bike race in which the competitors start together and compete on an off-road course. The first to cross the finish line wins.

CYCLE LANE Demarcated area of a road designated for cyclists.

CYCLO-CROSS An off-road race in which competitors start together to race on a multi-lap course; the first to cross the finish line, after the designated number of laps, is the winner. At international level, riders must compete on special cyclo-cross bikes. At a local level, mountain bikes are often used.

D

CYCLO-SPORTIF The French term for a semicompetitive event that any cyclist can enter; sometimes held over the same route as professional races.

DABBING The act of putting a foot down on the ground to steady yourself when riding.

DAMPING The regulated process by which suspension forks respond to uneven terrain.

DERAILLEUR Device that pushes the chain onto a larger or smaller *chainring* or *cog*.

DERAILLEUR GEARS A system that shifts the chain between *cogs* on the rear wheel (rear derailleur) and between *chainrings* attached to *cranks* (front derailleur); it allows multiple gearing.

DOWNHILL A race on mountain bikes in which the competitors start at intervals and cover a downhill course. The rider with the fastest time wins.

DOWNSHIFT Term for using the gear-shift mechanism to shift the chain to a smaller *chainring* or *cog*.

DOWN TUBE The frame tube that connects the *bottom bracket* shell to the *head tube*.

DRAFTING A term for riding behind another cyclist to shelter from the effects of the wind. Even when there is no wind, the sheltering cyclist is dragged along in the front rider's *slipstream*, using less energy.

DRAG A term sometimes used to describe the retarding forces of air on a moving object. Drag is also referred to as air resistance or wind resistance.

DRIVETRAIN The assembly of pedals, *crankset*, chain, and *cogs* that drives the bike forward by transmitting leg power into rear wheel rotation. See also *Transmission*.

DRIVING LEG The leg that is pressing down on a pedal at a particular moment.

DROPOFF Any vertical or near-vertical change of gradient on an off-road trail.

DROPOUT A slotted plate found at the end of the fork legs and stays, into which a wheel is attached.

DROPS The bottom parts of a dropped handlebar, the type of handlebar found on road bikes.

E

ECHELON Describes the formation taken by a *pace line* on the road when riding in a side wind. French cyclists call these "bordures."

ENDURANCE The ability to keep up a certain level of physical output for a length of time.

EXPANDER BOLT A bolt that draws up a truncated cone or triangle of metal inside a metal tube in order to wedge the tube in place. Commonly found inside the *stem* of a threaded *headset*.

F

FIXED GEAR A *transmission* system in which the pedals turn whenever the bike is in motion.

FREEHUB A mechanism, part of the hub, that allows the rear wheel to rotate while the pedals are stationary.

FREEWHEEL A mechanism that does the same job as a *freehub* but can be screwed on or off the hub.

FRONTAL AREA The area any moving object presents to the retarding effects of *drag*.

G H

GEAR An expression of the *chainring* and *cog* combination, linked by the chain, that propels the bike.

GRAN FONDO The Italian equivalent of the *cyclo-sportif*.

Glossary

HALF-PIPE A half-cylindrical ramp used by *BMX* riders to perform the bicycle acrobatics of *BMX Freestyle*.

HEADSET The *bearing* unit that attaches the forks to a frame and allows them to turn. There are two varieties: threaded and threadless.

HEAD TUBE The frame tube through which the *steerer* runs.

HEART-RATE MONITOR (HRM) A device for counting the beats per minute (BPM) of the heart.

HOUR RECORD The distance a cyclist can travel unpaced (alone) in one hour on a cycle racing track.

HYDRAULIC A mechanical system that uses compressed liquid to move an object. In cycling, this system is found in disc brakes.

K L

KING OF THE MOUNTAINS The title sometimes given to the best hill climber in a race. The most famous competition that uses this title is the *Tour de France*.

LACTIC ACID A by-product of *anaerobic exercise* that accumulates in the muscles, causing fatigue and pain.

LANDING AREA The place you pick for your bike to land when executing a *trail jump*, *bunny-hop*, or *dropoff*.

LOCKNUT A nut used to tighten onto a threaded object and lock it in place.

LOCKUP Describes a wheel ceasing to turn under braking.

M N

MUDGUARDS Shields that prevent a bike's wheels from throwing water and mud onto the rider.

NIPPLE The piece of metal attached to the end of a cable that prevents the cable from being pulled all the way through a control lever.

P

PACE LINE A line of cyclists who share the pace by taking turn riding at the front of the line, thus sheltering those following from the wind and some of the effects of *drag*.

PACK The largest group of riders in a race; also called a *bunch* or *peloton*.

PAD COMPOUND The material used to make brake pads. Compounds vary in their braking properties.

PANNIERS Load-carrying bags that fit on either side of a rack that is bolted to a bike's frame.

PEDAL STROKE The action of performing a *revolution*.

PELOTON French name for the biggest group of cyclists in a road race; also called a *bunch* or *pack*.

PERIODIZATION Moving through separate periods of training—each one addressing a different aspect of physical performance—while working toward a goal.

PLACE-TO-PLACE RACE A road race from one place to another, usually between two towns or cities.

PLAY A term mechanics use to describe any looseness in mechanical parts.

PNEUMATIC TIRE A tire filled with air.

POTHOLE A shallow hole in the road or trail surface.

Q R

QUADRICEPS The group of muscles in the front of the thigh that delivers most power to each *pedal stroke*.

QUICK-RELEASE MECHANISM A lever device connected to a skewer that allows a component to be locked into or released from the bike frame.

RACING LINE Taking a corner by first moving out into the road, cutting straight across the *apex*, and exiting by moving back out into the road.

REFLECTOR A unit that reflects light falling on its face, but emits no light of its own.

REVOLUTION The act of rotating the crank through 360 degrees by applying pressure to the pedal.

RING An abbreviation of *chainring*.

ROAD RACE Any race on a road or special cycling circuit (airfields and auto racing circuits are also used) in which the riders start together. The first to cross the finish line wins. See also *Circuit race*; *Place-to-place race*; *Stage race*; *Time trial*.

ROLLING RESISTANCE The friction between a tire and the surface over which it is rolling. See also *Traction*.

S

SEAT POST A hollow tube that holds the saddle and inserts into the *seat tube*.

SEAT STAY Frame tube joining the top of the *seat tube* to the rear *dropout*.

SEAT TUBE The frame tube into which the *seat post* inserts.

SHIFTER The control mechanism, usually on the handlebar of a bike, used to initiate gear-shifts.

SIDEWALL The part of the tire between the *tread* and the rim.

SINGLETRACK Off-road *trail* that allows only one bike to pass along at any time.

SLIPSTREAM The pocket of calmer air behind a moving rider. In this area, the effects of *drag* are reduced. See also *Drafting*.

SNAKEBITE PUNCTURE Name given to a puncture caused by the inner tube being trapped between the tire bead and the wheel rim; a snakebite puncture can be caused by running tires at too low a pressure.

SPINNING A term for pedaling; it usually implies that the pedaling is quick or easy.

STAGE RACE A road or off-road race that is split into several parts, which tend to be held on separate days. The rider who covers the whole course in the shortest time is the winner. The most famous example of a stage race is the *Tour de France*.

STEERER The tube that connects the forks to the *stem* and handlebar.

STEM The bike component that connects the handlebar to the *steerer*.

STOPPER PIN The end of a cantilever or V-brake return spring that fits into a locating hole on the bike's brake mounting *bosses*.

SUSPENSION An air/oil, coil/oil, or elastomer (rubber) spring system designed to absorb bumps from the trail or road. The system is either integrated into the forks or connected to the rear wheel via a linkage.

SWEET SPOT The place behind a cyclist that gives a following rider the most shelter from wind. See also *Slipstream*.

T

TAKEOFF The moment both wheels leave the ground—for example, in executing a *bunny-hop* or *trail jump*.

THREADS The spiral grooves cut into metal that allow separate parts to be screwed or bolted together.

TIME TRIAL A road race in which competitors start at intervals (usually of one minute) and cover the same course. The winner is the rider who covers the distance in the fastest time.

TOE CLIP A clip that attaches to a flat pedal and allows the rider to pull up on the pedal during each revolution.

TOE STRAP A strap that secures the rider's foot within the toe clip. This was how riders increased their pedaling efficiency before *clipless pedals* were invented, and the system is still found on some hybrid bikes.

TOP TUBE The frame tube that joins the *seat tube* to the *head tube*.

TORQUE A degree of rotary force. In cycling, the force the rider can apply to the back wheel through the *transmission*. Also, the amount of pressure applied to a tool to tighten a nut or bolt correctly.

TOUR DE FRANCE The oldest and most famous cycle race. Racers compete in teams on a different stage each day, circumnavigating France over a period of three weeks. The racer with the fastest overall time from all stages combined is the winner.

TRACK LEAGUE Race series held at cycle tracks where the beginner can gain racing experience.

TRACTION The amount of grip that a tire has on the road or *trail*. Varies with different *tread* patterns.

TRAIL Off-road path.

TRAIL JUMP An exaggerated *bunny-hop* performed to negotiate obstacles, or just for fun.

TRANSMISSION A bike's transmission is made up of those parts that transfer the rider's energy into forward motion—the pedals, crankset, chain, and cogs. See also *Drivetrain*.

TREAD The central part of a tire that makes contact with the ground.

TRIALS Tests of bicycle control in which the competitors ride over a series of obstacles and are penalized if they place a foot on the ground.

TRIATHLON A sport with three racing stages: swimming, cycling, and running. The competitor with the fastest time is the winner. Offshoots are duathlon (cycling and running), quadrathlon (swimming, canoeing, cycling, and running), and off-road triathlon (rough-water swimming, off-road cycling, and hill running).

TRI-BAR An attachment to the handlebar that allows a cyclist to ride in a lower body position and keep the hands and arms close to the body's centerline, reducing the effects of *drag*.

TUBULAR TIRE A tire whose outer part is sewn together around an inner tube, forming one unit. This enables it to hold more pressure than a separate removable tire and tube.

TURBO TRAINER A resistance unit and stand, in which a bike is mounted, that allows a rider to train indoors.

U V

UPSHIFT Term for using the gearshift mechanism to shift the chain to a larger *chainring* or *cog*.

VELODROME A stadium that contains a banked cycle-racing track.

VISUALIZATION Picturing in your mind how a situation might unfold before you go into it.

W

WARM-UP The process by which body temperature is raised and the muscles are exercised to bring your physical processes up to a level ready for optimum performance.

WASHOUT A slide that occurs when a tire loses *traction* with a surface during a turn.

WEIGHT TRAINING Any form of exercise in which the muscles push against the resistance of weights.

WICKING The unimpeded movement of body perspiration through a clothing fabric into the open air, a feature of certain items of specialty sportswear.

Directory

Organizations and websites

Cycling organizations exist for many purposes. There are political bodies campaigning for a wider appreciation of cycling and better cycling facilities; figurehead organizations for all cycling sports and recreational activities; and thousands of national and local cycling clubs. Most organizations have their own websites, all of which have something to offer. Also included here are independent websites that offer further information for cyclists. All details were correct at press time.

ORGANIZATIONS

Adventure Cycling Association
150 East Pine Street
PO Box 8308
Missoula, MT 59807
(800) 755-2453
www.adv-cycling.org
> This is a bicycle-touring association that produces maps, tour itineraries, and a magazine for members.

Afribike
Unit 16c Sanlam Industrial Park
Nadine Road, Robertville
Roodepoort, Johannesburg
South Africa
www.afribike.org
> Organization committed to increasing the use of bikes for low-cost, easily repairable transport across Africa.

America Bikes
1612 K Street, NW, Suite 800
Washington, DC 20006
(202) 833-8080
www.americabikes.org
> America Bikes is a coalition of eight major national bicycling organizations working to support a Safe Routes to School program, help develop a seamless bicycle transportation network, and insure that new road projects are safe for bicyclists and pedestrians.

Bicycle Federation of America
1506 21st Street NW, Suite 200
Washington, DC 20036
Phone: (202) 463-6622
Fax: (202) 463-6625
Email: mailto:info@bikewalk.org
http://www.bikewalk.org
> This organization is involced in bicycle advocacy, public policy, planning and facilities.

European Cyclists Federation (ECF)
Rue de Londres 15 (b. 3)
B-1050 Brussels
Belgium
www.eurovelo.org
> The ECF is developing the European Cycle Network, 12 long-distance cycle routes across the continent.

International Cycling Union (UCI)
CH 1860 Aigle
Switzerland
www.uci.ch
> The UCI governs competitive cycling worldwide. It is split into federations, the details of which are on the UCI web site. Here is a selection:

USA Cycling incorporating
United States Cycling Federation (USCF)
National Off-Road Bicycle Association (NORBA)
US Professional Racing Organization (USPRO)
All are based at:
One Olympic Plaza
Colorado Springs, CO 80909
(719) 866-4581
www.usacycling.org

Canadian Cycling Association
2197 Riverside Drive, Suite 702
Ottawa
Ontario K1H 7X3
Canada
(613) 248-1353
www.canadian-cycling.com

British Cycling
National Cycling Centre
Stuart Street
Manchester M11 4DQ
UK
www.britishcycling.org.uk

Australian Cycling Federation
PO Box 7183
Bass Hili
NSW 2197
Australia
www.cycling.org.au

Cycling New Zealand Federation
PO Box 1057
Wellington
New Zealand
www.cyclingnz.org.nz

International Mountain Bicycling Association (IMBA)
1121 Broadway, Suite 203
PO Box 7578
Boulder, CO 80306
(303) 545-9011
www.imba.com
> This body works to keep trails open for mountain bikes by encouraging responsible riding and supporting volunteer trail work. It produces an excellent trail-building manual.

International Triathlon Union (ITU)

7-1786 Esquimalt Avenue
West Vancouver
British Columbia V7U 1R8
Canada
(604) 926-7250
www.triathlon.org

The ITU is the governing body of the sports of triathlon and duathlon. It comprises different national federations, the details of which can be obtained from its website.

League of American Bicyclists

1612 K Street NW, Suite 800
Washington, DC 20006-2082
(202) 822-1333
www.bikeleague.org

Organization campaigning to make the US a more bike-friendly place.

National Trails Training Partnership

701 Ivanhoe Street, Denver, CO 80220
www.nttp.net

The National Trails Training Partnership (NTTP) is a forum of diverse trail organizations and agencies whose mission is to improve opportunities for training for the nationwide trails community. It maintains an extensive calendar of classes, workshops, and training sessions online and a database of a wide variety of trail-related resources.

Thunderhead Alliance

P.O. Box 3309
Prescott, AZ 86302
928-541-9841
www.thunderheadalliance.org

The Thunderhead Alliance is a national coalition of state and local bicycle advocacy organizations working in unison to break down the barriers to safe bicycling in American communities.

Trent Fleming Trail Studies Unit

Environmental Sciences Building ESB204
Trent University
Peterborough
Ontario K9J 7B8
Canada
(705) 748-1011, ext 1419
www.trentu.ca/academic/trailstudies

This unit studies eco-tourism and trail use in all their forms. The website has links to many trails in Canada and around the world.

Trips for Kids

610 4th Street
San Rafael, CA 94901
(415) 459-2817
www.tripsforkids.org

Based on the Trips for Kids Model Program in Marin County, California, Trips for Kids ride programs across the United States and Canada provide mountain bike outings and environmental education for children across the country who would not otherwise have these opportunities. The goal is to combine lessons in personal responsibility, achievement and environmental awareness through the development of practical skills and the simple act of having fun.

WEBSITES FOR CYCLING NEWS

www.usa.cycling.org
USA Cycling Online lists local, regional, and national racing events.

www.cyclingnews.com
An Australian cycling news site.

www.velomania.net
A French site dedicated to professional cycle racing worldwide and French cycle racing at all levels.

www.dailypeloton.com
A news service concerned primarily with professional road racing.

www.bikeamerica.info
A guide to annual cycling events across the US.

WEBSITES FOR CYCLING ADVOCACY

www.bicycling.about.com
Information on bike advocacy, with links to other bike advocacy sites.

www.crankmail.com
A directory of sites concerning cyclists and the law in the US.

WEBSITES FOR REGIONAL GROUPS

California Bicycle Coalition
www.calbike.org

Bicycle Trails Council of the East Bay
www.btceastbay.org

Mid-Atlantic Off-Road Enthusiasts
www.more-mtb.org

Southern Off-Road Bicycle Association
www.sorba.org

New England Mountain Bike Association
www.nemba.org

Texas Bicycle Coalition
www.biketexas.org

WEBSITES FOR CYCLING CLUBS

www.geocities.com/colosseum/6213
Web site of bicycle clubs in the US; it supplies club details.

www.cyclecanada.com
Contains listings of Canadian cycle clubs.

www.timeoutdoors.com/clubfinder
Clubfinder can locate bike clubs in all areas of the UK.

Books, magazines, and videos/DVDs

Whether you are a beginner cyclist requiring general tips on safe cycling, or an advanced cyclist wanting to improve your performance through training, there are books and magazines to help you. There are also numerous publications to guide cyclists touring unfamiliar countries, as well as inspirational accounts of the great sports personalities of cycling. Do not overlook the videos and DVDs made for the cycling market—many of them cover the top events of the cycling calendar.

GENERAL BOOKS

Access All Areas: BMX
Robin Reeve (Michael O'Mara)
   A book that contains flick animations of freestyle BMX moves.

The Art of Wheelbuilding
Gerd Schraner (Buonpane Publications)
   This book explains the mystique of the wheelbuilding craft.

Cyclecraft: Skilled Cycling Techniques for Adults
John Franklin
(British Stationery Office Books)
   A guide to cycling techniques and tips for cyclists who ride in traffic.

French Revolutions: Cycling the Tour de France
Tim Moore (St. Martin's Press)
   The account of a journalist's attempt to ride the route of the 2000 Tour de France. Emotional and funny.

Kings of the Mountains
Matthew Rendell (Aurum Press)
   A fascinating study of Colombian cycling and its fanatical following.

Mountain Bike Like a Champion
Ned Overend and Ed Pavelka
(Rodale Press)
   Tips from Ned Overend, mountain biking's first World Champion.

The Tour de France: the History, the Legend, the Riders
Graeme Fife (Mainstream Publishing)
   Stories covering some of the famous and not-so-famous men and incidents of the Tour de France.

TRAINING BOOKS

The Cyclist's Training Bible
Joe Friel, Tudor Bompa (VeloPress)
   A practical guide to constructing your own training plan.

Serious Cycling
Edmund R. Burke
(Human Kinetics)
   An insight into training and physiology, backed by the personal experiences of well-known cyclists.

Training Lactate Pulse-Rate
Peter GJM Janssen
(Polar Electro Oy)
   An explanation of the science behind training with a heart-rate monitor.

BIOGRAPHIES AND AUTOBIOGRAPHIES

It's Not About the Bike
Lance Armstrong
(Putnam Publishing Group)
   An award-winning book that charts Armstrong's fight with cancer, his recovery, and his subsequent victory in the Tour de France.

Miguel Indurain: A Tempered Passion
Javier Garcia Sanchez
(Mousehold Press)
   Biography of the great Spanish cyclist, the first sportsman ever to win the Tour de France five times in succession.

The Ride of My Life
Matt Hoffman (Regon Books)
   The autobiography of the greatest BMX rider ever.

TRAVEL AND TOURING BOOKS

A Bike Ride: 12,000 Miles Around the World
Anne Mustoe (Virgin Books)
   The account of a 54-year-old former teaching professional who, despite having had no previous cycling experience, bought a bike and cycled around the world.

A Ride in the Neon Sun: A Gaijin in Japan
Josie Dew
(Trafalgar Square)
   A guide to cycling in Japan, and to the country itself, written by an experienced cycling explorer.

MAGAZINES

Bicycling Magazine
1612 K Street NW, Suite 800
Washington, DC 20006-2082
(202) 882-1333
www.bikeleague.org
   Supplied to members by the League of American Bicyclists, which fights for cyclists' rights in the US.

BMX Plus!
Hi-Torque Publications
Subscriptions: (661) 295-1910
www.hi-torque.com
   Covers freestyle and racing BMX. Bike tests, track visits, interviews.

Cycle Sport, Cycling Weekly, and *Mountain Bike Rider* (see next page)
IPC Media
5th Floor, Focus House
9 Dingwall Avenue, Croydon CR9 2TA
UK
www.ipc.co.uk

Cycle Sport
Covers professional road, track, and cyclo-cross racing worldwide.

Cycling Weekly
Covers British and European road and track racing, as well as cyclo-cross and general cycling news. It includes tests and reviews, riding tips, and event listings.

Mountain Bike Rider
Covers all aspects of mountain biking. Provides routes to ride in the UK and elsewhere. It includes tests and reviews of bikes and other products, riding tips, and event listings.

Cycling Plus, Mountain Biking UK, and **What Mountain Bike?** (see below)
Future Publishing
Beauford Court
30 Monmouth Street, Bath BA1 2BW
UK
Subscriptions: 011 44 870 444 8470

Cycling Plus
Covers all aspects of road cycling. Tests and reviews bikes and other equipment. Includes cycling news, riding tips, and event listings.

Mountain Biking UK
Tests and reviews bikes and other equipment. Includes route suggestions, rides around the world, tips, and event listings.

What Mountain Bike?
A consumer's guide that tests and reviews bikes and equipment. Contains up-to-date listings of bike specifications, and riding tips.

Mountain Bike
2509 Empire Avenue
Suite 2
Burbank, CA 91504
mountainbike.com
Tests and reviews bikes and other equipment. Includes rides, tips, and event listings.

Procycling
Cabal Communications
374 Euston Road
London NW1 3BL
UK
www.procycling.com
Covers professional road, track, and cyclo-cross racing around the world. Tests and reviews road-race bikes.

Ride BMX
Transworld Media
Subscriptions: (850) 682-7644
www.bmxonline.com
Covers freestyle BMX. Bike tests, interviews, access campaigning.

Ride: Cycling Review
www.ridemedia.com.au
Covers road and track cycling from Australia and around the world. Also includes product reviews and advice.

Ride Magazine
PO Box 48291
Roosevelt Park 2129
South Africa
www.ride.co.za
Covers road, track, and mountain-bike racing both in South Africa and worldwide. Includes product reviews and riding and training advice.

220 Triathlon
Origin Publishing
Tower House, Fairfax Street
Bristol BS1 3BN
UK
www.220magazine.com
Covers triathlon and duathlon events worldwide. Includes training articles and reviews of bikes and equipment.

VeloNews
Inside Communications
1830 N 55th Street
Boulder, CO 80301
(303) 442-4966
www.velonews.com
Covers road, track, mountain-bike and cyclo-cross racing in North America and worldwide, plus product reviews and training advice.

VIDEOS/DVDS

Forward (Etnies)
This film documents some great BMX riders as they tour North America.

Tour de France '89: Never So Close (Beckmann Visual Publishing)
Covers Greg Lemond's comeback from a shooting accident to win the 1989 Tour de France by the narrowest-ever margin.

Road to Paris (World Cycling Productions)
A film that offers fascinating insights into Lance Armstrong's preparation for the 2002 Tour de France.

Search for the Holey Trail (Redline Entertainment)
A mountain-bike video that tours the world's most exciting places to ride.

Sprung 05 (Chilli Productions)
This DVD contains a good blend of mountain-bike and BMX action.

A Sunday in Hell: Paris–Roubaix 1976 (World Cycling Productions)
This is an excellent film about the classic Paris–Roubaix road-race.

AUTHOR'S ACKNOWLEDGMENTS

The author would like to thank:
Neil Lockley, Richard Gilbert, and Kevin Ryan of DK, Phil Hunt of Phil Hunt Editorial, Simon Murrell and David Tombesi-Walton of Sands Publishing Solutions, and Paul Reid and Pia Hietarinta of cobalt id for holding my hand and patiently guiding me at every stage of writing and putting together this book.

Luke Evans and Arthur Brown for suggesting my name as the writer in the first place.

Dave Marsh of the Universal Cycle Centre, Wayne Bennett of Don't Push It Mountain Bikes, Tim Flooks, Dave Lloyd of Dave Lloyd Bikesport, Andrew Dodds of *MBUK*, and Phil Axe and Michael Slack of JE James Cycles for help with technical matters.

Gerard Brown for his stunning photography, and Guy Andrews for getting all the equipment together for photo shoots.

All the models who interpreted so professionally what was needed of them to demonstrate the various techniques in the book.

All the professional cyclists for giving so freely of their pro tips in the Better Cycling section. And special thanks to Giles Wolf of M-A-D, Craig Robertson of Ride-On, and Russell Carty of Kona, who helped me contact some of them. Sustrans, The Cyclists Touring Club, and The National Byway for information on a wide range of matters. Karen McDonald of Endurance Events, Gordon Steer of World Expeditions, and Phil Hennem of MBMB for providing the information for maps.

All the companies who lent equipment, especially those who allowed their beautiful bikes be used in the location photo shoots.

Marguerite Lazell, the editor of *Cycle Sport*, for patience while I was writing this book.

PUBLISHER'S ACKNOWLEDGMENTS

Dorling Kindersley would like to thank the following for their help and participation:
Editorial: Jude Garlick, Mary Lambert, Sharon Lucas, Frank Ritter.
Index: Margaret McCormack.
Design: Isabel DeCordova, Janice English, Elaine Hewson, Marianne Markham, Jenisa Patel, Smiljka Surla, Simon Wilder, Dawn Young.
Additional photography: John Davis, Philip Gatward.
Photo montages: Iain Hazlewood at construct id.
Illustrator: Patrick Mulrey.
Picture research: Jo Walton.
Administrational help: Georgina Garner.
Photo-shoot help and accommodation: Rob and the staff at Le Renard hotel, Chatel, France.

Models:
Chris Hopkins, James Millard, Simon Oon, Simon Richardson, Vera Rodrigues.

Cycling models:
Hsu Min Chung, Jamie Newall, Claire Paginton, Hannah Reynolds, Helen Rosser, Kelli Salone, Ross Tricker, Deusa Vitoriano, Russell Williams.

Accessory, component, and bicycle suppliers:
Special thanks to Ross Patterson at ATB Sales for Hind clothing and Marin bikes; Caroline Griffiths at Madison for Colnago, Ridgeback, and Rocky Mountain bikes, and Shimano, Giro, Rock Shox, Park, and many more components and accessories; Brian at Yellow for Assos and Castelli clothing, and Rudy Project sunglasses; Bikepark cycles for Litespeed and Tomac bikes; Brompton bicycles; Chas Roberts bicycles; Pasq Bianchi at Cycleurope for Bianchi bike; Condor cycles; Cycles Dauphin; Evans cycles; Collette Clensy at Giant bicycles; Hope Technology hubs and disc brakes; Russell Carty at Kona bicycles; Ian Young at Moore Large for Haro bikes; Sean Moulton at Moulton bicycles; Adrian at Pashley bicycles; RJ Chicken and sons for Mavic wheels; Sigmasport cycles; Brian Buckle at Trek UK for Trek bike; Steve Wassell at TWT for Dawes tandem; Dominic Mason at Upgrade for DMR bike and pedals, USE seatposts; Dave Yates bicycles; Brian at Yellow for Pinarello bike.

Acknowledgments

PICTURE CREDITS

The publisher would like to thank the following for their kind permission to reproduce their photographs:
(Key: t=top, b=bottom, r=right, l=left, c=center)

4–5 Getty Images; 6–7 Getty Images; 10 Corbis: tl; Bettmann bl; 10–11: Hulton-Deutsch Collection; 10 Stockfile: br; 11 Corbis: bl; 11 Stockfile: bc, br; 12 Courtesy of Campagnolo: bc; 12 Corbis: Swim Ink tl; 12 Empics Ltd: Topham Picturepoint br; 13 Empics Ltd: Presse Sports t; 13 Getty Images: bl, bc, br; 14 Phil O'Connor: br; 15 Gerard Brown: bl; 15 Corbis: Russell Underwood br; 15 Stockfile: Jason Patient c; 17 Getty Images; 20 ATB Sales Ltd: b; 21 ATB Sales Ltd: bc; 21 Corbis: David Stoecklein bl; Earl and Nazima Kowall br; 26 Gerard Brown: t; 30 Stockfile: Paul Carpenter; 31 Stockfile: Steven Behr bl; 32 Corbis: Roger Ressmeyer; 33 Stockfile: Seb Rogers br; 34 Corbis: Tom and Dee Ann McCarthy bl; 36 Corbis: Tom Stewart; 37 Corbis: Ariel Skelley br; Michael DeYoung bl; 38 Stockfile: Seb Rogers b; 41 Stockfile: Jamie Carr bl, br; 42 Stockfile: Steven Behr; 43 Gerard Brown: r; 48 Getty Images: l; 52 Gerard Brown: l; 54 Getty Images: l; 56 Empics Ltd: Tony Marshall l; 62 Gerard Brown: l; 64 Gerard Brown: l; 70 Gerard Brown: bl; 70 Gerard Brown: l; 76 Gerard Brown: l; 78 Stockfile: Seb Rogers l; 80 Stockfile: Steven Behr l; 82 Stockfile: Steven Behr l; 139 Stockfile: Steve Thomas br; Steven Behr bc; 153 Phil O'Connor; 156–57 Corbis: Jean-Yves Ruszniewski; 159 Phil O'Connor: l; 159 Gerard Brown: r; 160 Getty Images: l, r; 161 Phil O'Connor; 162 Getty Images: l, r; 163 Getty Images; 164 Empics Ltd: Neal Simpson l; Tony Marshall r; 165 Empics Ltd: Jon Buckle l; 165 Getty Images: r; 166 Phil O'Connor: l, r; 167 Getty Images; 168 Stockfile: Steven Behr l; 168–69 Getty Images; 170 Gerard Brown: l; 170 Getty Images: r; 171 Gerard Brown: l; 171 Stockfile: Steven Behr r; 172 Stockfile: Steven Behr l, r; 173 Getty Images; 174 Getty Images; 175 Stockfile: Steven Behr bl, br; 176 Stockfile: Steven Behr bl, br; 177 Stockfile: Steven Behr l, r.

All other images © Dorling Kindersley.

For further information see www.dkimages.com

PLEASE NOTE

Road and off-road riding are, by their very nature, potentially hazardous. All participants in such an activity must assume responsibility for their own actions and safety. The information contained in this book cannot replace sound judgment and decision-making that can help reduce risks, nor does the scope of this book allow for an explanation of all the potential hazards and risks involved in such an activity. Neither the author nor the publisher can be held responsible for any accidents resulting from following any of the activities shown in this book. Always prepare for the unexpected and be cautious.